British Romanticism and the *Edinburgh Review*

Also by Duncan Wu

ROMANTICISM: An Anthology (editor)

SELECTED WRITINGS OF WILLIAM HAZLITT (editor)

WORDSWORTH: An Inner Life

British Romanticism and the *Edinburgh Review*

Bicentenary Essays

edited by

Massimiliano Demata
Postdoctoral Fellow
University of Bari

and

Duncan Wu
Lecturer in English and Fellow of St Catherine's College
Oxford

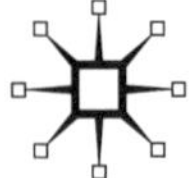

First published 2002 by
PALGRAVE MACMILLAN
Houndmills, Basingstoke, Hampshire RG21 6XS and
175 Fifth Avenue, New York, N. Y. 10010
Companies and representatives throughout the world

PALGRAVE MACMILLAN is the global academic imprint of the Palgrave
Macmillan division of St. Martin's Press, LLC and of Palgrave Macmillan Ltd.
Macmillan® is a registered trademark in the United States, United Kingdom
and other countries. Palgrave is a registered trademark in the European
Union and other countries.

ISBN 0–333–96349–0 hardcover

This book is printed on paper suitable for recycling and
made from fully managed and sustained forest sources.

A catalogue record for this book is available
from the British Library.

Library of Congress Cataloging-in-Publication Data

British Romanticism and the Edinburgh review: bicentenary essays/edited by
Massimiliano Demata and Duncan Wu.
      p.   cm.
   Includes bibliographical references and index.
   ISBN 0–333–96349–0
   1. English literature—19th century—History and criticism—Theory, etc.
   2. Criticism—Scotland—History—19th century.   3. Scotland—Intellectual
   life—19th century.   4. Romanticism—Great Britain.   5. Romanticism—
   Scotland.   6. Edinburgh review (1802)   I. Demata, Massimiliano, 1967–
   II. Wu, Duncan.

PR457 .B747 2002
820.9′007—dc21

                                                      2001058647

10   9   8   7   6   5   4   3   2   1
11   10   09   08   07   06   05   04   03   02

Printed and bound in Great Britain by
Antony Rowe Ltd, Chippenham and Eastbourne

Contents

Acknowledgements

The editors wish to thank Roy Park, whose idea this book was; the anonymous readers, who so kindly assessed its contents at various stages (and in so doing much improved it); and Eleanor Birne and Rebecca Mashayekh at Palgrave, who nurtured it through its various stages. Our wives, Jole and Caroline, helped mitigate our labours on it during the summer and autumn of 2001.

Abbreviations

Atkinson and Jackson	*Brougham and his Early Friends: Letters to James Loch 1798–1809*, collected and arranged by R. H. M. Buddle Atkinson and G. A. Jackson (3 vols, 1908)
BLJ	*Byron's Letters and Journals*, ed. Leslie A. Marchand (13 vols, 1973–94)
Bromwich	David Bromwich, *Hazlitt: The Mind of a Critic* (1983)
Bryson	Gladys Bryson, *Man and Society: The Scottish Inquiry of the Eighteenth Century* (1945)
CC	*Collected Coleridge Series*, Bollingen Series 75
CC *Biographia*	*Samuel Taylor Coleridge: Biographia Literaria*, ed. James Engell and Walter Jackson Bate (2 vols, 1983)
CC *Essays*	*Samuel Taylor Coleridge: Essays on his Times* ed. David V. Erdman (3 vols, 1978)
CC *Friend*	*Samuel Taylor Coleridge: The Friend*, ed. Barbara Rooke (2 vols, 1969)
CC *Literature*	*Samuel Taylor Coleridge: Lectures 1808–19 on Literature*, ed. R. A. Foakes (2 vols, 1987)
CC *Marginalia*	*Samuel Taylor Coleridge: Marginalia*, ed. George Whalley and Heather Jackson (6 vols, 1980–2001)
Cockburn	Henry Thomas, Lord Cockburn, *Life of Lord Jeffrey* (2 vols, 1852)
Contributions	Francis Jeffrey, *Contributions to the Edinburgh Review* (1844)
Cornell *LB*	*William Wordsworth: Lyrical Ballads and Other Poems, 1797–1800*, ed. James Butler and Karen Green (1992)
Dowden	*The Letters of Thomas Moore* ed. Wilfred S. Dowden (2 vols, 1964)
ER	*Edinburgh Review*
EY	*Letters of William and Dorothy Wordsworth: The Early Years, 1787–1805*, ed. Ernest De Selincourt, rev. Chester L. Shaver (1967)

Ferguson	Adam Ferguson, *An Essay on the History of Civil Society*, ed. Fania Oz-Salzberger (1995)
Flynn	Philip Flynn, *Francis Jeffrey* (1978)
Greig	James Greig, *Francis Jeffrey of the Edinburgh Review* (1948)
Grierson	*The Letters of Sir Walter Scott*, ed. H. J. C. Grierson (12 vols, London: Constable, 1932–79)
Griggs	*The Letters of Samuel Taylor Coleridge*, ed. E. L. Griggs (6 vols, 1956–71)
Hewitt	*Scott on Himself*, ed. David Hewitt (1981)
Jones	Stanley Jones, *Hazlitt: A Life* (1991)
Howe	*The Works of William Hazlitt*, ed. P. P. Howe (21 vols, 1930–4)
Marrs	*The Letters of Charles and Mary Anne Lamb 1796–1817*, ed. Edwin W. Marrs, Jr. (3 vols, 1975–8)
McGann and Weller	*Lord Byron: The Complete Poetical Works*, ed. Jerome J. McGann and Barry Weller (7 vols, 1980–93)
Meek	Ronald L. Meek, *Social Science and the Ignoble Savage* (1976)
Morley	*Henry Crabb Robinson on Books and Their Writers*, ed. Edith J. Morley (3 vols, 1938)
MY	*The Letters of William and Dorothy Wordsworth: The Middle Years*, ed. Ernest De Selincourt, *i: 1806–11*, rev. Mary Moorman (1969); *ii: 1812–20*, rev. Mary Moorman and Alan G. Hill (1970)
Nicholson	*Lord Byron: The Complete Miscellaneous Prose*, ed. Andrew Nicholson (1991)
Notebooks	*The Notebooks of Samuel Taylor Coleridge*, ed. Kathleen Coburn (5 vols, 1957–)
Nowell Smith	*The Letters of Sydney Smith*, ed. Nowell C. Smith (2 vols, 1953)
O'Brien	Edmund Burke, *Reflections on the Revolution in France*, ed. Conor Cruise O'Brien (1969)
On Longing	Susan Stewart, *On Longing: Narratives of the Miniature, The Gigantic, the Souvenir, the Collection* (1999)
Owen and Smyser	*The Prose Works of William Wordsworth*, ed. W. J. B. Owen and Jane Worthington Smyser (3 vols, 1974)
Sadler	*Diary, Reminiscences and Correspondence of Henry Crabb Robinson*, ed. Thomas Sadler (3 vols, 1869)

Sikes   *The Letters of William Hazlitt*, ed. Herschel More-
                        land Sikes, assisted by Willard Hallam Bonner
                        and Gerald Lahey (1979)
Stewart   *The Collected Works of Dugald Stewart, Esq.*, ed.
                        Sir William Hamilton (11 vols, 1834–6)
Sutherland   Kathryn Sutherland, 'Fictional Economies: Adam
                        Smith, Walter Scott and the Nineteenth-Century
                        Novel', *English Literary History* 54 (1987) 97–127
Sydney Smith   *The Works of the Rev. Sydney Smith* (3 vols, 1839)
Winch   Donald Winch, 'The System of the North: Dugald
                        Stewart and His Pupils', in Stefan Collini, Donald
                        Winch and John Burrow, *That Noble Science of
                        Politics: A Study in Nineteenth-Century Intellectual
                        History* (1983), pp. 23–61
Wu   *Selected Writings of William Hazlitt*, ed. Duncan
                        Wu (9 vols, 1998)

Notes on the Contributors

Stuart Curran is Vartan Gregorian Professor of English at the University of Pennsylvania and has interests in European Romantic culture and gender studies. Author of numerous essays on the contributions of women poets to the Romantic Age, he has also edited Charlotte Smith's *Poems* and Mary Shelley's second novel, *Valperga*.

Massimiliano Demata has worked for Mansfield College, Oxford, and is currently a postdoctoral fellow at the University of Bari, Italy. He has published articles on Byron, the Gothic novel, Orientalism and Scottish literature. He is currently completing an anthology of texts of Romantic Orientalism and a book on eighteenth- and nineteenth-century literary translations.

Philip Flynn is Professor of English at the University of Delaware, where he teaches British, classical and biblical literature. He is the author of *Francis Jeffrey*, a study of the first editor of the *Edinburgh Review*, and of *Enlightened Scotland: A Study and Selection of Scottish Philosophical Prose from the Eighteenth- and Early Nineteenth Centuries*.

Paul H. Fry is William Lampson Professor of English and Master of Ezra Stiles College at Yale University. With emphasis on British Romanticism and the history of literary criticism, and with additional interests in literary theory, the history of genres, and art history, he has published the following books: *The Poet's Calling in the English Ode* (1980); *The Reach of Criticism: Method and Perception in Literary Theory* (1984); *William Empson: Prophet against Sacrifice* (1990); *A Defense of Poetry: Reflections on the Occasion of Writing* (1995); and a critical edition, with commentaries, on *The Rime of the Ancient Mariner* (1999). He is currently working on a book to be called *Wordsworth and the Anthropology of Poetry*.

Susan Manning is Grierson Professor of English Literature at the University of Edinburgh. Her primary research interests lie in the fields of the Scottish Enlightenment and Scottish–American literary relations, the subject of her books *The Puritan-Provincial Vision* (1990), and the transatlantic study, *Fragments of Union* (2001). She has edited the works of Henry Mackenzie, including a new edition of *Julia de Roubigné* (1999), Walter Scott's *Quentin Durward*, Washington Irving's *The Sketch-Book of Geoffrey Crayon, Gent.*, and Hector St. John de Crèvecoeur's *Letters from* *an American Farmer*. Her edition of Nathaniel Hawthorne's *The Marble Faun*, for Oxford University Press, was published in 2001. She is a Board Member and Past President of the Eighteenth-Century Scottish Studies Society, and serves on the editorial boards of several journals, including the Anglo-American *Symbiosis*.

Jane Stabler is a Lecturer in English Literature at the University of Dundee, Scotland. She has published the Longman Byron Critical Reader and is the author of *Byron, Poetics and History* (2002) and co-editor of *British Women in Italy in the Nineteenth Century* (2002).

Fiona Stafford is Lecturer in English at the University of Oxford, and a Fellow of Somerville College. She is the author of *Starting Lines in Scottish, Irish, and English Poetry: From Burns to Heaney* (2000) and *The Last of the Race: The Growth of a Myth from Milton to Darwin* (1994). Her first book was *The Sublime Savage: James Macpherson and the Poems of Ossian* (1988). She has also published articles on Ossian, Celticism, Romanticism, Robert Burns, James Hogg, Jane Austen and Mary Shelley.

Timothy Webb is Winterstoke Professor at the University of Bristol where he was Head of the Department of English from 1990 to 1999. His books include *The Violet in the Crucible: Shelley and Translation* (1976), *Shelley: A Voice Not Understood* (1977), *English Romantic Hellenism* (1982), *Shelley's 'Devils' Notebook* (with P. M. S. Dawson, 1993), *Shelley's 'Faust' Draft Notebook* (with Nora Crook, 1997), and editions of *W. B. Yeats: Selected Poetry* (1991) and *Shelley's Poetry and Prose* (1976, 1995). He is currently working on a number of projects including *Bristol: Romantic City* (joint editor), *The Book of Stones*, an edition of Leigh Hunt's *Autobiography*, and books on Ireland and the English Romantics, Byron, and the Romantic City.

Duncan Wu is University Lecturer in English Literature at the University of Oxford and a Fellow of St Catherine's College. He is the editor of *Romanticism: An Anthology* (1994, 1998), *Selected Writings of William Hazlitt* (9 vols, 1998), and the author of *Wordsworth: An Inner Life* (2002).

Introduction

Massimiliano Demata and Duncan Wu

The bicentenary of the foundation of the *Edinburgh Review* provides the contributors to this volume with a welcome opportunity to reassess the periodical's significance and influence. Over the years a number of works and essays on the *Edinburgh* have appeared. The monographs of Thomas Crawford, James Greig, John Clive, George Pottinger and Philip Flynn have focused mainly on Jeffrey and the influence of his Scottish philosophical background on his literary criticism, especially in relation to his attack on the Lake Poets.[1] Peter Morgan's useful collection of *Jeffrey's Criticism* has provided those without access to the original run of the *Edinburgh* with up-to-date texts of his finest essays.[2] This commemorative volume aims to capture the vision of the *Edinburgh* through the investigation of two related areas: first, the redefinition of the role of Scotland in terms of national 'community' within the Union and its intersection – on philosophical, political and literary levels – with Great Britain; second, the new awareness of the role of reviews in the larger sociological and cultural context of British Romanticism, and the centrality of the *Edinburgh* in that context.

In his biography of Francis Jeffrey, Henry Cockburn remembers the impact of the publication of the first issue of the *Edinburgh Review* in October 1802:

The effect was electrical. And instead of expiring, as many wished, in their first effort, the force of the shock increased on each subsequent discharge. It is impossible for those who did not live at the time, and in the heat of the scene, to feel, or almost to understand, the impression made by the new luminary, or the anxieties with which its motions were observed. It was an entire and instant change of every thing that the public had been accustomed to in this sort of composition. The old periodical opiates were extinguished at once. The learning of the new journal, its talent, its spirit, its writing, its independence, were all new. And the surprise was increased by a work so full of public life springing up, suddenly, in a remote part of the kingdom.[3]

Even allowing for partiality on Cockburn's part (he was a close friend of Jeffrey's), one thing about the *Edinburgh Review* upon its appearance in 1802 was clear: it opened a new chapter in the history of literary criticism. Whether or not Jeffrey was, as Cockburn puts it, 'the greatest of British critics', or, according to Macaulay, 'more nearly an universal genius than any man of our time', the man who was primarily responsible for the success of the *Edinburgh* gave new meaning to the concept of periodical literature and reshaped the world of letters.

Several respectable review publications flourished during the late eighteenth century (such as the *Monthly Review* and the *Critical Review*), but none had given such prominence to the reviewing of current research and creative writing across the spectrum of the arts and sciences. Good though some of the late eighteenth-century periodicals had been, none had been so influential as to shape the taste of the reading public or to determine the agenda followed by writers themselves. The *Edinburgh* would change all that. Its founding in 1802 began a tradition that lasted well into the twentieth century (until 1929), and provided a model for subsequent periodical publications. Rigorous selection criteria, announced in the 'Advertisement' to the first issue, accounted for its policy:

> It will be easily perceived, that it forms no part of their [the editors'] object, to take notice of every production that issues from the Press: and that they wish their Journal to be distinguished, rather for the selection, than for the number, of its articles.[4]

At the same time, the proposal to publish on a quarterly basis, rather than monthly, was designed to permit the editors 'a greater variety for selection', and to allow them to be 'occasionally guided in their choice by the tendencies of public opinion'.[5] It was a complex but well-considered policy. The editors aimed at a careful selection of titles, while striving to reflect the full range of the intellectual endeavour of the time. In addition, they wished to follow (to an extent) the interests of the reading public. That educational function was clear from the outset. Including a review of Southey's *Thalaba* (the first of Jeffrey's many scathing attacks on the Lake Poets), the first number of the *Edinburgh* carried no fewer than

29 reviews within 252 pages. Topics included poetry, natural history, travel literature, philosophy, politics, and antiquarianism. Its range was preserved in subsequent issues, although articles decreased in number and accordingly expanded to become lengthy pieces of 20–30 pages, sometimes more.

The *Edinburgh* quickly established itself as the most important review of its day. The first issue of October 1802 had an initial run of 750 copies, and a second edition was called for within the month. By the end of 1803, 2150 copies of the first number had been sold in Edinburgh alone, many passing through several hands. Printings of subsequent numbers were expanded, and Longman acquired publication rights in London. A steady progression ensued: the print run had risen to 9000 by 1809 and 13 000 by 1815. It claimed to draw readers from the lower clergy, shopkeepers, teachers and lesser professionals who composed the middle classes. Walter Scott, one of the most distinguished of its early contributors, observed that 'No genteel family can pretend to be without it, because independent of its politics, it gives the only valuable literary criticism that can be met with.'[6]

This early success was a surprise to everyone involved. Its founders were a circle of intellectually aggressive young Whigs – (besides Jeffrey) Francis Horner, Henry Brougham and Sydney Smith.[7] They felt like outsiders; not just because they were young (most were in their twenties) and unknown, but because of their politics. In Scotland at the time the *Edinburgh* was established there were no newspapers or periodicals representing Whig opinion; cases argued by Whig lawyers were consistently defeated; and Church livings were in the hands of the Crown and its associates. Scotland was little more than a Tory constituency, with no effective opposition voice. There was an overwhelming need for a publication unafraid of expressing views contrary to received opinion. Against that background Jeffrey may have seemed extreme to some, but he was actually a moderate. Having witnessed the French Revolution and its consequences he was disinclined to follow radical lines of thought; at the same time, he was unhappy with the Tory stranglehold on Scottish affairs. By 1800 he had 'outed' himself as a Whig and was resigned to suffer the consequence – to be passed over in his legal career. It was usual for Whig lawyers from Scotland to go to London where advancement was easier to come by, as did Horner (in 1803) and Smith (in 1804). Of his colleagues, Henry Brougham remained most closely involved with editorial process. By 1825 he was the most prolific of the *Edinburgh*'s contributors (responsible for over 200 articles), writing principally on science, travel, economics and politics. Like Horner and Smith, Brougham went to London (in 1804) to pursue a career at the English bar, where he became involved with the abolition-ist movement. In 1810 he became a Whig MP, beginning a momentous career in politics.

From the third number, in 1803, Jeffrey was sole editor (except for numbers 33 and 34 during the winter of 1813–14, which Jeffrey spent in America), and remained so until the 98th in 1829 when he was made Dean of the Faculty of Advocates, and resigned. It was arduous work, but Jeffrey clearly had a talent for it. It involved revising and arranging each issue when contributors had delivered, as well as the more delicate tasks of finding and training reviewers, commissioning, and either rejecting or revising articles when they arrived. Everyone who knew him believed him to be the best qualified man for the job; as Cockburn remarked, 'There was not one of his associates who could have held these elements together for a single year.'[8] This volume necessarily focuses on his editorship for the journal.

As time passed the *Edinburgh* became more determined in its political convictions and by 1808 was confirmed in its opposition to the govern-ment. In that year Jeffrey and Brougham published a review of Don Pedro Cevallos' *Exposition of the Practices and Machinations Which Led to the Usurpation of the Crown of Spain* proposing that a successful outcome to the popular uprising in Spain would lead to reform throughout the Spanish political system – and perhaps throughout other parts of Europe, including England:

> We sincerely believe, that the success of that cause would not only save the rest of the Continent from France, – from the enemy of both national independence and civil liberty, but would infallibly purify the internal constitution both of this and other countries of Europe. Now, if any man thinks, that we should not extravagantly rejoice in any conceivable event which must reform the constitution of England, – by reducing the over-grown influence of the Crown, – by curbing the pretensions of the privileged orders, in so far as this can be effected without strengthening the Royal influence, – by raising up the power of real talents and worth, the true nobility of a country, – by exalting the mass of the community, and giving them, under the guidance of that virtual aristocracy, to direct the councils of England, according to the spirit, as well as the form of our invaluable constitution; – whoever believes, that an event, leading to such glorious conse-quences as these would not give us the most heartfelt joy, must have read but few of the pages of this Journal, or profited but little by what he has read.[9]

This was strong stuff, even for liberals. As Hazlitt pointed out in *Spirit of the Age* (1825), such enthusiasm for a 'glorious consequence' 'stung the Tories to the quick by the free way in which it spoke of men and things'.[10] The article precipitated a storm of indignation and outrage from Tory newspapers and journals, and even the Whig Holland House set in London expressed alarm. Subscribers resigned, and a number of contributors felt distinctly uneasy in the *Edinburgh*'s pages. Scott was sufficiently discomfited to break off relations with Jeffrey and initiate the founding of the rival Tory *Quarterly Review*.[11] Edited by William Gifford, formerly the star satirist of *The Anti-Jacobin*, it was funded at its inception by the Tory government. George Canning, George Ellis (both of whom had also been involved with *The Anti-Jacobin*), John Wilson Croker and Robert Southey were quickly enlisted as contributors and after an uncertain start the *Quarterly* proved a success, with circulation figures that were to surpass those of the *Edinburgh*. Its links with the government were strong, but its founders believed that the *Quarterly* should be independent. The Tories were in power from 1809 to 1830, but the *Quarterly* did not unswervingly support them throughout that period. Its primary function was to counter the Whig principles of the *Edinburgh*.

The *Quarterly* lifted its format and technique from the *Edinburgh* – a fact that accounts in part for its popularity. There were other similarities: both were partisan productions that aspired to a degree of independence. For that reason it would be incorrect to think of them as deadly rivals representing, without question, their respective party lines; competitors they may have been, but Jeffrey, Brougham and Horner were no more unthinking hacks than were Gifford, Ellis and Southey. It was unfair for Hazlitt (no impartial judge) to condemn the *Quarterly* as 'a mere mass and tissue of prejudices on all subjects'.[12]

Another competitor appeared in April 1817: *Blackwood's Edinburgh Magazine*. Blackwood was a former associate of John Murray and just as conservative in his politics. Blackwood had two competitors in the *Edinburgh* and the *Quarterly*, but aimed to be more adventurous in his editorial policy than either. *Blackwood's* would contain a mixture of satire and reflective pieces by some of the greatest writers of the day – Thomas De Quincey, James Hogg, J. G. Lockhart, John Wilson, William Maginn and, briefly, S. T. Coleridge. The two most important editors were Lockhart and Wilson, who contributed almost all the important literary reviews between 1817 and 1825. No one person seems to have exercised complete editorial control; from August 1818 onwards Lockhart and Wilson seem to have acted as literary editors, with Blackwood operating a power of veto when contentious issues arose. The trio worked in collaboration until Lockhart went to London in 1825 to edit the *Quarterly*. *Blackwood's* was always a partisan Tory publication ready to launch wild attacks on those it saw as enemies – although it could be unpredictable when it came to deciding who they might be. Wordsworth was one of several writers who were alternately damned and praised in successive issues during the course of 1817. Nor was it slow to initiate feuds. The most obvious example is its campaign against what it dubbed 'the Cockney School of Poetry', which began with attacks on Leigh Hunt and John Keats,[13] and went on to include libellous criticisms of Hazlitt. Hazlitt sued and won an out-of-court settlement. But that didn't discourage the *Blackwood's* men (the 'Mohawks' as they were known): they continued to vilify their English colleagues, who eventually struck back. The result was a duel between John Scott, editor of the *London Magazine* (and friend of Keats and Hazlitt) and Jonathan Christie, an associate of Lockhart. Scott was wounded and died on 27 February 1821, leaving a young family.[14] There were many differences between the Mohawks and Jeffrey, but it is worth noting that Jeffrey was not immune from this sort of disagreement. In 1806 his criticisms of Thomas Moore's *Epistles, Odes, and Other Poems* led to a farcical duel in which neither Moore nor Jeffrey fired a shot; in fact, it brought them together and they became fast friends.[15]

What distinguishes the *Edinburgh* from *Blackwood's* and the *Quarterly* is that it was one of the last articulations of Scottish Enlightenment thinking. Empirical and inquisitive in philosophy and science, liberal in politics, Enlightenment thought had flourished during the eighteenth century and its effects could still be strongly felt in Scotland when the *Edinburgh* was founded. The writings of Hume, Ferguson, Adam Smith, Lord Kames, William Robertson, Thomas Reid, Archibald Alison and Dugald Stewart provided Jeffrey and his reviewers with a 'common-sense' view on human nature, ethics and language on which the *Edinburgh*'s criticism was based. This gave it the status almost of an institution from an early point in its development. 'To be an Edinburgh Reviewer is, I suspect, the highest rank in modern literary society,' declared Hazlitt, and however humorous his comment might be (or perhaps proudly self-congratulatory, given that Hazlitt was an 'Edinburgh Reviewer' himself), it reflected the journal's importance to an expanding and socially respectable readership. Indeed, the definition of what Hazlitt calls 'modern literary society' is crucial to our understanding of the *Edinburgh*'s actual impact and influence. As Jon P. Klancher has shown, towards the end of the eighteenth century the shaping of a reading audience went side by side with the emergence of social classes in the modern sense. The 'reading public' had outgrown numerically and socially narrow boundaries, but could not find any kind of social or cultural unity as a whole. Social divisions encouraged the creation of cultural areas which realised cohesion and dialogue within them but which in a broader social frame were also divisive. The *Edinburgh* was the first of many periodicals which found their readership in what may be called 'unity in division': periodicals addressed the interests of *their* community in contrast or opposition to other interests or groups.

The *Edinburgh* was established at a time when other key Romantic texts, which also had an educative purpose, were appearing. *Lyrical Ballads* had been published in 1798, and volume 2 had followed in early 1801[16] with its famous 'Preface' setting out Wordsworthian poetic theory. In some ways closely aligned with the emergence of Romanticism, the *Edinburgh* enables us to question and debate that phenomenon. Jeffrey's opposition to the Lake School has on occasion encouraged the mistaken view that he was antipathetic to Romantic literature. As some of the contributors to this volume demonstrate, that does no justice to the more complex, and intriguing, reality. One could argue that the tradition that bound Jeffrey and his colleagues to Scottish enlightenment thought makes his criticism of the Lakers predictable. He could be trenchant in his remarks, and occasionally intemperate, if not bloody-minded (as for instance in the review of *Christabel* which he co-authored with Hazlitt[17]), but he remained true to the intellectual system he had been taught as a young man at Glasgow. In that sense, Jeffrey was a representative of eighteenth-century Enlightenment values.

On the other hand, Jeffrey was capable of championing the work of Felicia Hemans – a Romantic poet who looked to Wordsworth for inspiration. He wrote kindly of Keats and – more strikingly – employed Hazlitt (a former associate of the 'Lake School'). There was nothing exclusive or limiting about his editorial policy. He was open to new writing and the values it represented, but at the same time remained keenly aware of his own intellectual roots. The essays in this volume offer new opportunities to assess these two sides of Jeffrey's make-up – the Enlightenment thinker on the one hand, and the forward-looking literary analyst on the other. That combination of qualities, we would argue, made Jeffrey one of the most provocative and intriguing critics of his day. He may not always have been right (*The Excursion* wasn't an outright failure, as Jeffrey thought), but he frequently found himself attempting to resolve the tensions between Romanticism and the eighteenth-century culture of which he was a product. If that makes him fallible it also makes him exemplary, because that tension lies at the heart of what we now call Romanticism, and has inspired much of the analysis in the present volume.

British Romanticism and the Edinburgh Review begins with five essays that discuss how the *Edinburgh* saw itself in relation to the outside world. Eighteenth-century Scotland provided the philosophical foundation for the *Edinburgh Review*. Philip Flynn analyses in detail the philosophical and aesthetic threads that were current before and during Jeffrey's time. He outlines the *Edinburgh*'s indebtedness to the philosophical tradition which developed during the eighteenth century in Scotland, its education system, debating societies and political context. Flynn shows how the most remarkable qualities of the *Edinburgh*'s literary criticism – inquisitive and empirical, rigorous and prescriptive – maintained the tradition of common-sense philosophy. As Jeffrey acknowledged, while literature had a prominent role in the *Edinburgh*, its '*Right* leg' was politics. This was the *raison d'être* of all the early quarterlies, each of which carried a strong political connotation on which even their literary criticism was founded.

From the outset, the *Edinburgh Review* was defined by its Scottishness. Unlike his colleagues Jeffrey chose not to migrate to London, but remained in Edinburgh, consolidating a northern centre of British culture. It was partly in defiance of a London-centred literary milieu that the journal was established, and this accounts for its sense of fellow-feeling with those it regarded as oppressed. As Fiona Stafford demonstrates, it identified itself from the outset with opposition to the slave trade, harshness of the laws of libel and the Corporation and Test Acts. And in selecting books to review, it chose publications that would permit direct and broadly Whiggish comment on current affairs. This in itself was an act of nationalistic assertion; the perspective of the Edinburgh Whig, it argued, was as valid as any from which to discuss issues of the day. But Stafford goes further. It is clear from her findings that Jeffrey's enthusiasm for the newly United Kingdom was part and parcel of a belief in Scotland and its place in an international culture. That understanding of Scotland's place within the larger community of nations is key to the *Edinburgh*'s vision of itself, and is reflected in its adventurous attitude towards travel literature, the subject explored by Massimiliano Demata. Like any young nation that understands itself to have something to offer to the rest of the world, the *Edinburgh* had a voracious appetite for information about foreign parts. Its editors constructed an aesthetic by which such literature could be evaluated – one that was based on the empirical methods and utilitarian functions associated with the genre by the philosophers of the Scottish Enlightenment; it was an aesthetic that prized lack of prejudice above all other qualities.

A similarly unprejudiced view characterized its evolving opinion of Ireland. Timothy Webb demonstrates that readers of the *Edinburgh* were taught to assess Irish problems in an impartial manner. Editorial policy was one of genuine, open enquiry, in the sense that unlike other journals such as the *Quarterly*, it did not make negative prejudgements. Jeffrey and his contributors were capable of sympathizing with the plight of Irish people and the oppression they suffered from what Sydney Smith could describe as 'the long wickedness of the English Government'. As Webb observes, the sensitivity of the *Edinburgh*'s reviewers to Irish problems had much to do with their experiences as Scotsmen.

At the same time Jeffrey was clearly anxious about appearing nationalistic in a narrow, parochial sense. This is what makes the appearance of essays on antiquarianism so important, at least in the journal's earlier years. As Susan Manning argues, those articles – half of them by Walter Scott (no friend to Whiggishness) – provided 'a means to articulate Scottishness without compromising the journal's enlightened and cosmopolitan stance'. This was, in part, because Jeffrey and his colleagues were acutely conscious of the need to identify Scotland's place within a historical and geopolitical context. Antiquarianism, travel books, books about Ireland – all provided a means of doing that.

Manning also prompts us to consider the other side of Jeffreyan aesthetics – his attitudes towards contemporary writers. The relationship with Scott was a particularly problematic one. Scott was originally a friend and collaborator, but also a Tory – who, as Manning observes, was intent on peddling a vision of disjunctive Toryism for profit. This was bound to lead to strains which manifested themselves with Jeffrey's review of *Marmion* in 1808, expressing impatience with Scott's unreconstructed antiquarian stances. The final break between the two men took place in the wake of the Don Pedro Cevallos article, which prompted Scott to establish the *Quarterly Review*.

The *Edinburgh* discussed poetry for the benefit of a large and discerning public. No other topic caught the attention of literary criticism (and polemics) more than the discussion of the 'new' poetry of Romanticism. In this sense, the interaction between the *Edinburgh*, Wordsworth, Coleridge, Hazlitt and Byron constituted the forum of much of the discussion on poetic matters of the age.

The *Edinburgh* is at present known and discussed in literary circles because of its controversial interpretation of the Lake Poets. Indeed, Jeffrey's attack on Wordsworth and his dislike of what he considered to be a vulgar or, at best, unintelligible poetry has been seen as the dividing line between two centuries and two diverging ways of interpreting the nature and function of poetry. Paul H. Fry discusses this phase of the history of criticism by focusing on the most overt point of difference between Jeffrey and Wordsworth: the nature of the 'non-human' and its relationship with the 'human'. Fry delves into Jeffrey's and Wordsworth's interpretations of nature to trace a dialogue between the two men comprising some unobtrusive points of agreement and a number of irreconcilable differences in their attitudes to nature, the sublime, and the beautiful.

While Fry shows that in his dislike of Wordsworth Jeffrey found Byron a valuable supporter, Jane Stabler demonstrates that the alliance of the critic and the poet went deeper than their joint attack on the Lakers. Jeffrey and Byron relished their cultural sovereignty as chief critic and poet of the day. They influenced each other both in the development of their public personae and in literary matters – Byron respectfully acknowledging the honesty and acute reasonableness of Jeffrey's judgements, and Jeffrey adding the innovative, 'irregular' and often subversive character of Byron's verse to his own allegedly 'conservative' criticism. Furthermore, while Jeffrey was alert to the misanthropic and morally equivocal character of Byron's poetry, he alone amongst critics of his time considered it an essential component of the poet's genius. Jeffrey criticized Byron's recourse to the classical 'Unities' in his drama, arguing that this was a limitation when compared with his earlier poems.

Jeffrey's response to Byronic Romanticism heightens our awareness of the dual nature of his attitude to Romantic literature more generally – something reiterated by his relationship with William Hazlitt. Duncan Wu attempts to resolve the strange paradox that Hazlitt, who started out as a close associate of Wordsworth and Coleridge, could find himself as a mature journalist voicing his most fierce and indignant criticism of those writers (particularly Coleridge) in the pages of the *Edinburgh*. It is a significant paradox because Hazlitt's outwardly contradictory stance exemplifies the tension between eighteenth-century thinking and Romanticism. What makes it difficult to understand is the fact that Hazlitt was no conservative. Few men were so well informed when it came to what Wordsworth and Coleridge were attempting to achieve, and Hazlitt was ideally placed to write searching, perceptive criticism of their work. Instead, he chose to attack them in as destructive and public a manner as he could.

It is one of the arguments of this book that Jeffrey was both an enlightenment thinker and a keen follower of Romantic literature; Wu's argument is that much the same can be said of Hazlitt. As Wu points out, Hazlitt's father attended the Old College in Glasgow and was thus the product of the same intellectual tradition as Jeffrey. Almost by proxy, therefore, Hazlitt was a product of that tradition (he was, indeed, taught for some years by his father at home). So that, even in 1798, when he first met Wordsworth and Coleridge, Hazlitt would have had his own perspective – one quite distinct from theirs – on the grandiose, and ultimately failed, project of *The Recluse*. It would be tempting to argue, in fact, that in 1798 Hazlitt's grasp of the philosophical issues was as far-reaching, if not more so, than that of his mentors. At all events, his inheritance of the Scottish tradition would have meant that he was innately predisposed to the values of the *Edinburgh*.

Given the journal's Whiggish inclinations, as in its sympathy with the Irish, one would expect it to have been supportive of the many women writers who appeared during the Romantic period. But as Stuart Curran demonstrates, that was one manifestation of Romanticism that the journal was slow to accept. It is clear from Curran's findings that the *Edinburgh* had a blind spot, in its early years, when it came to women writers: 'In its early days women were simply beyond the pale of the periodical's intellectual authority.' But in time Jeffrey became more thoughtful in his judgements, and found words of praise for Joanna Baillie and Maria Edgeworth – both members of two other oppressed groups: the Scots and Irish.

That important observation returns this volume to where it began. The periodical commemorated by this volume was the brainchild of a man – Francis Jeffrey – who may have felt marginalized not just because he was a Whig in a world ruled by Tories, but by the distinct perspective of those north of the border. Its founding was a means of asserting a new perspective – one different from the metropolitan bias of newspapers and periodicals produced from London. It did so in a thoroughly persuasive fashion and, in so doing, incited opposing literary and political interests to establish rival journals. We hope that this collection of new essays will restore the *Edinburgh Review* to a comparably prominent position in twenty-first-century accounts of eighteenth-century and Romantic culture.

Notes

1. Thomas Crawford, *The Edinburgh Review and Romantic Poetry (1802–29)* (Auckland University College, Bulletin no. 47, English Series 8, 1955); James A. Greig, *Francis Jeffrey and the Edinburgh Review* (Edinburgh: Oliver and Boyd, 1948); John Clive, *Scotch Reviewers. The Edinburgh Review, 1802–1815* (London: Faber and Faber, 1957); Philip Flynn, *Francis Jeffrey* (Newark: University of

Delaware Press; London: Associated University Presses, 1978); George Pottinger, *Heirs of the Enlightenment. Edinburh Reviewers and Writers 1800–1830* (Edinburgh: Scottish Academic Press, 1992).

2. Peter F. Morgan, *Jeffrey's Criticism* (Edinburgh: Scottish Academic Press, 1983).
3. Cockburn, i 131.
4. *Edinburgh Review* 1 (October 1802), 'Advertisement' (no page number).
5. Ibid.
6. Grierson, ii 121.
7. Identification of contributors to the *Edinburgh Review* throughout this volume is based on the attributions provided in the *Wellesley Index to Victorian Periodicals*.
8. Cockburn, i 301–2.
9. *Edinburgh Review* 13 (October 1808) 223, 225.
10. Wu, vii 192.
11. See Susan Manning's essay, pp. 117–18, below.
12. Wu, vii 195.
13. See Nicholas Roe, *John Keats and the Culture of Dissent* (Oxford: Clarendon Press, 1997), chapter 8, and Duncan Wu, 'Keats, and the "Cockney School"', *The Cambridge Companion to John Keats,* ed. Susan Wolfson (Cambridge: Cambridge University Press, 2001), pp. 37–52.
14. Further details can be found in Patrick O'Leary, *Regency Editor: Life of John Scott* (Aberdeen: Aberdeen University Press, 1983), chapter 9, and Duncan Wu, 'John Scott's Death and Lamb's "Imperfect Sympathies"', *The Charles Lamb Bulletin* NS 114 (April 2001) 38–50.
15. Jane Stabler discusses Byron's treatment of the affair, pp. 147–8, below.
16. It was published 25 January 1801, despite having '1800' on its title-page.
17. For further discussion see Duncan Wu's essay, especially pp. 175–6 below.

1
Francis Jeffrey and the Scottish Critical Tradition

Philip Flynn

From the late seventeenth- through the mid-eighteenth century lowland Scotland's intellectual life was influenced by Jacobite, Episcopalian Scotsmen whose learning and activities were rooted in the Renaissance tradition of Humanist scholarship. Prominent among these Scottish Humanists were Sir Robert Sibbald, Sir George Mackenzie, Archibald Pitcairne and Sir John Clerk of Penicuik – men whose interests and activities included poetry, law, medicine, classical scholarship, antiquarianism, agricultural reform, the foundation of the Royal College of Physicians in Edinburgh and the codification of Scotland's criminal law. In the early eighteenth century this Humanist-Jacobite-Episcopalian tradition was promoted through the editorial and publishing activities of Thomas Ruddiman and Robert Freebairn, who attempted to preserve the Renaissance Scoto-Latin literary heritage while encouraging the adoption of Latin as eighteenth-century Scotland's international literary voice.

Their aspirations and traditions were not to prevail. After the Act of Union of 1707, with the defeat of the Jacobite rebellions, and with the emergence of the Moderate Party within the Church of Scotland, several generations of Whig-Presbyterian thinkers began to define the mainstream of Scottish intellectual culture. Among these were moderate clergy such as William Robertson; university professors such as Francis Hutcheson, Thomas Reid, Adam Smith and John Millar; physicians, chemists, lawyers, men of letters and of public affairs. From the 1720s through the 1820s this community found its primary expression through the medium of expository and analytical prose, and most members of this community were products of the courses in Moral Philosophy taught at the Scottish universities. The curricula of those courses included natural religion, moral and mental processes, political rights and social organization; and the writings of Hutcheson, Hume, Smith, Lord Kames, Reid, Adam

Ferguson and Dugald Stewart covered a broad range of psychological and socio-political subjects. They were profoundly influenced by the accomplishments and methodology of natural philosophy. At the same time, with the notable exception of Hume, they were determined to preserve a religious and teleological interpretation of human nature and the physical universe. Concentrated in the university cities of Edinburgh, Glasgow and Aberdeen – bound by a network of progressive clubs and personal friendships – this community constituted a large part of that cultural phenomenon known as the Scottish Enlightenment.

Francis Jeffrey and the *Edinburgh Review* were late children of that Enlightenment. Born in Edinburgh in 1773, a few months after the North Bridge had joined the medieval Old Town that Hume had known with the neoclassical New Town, 'the Athens of the North', Jeffrey was educated at the High School of Edinburgh, under the rectorship of Alexander Adam, the educational reformer whose students included Henry Brougham, Walter Scott and Henry Cockburn. He then matriculated at the 'Old College' in Glasgow, coming under the influence of its Professor of Logic and Rhetoric, George Jardine. Jardine's First Class of Philosophy – which Henry Cockburn would describe as 'the intellectual grindstone of the college'[1] – was a rigorous regimen of readings in primary philosophic texts and almost daily composition. Jardine's intention, as he explained in his *Outlines of Philosophical Education* (1818), was 'the formation of those intellectual habits of thinking, judging, reasoning, upon which the farther prosecution of Science, and the business of active life almost entirely depend'. To form those intellectual habits he introduced his students to 'the elements of the science of mind, with an analysis of the different intellectual powers, in the order of their connexion and dependence – the theory of language, as illustrative of human thought – the principles of taste and criticism – and the means of improving the powers of communication by speech and writing, as exhibited in the best models of ancient and modem composition.' Among the authors read and analysed in connection with 'the science of mind' were Aristotle, Aquinas, Bacon, Locke, Hume and Reid. To demonstrate the various 'principles of taste and criticism' Jardine assigned the works of Horace, Quintilian, Addison, Hutcheson and Burke. In their critical essays on imaginative literature Jeffrey and his classmates were taught to consider 'the Object, or Purpose, of the Author – the Quality of the Materials which he brings forward to accomplish his End – and the Skill which he displays in their Arrangement; together with the Propriety and Eloquence, of the Language in which they are Embodied'.[2]

For Jeffrey, soon to be an essayist and editor, Jardine's course was the most practical of educations. It introduced him to the western traditions of moral, epistemological and aesthetic inquiry, schooled him in analysis, taught him the relevant questions to ask when studying the methodology of a political scientist, moral psychologist or aesthetician. It taught him to sustain and discipline his intellectual growth through the regular exercise of analytical essays. Jardine's classroom was a school for critics. Years later, when Jeffrey became Rector of Glasgow College, he acknowledged his debt to Jardine in his inaugural address: 'the individual of whom I must be allowed to say *here*, what I have never omitted to say in every other place, that it is to him, and his most judicious instructions, that I owe my taste for letters, and any little literary distinction I may since have been enabled to attain.'[3]

After Glasgow, Jeffrey returned to Edinburgh to study Scottish and civil law at the university. He spent his spare time writing poetry, investigating chemistry and maintaining his Glasgow College regimen of philosophical reading, critical essays on that reading, and original essays on a broad range of subjects – some of which he later would expand into essays in the *Edinburgh Review*. In 1791–2 he spent ten desultory months at the Queen's College, Oxford, where instruction was the bored leading the bored and where the languid undergraduate dinner parties seemed to the effervescent Scotsman a 'complete abuse of time, wine, and fruit'.[4] Escaping back to Edinburgh he completed his legal studies and was called to the Scottish bar. With few briefs to plead he attended Dugald Stewart's lectures on political economy, studied Spanish and made translations from the Greek 'with a fine poetical fury'.[5] He was also reading current political books and controversial pamphlets, developing a liberal but pragmatic temper that distrusted both doctrinaire egalitarians and autocratic Tories. He was able to refine that position at meetings of the Speculative Society, a descendant of the earlier clubs of Smith and Hume, and now the most distinguished of Edinburgh's literary forums. There he listened to speeches by Dugald Stewart, Walter Scott, William Smellie, editor of the *Encyclopaedia Britannica*; James Mackintosh, whose *Vindiciae Gallicae* (1791) had recently appeared; and Henry Erskine, leader of the Scottish Whigs and Dean of the Faculty of Advocates.

Among the younger Scottish Whigs and members of 'the Spec' were Henry Brougham and Francis Horner – like Jeffrey, still struggling members of that Faculty of Advocates whose conversation Lockhart described as 'brilliant disquisition – such as might be transferred without alteration to a professor's notebook, or the pages of a critical Review'.[6]

It was such a Review that Sydney Smith suggested when he met Jeffrey, Horner, Brougham and Thomas Brown at the Academy of Physics, where those polymaths were deep in 'the investigation of nature, the laws by which her phenomena are regulated, and the history of opinions concerning these laws'.[7] Through the winter of 1801–2 plans for the new review were developed: there would be Thomas Brown for metaphysical subjects, Homer for political economy, Brougham for mathematics and colonial administration, Thomas Thomson for antiquarian subjects – and Jeffrey, '*facile princeps* in all kinds of literature', *de omni scribili* for everything else.[8]

In time, Jeffrey would write over 200 essays for the *Edinburgh Review*, carrying the tradition and training of late eighteenth-century Scotland into the early nineteenth century. In an atmosphere of Jacobin extremism and Tory reaction, Jeffrey and his *Review* kept alive that spirit of analytical philosophy that Adam Smith had prescribed as 'the great antidote to the poison of enthusiasm and superstition'.[9] His essays on epistemology and politics were lessons learned from Hume and John Millar. His writings on aesthetics and on moral psychology were applications and reappraisals of the work of Archibald Alison, Francis Hutcheson, Lord Kames and Adam Smith.

Jeffrey's sceptical position on those epistemological issues that loomed large in Scotland's 'science of mind' was revealed through his reviews of works by members of the Scottish School of Common Sense, whose writings he had encountered in Jardine's classroom at Glasgow and among the students of Dugald Stewart in Edinburgh.[10] That position was the 'mitigated scepticism' advocated by Hume.[11] In his *Treatise of Human Nature* (1739–40) and *Enquiry concerning Human Understanding* (1748) Hume had denied that empirical reason can validate our beliefs on many basic subjects – for example, our belief in a continuing substratum of personal identity; our belief that our perceptions are caused by a material world that exists independently of our perceptions; our beliefs in the uniformity of nature, in necessary connection, in causal relationship – beliefs basic to Christian eschatology, natural theology and scientific induction. Moreover, Hume's reduction of these beliefs to feelings, to the sensitive rather than the cognitive level of our nature, raised basic problems of subjectivism. If our sensitive organization were different, would we not have different feelings and, thus, different beliefs? Perhaps we would, but Hume did not press the point. He recognized that our beliefs in personal identity, in the existence of a material world and in causal relationship are part of the basic common sense of mankind and that the practical demands of life force us to proceed as if those beliefs are true.

Hume's writings were studied closely by members of the Aberdeen Philosophical Society, whose members included Thomas Reid, George Campbell, Alexander Gerard and James Beattie; and several papers read by members of the Society were later published as formal responses to different aspects of Hume's thought. Among those publications were Campbell's *Dissertation on Miracles* (1763), Beattie's *Essay on the Nature and Immutability of Truth* (1770), and – most influential – Reid's *Inquiry into the Human Mind, on the Principles of Common Sense* (1764). In the *Inquiry* Reid accused Hume of accepting, without experimental proof, tenets of what Reid called 'the ideal system' – a model of our mental life that confines human knowledge to the subjective world of its own impressions and ideas. While he rejected that system as a flawed hypothesis, Reid denied that he had any ambition of constructing a mental model of his own. None the less, in his subsequent *Essays on the Intellectual Powers of Man* (1785), Reid identified a series of intuitive judgments – 'first principles, principles of common sense, common notions, self-evident truths' – including our belief in a continuing personal identity, our belief in the uniformity of nature and our belief that whatever exists must have had a prior cause.[12] Like Hume, Reid acknowledged that these natural beliefs cannot be validated through discursive reasoning. Rather, these beliefs are the first principles of reasoning. Unlike Hume, Reid concluded that these natural beliefs are not reducible to feelings. They are real judgements – 'determinations concerning what is true and what is false' – and the 'inspirations of the Almighty'.[13]

In formal philosophy Jeffrey was wary of inspirations of the Almighty. He sought for the empirically verifiable content of any philosophical system. He was suspicious of mysticism in any form, be it the Quaker doctrine of Inner Light or the 'misty metaphysics' of Goethe's *Wilhelm Meister's Apprenticeship*.[14] He believed that a valid epistemology must confine itself to the description and classification of the phenomena of common consciousness, 'those primary functions of the mind, which are possessed in common by men of *all* vocations and *all* conditions'.[15] We have experiential knowledge of those functions, and epistemologists may observe and describe the laws by which they appear to be governed. However, 'we only know the existence of mind by the exercise of its functions', so the question of 'the essence of the thinking principle' remains an area 'of mere conjecture and uncertainty', and the teleology of mental activity is 'a domain into which our limited faculties do not permit us to enter'.[16] Reviewing the work of Reid, Beattie and Stewart, he concluded that their arguments concerning the uniformity of nature, the evidence of distinct memory and the existence of a material world are, as Hume maintained, vulnerable to sceptical objections. A candid man will admit the theoretical value of Hume's mitigated scepticism; a wise man will live his life as if those beliefs common to our species are true. 'As this speculative scepticism neither renders us independent of the ordinary modes of investigation, nor assists us materially in the use of them, it is inexpedient to dwell long upon it in the course of our philosophical inquiries, and much more adviseable to proceed upon the supposition that the real condition of things is conformable to our natural apprehensions.'[17] Life – even the examined life – goes on.

Jeffrey's study of Scotland's philosophical activity convinced him that a consistently empirical epistemology has limitations that its practitioners had not always recognized. In 1802, Dugald Stewart published an *Account of the Life and Writings of Thomas Reid*, a version of which he had read earlier before the Royal Society of Edinburgh. In the *Account*, and in his later *Philosophical Essays* (1810), Stewart praised Reid's *Inquiry* as a product of the genuine spirit of inductive study, the first systematic attempt to study human faculties according to the plan of investigation that Bacon had outlined in the *Novum Organum* and that Newton had followed with success in physics. Reviewing the *Account* and the *Philosophical Essays*, Jeffrey noted Stewart's hopeful prediction that, should later thinkers follow Reid in a truly Baconian study of the mind, a science of human nature could be developed that would include grammar, rhetoric, logic, politics, natural theology and ethics. Jeffrey judged that hope to be a fond delusion common among metaphysicians. Stewart, Reid and Hume, for all the differences between them, had been misled by the same analogy: in comparing the study of the mind with contemporary physics they had confused the phenomena of mere observation with the phenomena of true experiment. As Bacon had written, knowledge is power, and the phenomena suitable to experiment 'are actually in our power, and the judgment and artifice of the inquirer can be effectually employed to arrange and combine them in such a way as to disclose their most hidden properties and relations'. Mental phenomena, however, are the subject of mere observation – phenomena 'the order and succession of which we are generally unable to controul, [and] as to which we can do little more than collect and record the laws by which they appear to be governed'.[18] The methodology and progress of the physical sciences could not be applied to or expected in the study of the mind:

> In reality, it does not appear to us that any great advancement of our knowledge of the operations of mind is to be expected from any improvement in the plan of investigation, or that the condition of

mankind is likely to derive any great benefit from the cultivation of this interesting but abstracted study.[19]

In thus distinguishing experimental science from a philosophy based upon observation, Jeffrey anticipated both the specific separation of experimental psychology from the academic philosophy of mind and the general separation of science from philosophy that would accelerate later in the nineteenth century.

As in epistemology, Jeffrey's thinking on moral psychology was influenced by his study of eighteenth-century Scottish moral philosophers. Rejecting the pessimistic views of human nature found in their native Calvinism and in the writings of Hobbes and Mandeville, the majority of those philosophers affirmed man's capacity for benevolent action and natural desire for harmonious relations with others. 'If any opinions deserve to be contended for', Francis Hutcheson stated in his *Inquiry into the Original of Our Ideas of Beauty and Virtue* (1725),

> they are those which give us lovely Ideas of the DEITY and of our *Fellow-Creatures*: If any Opinions deserve Opposition, they are such as raise Scruples in our Minds about the Goodness of PROVIDENCE, or represent our Fellow-Creatures as *base* and *selfish*, by instilling into us some ill-natur'd, cunning, shrewd Insinuations, 'that our most generous Actions proceed wholly from *selfish Views*'.[20]

Hutcheson' s *Inquiry* and *Essay on the Nature and Conduct of the Passions and Affections* (1728), Hume's *Treatise and Enquiry concerning the Principles of Morals* (1751), Lord Kames's *Essays on the Principles of Morality and Natural Religion* (1751) and Adam Smith's *Theory of Moral Sentiments* (1759) concurred in identifying the 'passions', 'sentiments' and 'feelings' as the motivating forces in human conduct and the source of our ideas of virtue and vice. Hutcheson and Kames argued that humans feel a natural attraction towards virtue, an attraction felt through a 'moral sense', while Hume and Smith explained our moral sentiments in terms of 'sympathy'. With the exception of Hume, these philosophers claimed that the study of man's moral life inexorably leads us to God: the evidence of moral design in the human frame is proof of the existence of a moral government, just as evidence of physical design in the external world proves intelligent design in that sphere. Kames described conscience or the moral sense as 'the voice of God within us'.[21] Reid believed that, in the study of human moral faculties, 'the noblest work of GOD that falls within our notice, we may discern most clearly the character of him who made us'.[22] At that point Hume parted company. Although he agreed that feelings are the basis of our moral distinctions, his moral analysis was naturalistic: different creatures with different feelings would develop different standards of virtue and vice, as natural and valid for them as human standards are for us. Hume did not find in our moral sentiments any evidence of divine design.

As Jeffrey knew, the early and mid-eighteenth-century theories that based moral distinctions upon feelings carried with them a danger of moral relativism, and Scottish thinkers of the later eighteenth and early nineteenth centuries had already recognized that danger. Looking back upon his century's progress in the science of morals, Dugald Stewart cited the concern with moral *theory*, as opposed to practical moral exhortation, as the feature that most clearly divided modern writings from the writings of moral philosophers before Hobbes.[23] But James Oswald, in his *Appeal to Common Sense in Behalf of Religion* (1767–72), had insisted that the fascination with moral theory had obscured the proper business of a moral writer: his elaboration of the moral duties of life.[24] James Beattie had devoted long sections of his *Elements of Moral Science* (1790), an abridgment of lectures delivered at Marischal College, Aberdeen, to warnings against metaphysical moralists and to direct moral exhortation. And Thomas Reid recognized that the subjectivistic emphasis of recent moral analysis had led logically to Hume's conclusion that men's moral judgements are not judgements of objective fact, but expressions of our subjective sentiments or feelings. Hume's conclusion, Reid believed, was potentially destructive to morality and natural religion:

> If what we call *moral judgment* be no real judgment, but merely a feeling, it follows that the principles of morals...have no other foundation but an arbitrary structure and fabric in the constitution of the human mind: So that, by a change in our structure, what is immoral might become moral.... It follows that, from our notions of morals, we can conclude nothing concerning a moral character in the Deity, which is the foundation of all religion, and the strongest support of virtue.[25]

For Reid, James Oswald, James Beattie and Dugald Stewart, Scottish theories from Hutcheson through Smith seemed milestones on a road to moral scepticism – the replacement of Right Reason by moral 'Taste', the denial of moral liberty in the name of determinism, the abandonment of stern duty in pursuit of the pleasures of benevolence, sympathy or recognized utility.[26]

Where did Jeffrey stand along that road? Close to Hume, whose moral theory, 'when rightly understood', he believed to be 'both salutary and true' in that it acknowledged the subjectivist confusion to which a rigorous empiricism may lead in the field of moral psychology.[27] Jeffrey believed that humans are motivated by the desire to enjoy pleasure and avoid pain; that the degree of pleasure or pain involved in any attitude of mind or course of conduct 'is ascertained by feeling, and not determined by reason or reflection'; that our feelings of moral approbation and disapprobation develop from these 'instinctive and involuntary' evaluations; and that our ideas of moral good and evil develop associatively through the repetition of pleasurable or painful experiences.[28] Unhappily for moral philosophers, the wide diversity of human pleasures – and the diverse feelings of moral approbation to which those diverse pleasures give rise – cannot always be explained as our appreciation of propriety or moral harmony or general utility, however appealing such explanations may be to philosophers who attempt to use empirical psychology to illustrate divine providence.

> Our feelings of approbation and disapprobation, and the moral distinctions which are raised upon them, are *facts* which no theory can alter, although it may fail to explain. While these facts remain, they must regulate the conduct, and affect the happiness of mankind, whether they are well or ill accounted for by the theories of philosophers.[29]

As in epistemology he entertained the more sceptical elements within eighteenth-century Scottish thought, Jeffrey accepted the more relativistic elements in eighteenth-century moral psychology. But he developed a pragmatic moral standard through a philosophical manoeuvre similar to that by which he developed a pragmatic position in epistemology. Noting that our natural beliefs concerning the existence of external objects and the accuracy of distinct memory cannot be fully verified by empirical reason, Jeffrey also noted that normal humans have such beliefs and must be guided by them in practical life and other areas of investigation. Noting the frequent diversity and disparity in human pleasures and moral judgements, Jeffrey also found 'common impressions of morality, the vulgar distinctions of right and wrong, virtue and vice'.[30] He believed those common impressions to be the record of humanity's collective experience of pleasure and pain, and simple pragmatism should lead us to consider that collective experience in shaping our own attitudes and actions.

Although he thought that teleological explanations of our moral sentiments are 'presumptuous and inconclusive',[31] Jeffrey used the experiential moral consensus as his standard in evaluating the programmes of reformers in his radical age. Reviewing Bentham's *Traités de legislation* (1802) he warned that even a brilliant reformer might overlook or undervalue important aspects of human happiness:

> It is in aid of this oversight, of this omission, of this partiality, that we refer to the *general rules* of morality; rules, which have been suggested by a larger observation, and a longer experience, than any individual can dream of pretending to, and which have been accommodated by the joint action of our sympathies with delinquents and sufferers to the actual condition of human fortitude and infirmity.... Such summaries of utility, such records of uniform observation, we conceive to be the *general rules of morality*, by which, and by which alone, legislators or individuals can be safely directed in determining on the propriety of any course of conduct.[32]

This was the pragmatic conservatism of a theoretical sceptic – the position of Montaigne and Hume.

The branch of philosophy known as aesthetics developed under several different titles in eighteenth-century Scotland, and studies of aesthetic psychology (books on 'taste', 'genius', 'rhetoric', 'criticism' or 'belles lettres') were closely connected with Scottish studies of moral psychology. As in moral psychology Scottish writers were determined to develop what Hume called the 'Science of Man', attempting to develop aesthetic principles through an inductive analysis of human responses. Although they often cited Aristotle, Quintilian and Longinus, they rejected what William Duff called the 'servile deference to antiquity'.[33] 'Criticism is founded wholly on experience,' Hugh Blair remarked, 'on the observation of such beauties...as have been found to please mankind most generally.'[34] Lord Kames's plan, as he explained in the introduction to his *Elements of Criticism* (1762), was 'to ascend gradually to principles, from facts and experiments; instead of beginning with the former, handled abstractedly, and descending to the latter'.[35] In describing a sound critical method, Alexander Gerard could use the language of contemporary science: 'it investigates those qualities in its objects which, from the invariable principles of human nature, must always please or displease; describes and distinguishes the sentiments which they in fact produce; and impartially regulates its most general conclusions according to real phenomena.'[36]

Admitting the vagaries of personal associations and the influence of disparate cultural environments, the majority of Scottish aestheticians attempted to establish a standard of taste. They believed that aesthetic responses are psychologically allied to moral sentiments – 'effects of the same cause, streams issuing from the same fountain', wrote Gerard[37] – and they recognized that relativism in aesthetic questions might lead to anarchy in moral matters. 'A taste in the fine arts goes hand in hand with the moral sense, to which indeed it is nearly allied,' Kames remarked.

> Both of them discover what is right and what is wrong: fashion, temper, and education have an influence to vitiate both, or to preserve them pure and untainted: neither of them are arbitrary nor local, being rooted in human nature and governed by principles common to all men.

If we once admit that there is no disputing about tastes, Kames warned, it must follow that 'there is not such a thing as a *good* or a *bad*, a *right* or a *wrong;* that every man' s taste is to himself an ultimate standard without appeal; and consequently that there is no ground of censure against anyone, if such a one there be, who prefers Blackmore before Homer, selfishness before benevolence, or cowardice before magnanimity'.[38]

Francis Hutcheson's *Inquiry* was the first important Scottish study of aesthetic psychology, and Hutcheson recognized the danger of aesthetic/ moral relativism. Defining beauty as an 'idea raised in us', he inquired 'what real quality' in external objects normally excites this idea. Influenced by both Shaftesbury and Locke, Hutcheson argued that men share an involuntary 'sense of beauty' – an internal sense capable of receiving stimuli from without and of subsequently raising the idea of beauty in our minds. But Hutcheson believed that 'original beauty' is excited by only one formal quality – the quality of uniformity amidst variety – as that uniformity is perceived in works of nature or of art. Thus Hutcheson was able to combine an essentially subjectivistic aesthetic theory with a common standard of beauty, a 'real quality'. If beauty is in the eye of the beholder, it is in the eye of every normal human beholder as he encounters uniformity amidst variety in geometric figures, pleasure gardens or poetic metre.[39]

In time Kames and Blair came to reject Hutcheson's standard of beauty as too narrow. Writing in the name of nature's 'economy' Hume and Adam Smith rejected Hutcheson's notion of a distinct aesthetic sense. The debt that these writers owed to Shaftesbury and Hutcheson was basic: the emphasis upon aesthetic response. But human responses and the formal qualities that excited them proved to be remarkably varied. As the century progressed Scottish aestheticians concerned themselves with a wide range of psychological effects – the effects of sublimity and novelty among them – and their attempt to establish a standard of taste was complicated by the Scottish interest in 'rude societies' and primitive literature. That interest itself was part of the strong Scottish tradition of sociological and anthropological study. Scottish historians, sociologists and anthropologists – Gilbert Stuart, William Robertson, James Dunbar, Adam Ferguson, Lord Monboddo, Adam Smith, David Hume, John Millar – had been exploring the shaping effect of environment upon both past and present peoples, developing a 'natural or theoretical history of society' that Dugald Stewart thought to be 'the peculiar glory of the latter half of the eighteenth century'.[40] This sociological/anthropological perspective was applied to literature in Thomas Blackwell's *Enquiry into the Life and Writings of Homer* (1735), William Duff's *Essay on Original Genius* (1767), Lord Kames's *Sketches of the History of Man* (1774) and Hugh Blair's *Critical Dissertation on the Poems of Ossian* (1763) and *Lectures on Rhetoric and Belles Lettres* (1783). By the end of the century Archibald Alison was willing to admit the relativistic implications of Scotland's search for a standard of taste. Aesthetic responses, Alison believed, are the products of association of ideas, and individual associations, he admitted, are inevitably shaped by our personal experience and temper.

In his *Essays on the Nature and Principles of Taste* (1790) Alison was careful to distinguish aesthetic emotions from the moral sentiments. With that distinction he freed 'taste' from its earlier connection with the 'moral sense', and was himself free to develop fully an associationist aesthetic. Nothing in nature or in art, he argued, is of itself sublime or beautiful. The terms *sublime* and *beautiful* should be understood as describing the emotions that we feel in contemplating works of nature or of art. These 'emotions of taste' are not produced directly by qualities intrinsic in landscape, sculpture, poetry or music. A mountain storm or landscape by Claude Lorrain moves us aesthetically only by suggesting some aspect of sentient life that is capable of raising a 'simple emotion' of pity, melancholy, gaiety or awe, and then by triggering a train of associated thoughts that are coloured by that simple emotion. The consequent and complex aesthetic emotions – the 'emotions of taste' – are eventually aroused through that process of associative activity that the work of art or nature has first prompted.[41]

Alison and Jeffrey were members of the Friday Club in Edinburgh, and they may have discussed aesthetics there. Jeffrey had applied associationist psychology to aesthetic matters in essays he wrote while in college,[42] and he had praised investigations of association as the most fruitful aspect of eighteenth-century epistemology.[43] When a second and enlarged edition of Alison's *Essays* appeared in 1810, Jeffrey gave the book a lengthy and approving review, in which he discussed the eighteenth-century debate about the standard of taste, referring indirectly to Burke, Hogarth, Hutcheson, Hume and other writers. Alison's theory, he thought, had carried that debate to its only possible conclusion. 'If things are not beautiful in themselves, but only as they serve to suggest interesting conceptions to the mind,' Jeffrey observed,

> then every thing which does in point of fact suggest such a conception to any individual, *is beautiful* to that individual; and it is not only quite true that there is no room for disputing about tastes, but that all tastes are equally just and correct, in so far as each individual speaks only of his own emotions.

That conclusion, at first reading, seemed to strip the critic of his basic role. But Jeffrey – adapting ideas expressed earlier by Beattie, Alison and Dugald Stewart – defined a working standard for applied criticism. He believed that it is the critic's function to distinguish between associative relations felt by all men and women, 'where the object is necessarily and universally connected with the feeling by a law of nature', and peculiar, accidental relations 'where this perception of beauty is not universal, but entirely dependent upon the opportunities which each individual has had to associate ideas of emotion with the object to which it is ascribed'. Poets and novelists should not speak only of their own emotions. It is the duty of the imaginative writer to employ 'only such objects as are the *natural* signs and *inseparable* concomitants of emotions, of which the greater part of mankind are susceptible; and his taste will *then* deserve to be called bad and false, if he obtrude upon the public, as beautiful, objects that are not likely to be associated in common minds with any interesting impressions'.[44]

This was Jeffrey's standard of aesthetic consensus, which he applied to the works of Wordsworth, Scott, Crabbe and other contemporary writers.[45] It was consistent with the standard of moral consensus that he used in evaluating the social panaceas proposed by writers such as Bentham and Godwin. Granting that our individual notions of virtue and vice develop from subjective, associational assessments of the pleasure or pain involved with any attitude of mind or course of conduct, there are, none the less, 'common impressions of morality, the vulgar distinctions of right and wrong' that may serve as a pragmatic moral standard. So, too, if individual ideas of beauty are based upon subjective associational responses, there are common associations that may serve as a practical aesthetic standard.

In practice, however, those common associations – the 'emotions of which the greater part of mankind are susceptible' – proved to be a vague point of reference. They might serve as a means of explaining the enduring appeal of established classics from the past. But which group's associational responses could represent our common human nature in the early nineteenth century? Reviewing works of Keats, Wordsworth and Scott at a specific moment in Britain's cultural development, Jeffrey often spoke for a limited consensus, equating 'the greater part of mankind' with the range of associative response to be expected among middle-class readers in Edinburgh and London. His very awareness of the factors contributing to relativism forced him to appeal, as his safest guide, to what men of his own class and education felt and thought.

Although Jeffrey is now remembered primarily for his criticism of imaginative literature, in his own time he and his *Review* were praised or damned primarily as a political force. Jeffrey's circle had inherited a stimulating heritage of eighteenth-century Scottish debate on political authority, economy and evolution – a debate that involved Hutcheson's *System of Moral Philosophy* (1755), Hume's *Three Essays, Moral and Political* (1748) and *Political Discourses* (1752), Smith's *Inquiry into the Nature and Causes of the Wealth of Nations* (1776) and Adam Ferguson's *Principles of Moral and Political Science* (1792) and *Essay on the History of Civil Society* (1767). Moreover, in his days as a student and struggling young lawyer, Jeffrey was exposed to two of the more liberal and charismatic figures in Scottish academic life. The first was John Millar, Professor of Civil Law at Glasgow and protégé of Kames, Smith and Hume. Millar's forceful presentation of a liberal Whig interpretation of history, published in his *Historical View of the English Government* (1787–1803), attracted to Glasgow the sons of English and Scottish Whig families – among them James Moncrieff and George Cranstoun, both to become prominent Whig lawyers and allies of the *Edinburgh Review*.[46] In his lecture-room and other public fora, Millar advocated a broad range of reforms: an extension of the electoral franchise, constitutional control of government's expenditure, abolition of the slave trade and improved education for the lower classes. In the process he made powerful enemies. Alexander Carlyle, speaking for many Scottish political conservatives, complained of the 'democratic principles and that sceptical philosophy which young noblemen and gentlemen of legislative rank carried into the world with them from his law class'.[47] In the mid-nineteenth century an Edinburgh Reviewer, discussing the impact of Millar's thought, suggested 'that the bold lines of thought on which the "Edinburgh Review" was afterwards constructed, were first laid down by his masterly hand'.[48]

The second of those teachers who influenced the political attitudes of Jeffrey's circle was Dugald Stewart, Professor of Moral Philosophy at Edinburgh, a man whose 'gentle and persuasive eloquence' has been described by James Mackintosh, Henry Cockburn and others.[49] Although his popularity as a teacher was pre-eminent at the university, Stewart's liberal political principles made him the target of angry criticism. His Edinburgh home was a social centre for Scottish and English liberals; his friendship with the French *philosophes* led him to welcome the first movements of the French Revolution; and his course in political economy drew many of the Scottish and English Whigs who would inaugurate the *Edinburgh Review* and, years later, push through Parliament the First Reform Bill. Jeffrey encountered Stewart's thinking in three contexts: as a student in Stewart's course in political economy, as a reader and reviewer of Stewart's writings, and as a member of Edinburgh's most respected club, the Speculative Society.

The *Edinburgh Review* was conceived of and conducted as a liberal Whig quarterly – the term *liberal* encompassing the beliefs that religious tolerance, representative government, security of private property and a sense of international community are necessary for social progress – the term *Whig* implying, not subservience to the Holland House circle or any other faction, but a respect for government on the basis of its secular utility rather than on the basis of Divine Right or reverence for ancient institutions. Within those guidelines Jeffrey as editor rode his anonymous reviewers with a loose rein, allowing them to argue positions on contemporary issues that Jeffrey himself was sometimes hard-pressed to defend. In a letter to Francis Horner, one of his more sober contributors, he tried to justify his editorial policy:

> Perhaps it would have been better to have kept more to general views. But in such times as we have lived in, it was impossible not to mix them, as in fact they mix themselves, with questions which might be considered as of a narrower and more factious description. In substance it appeared to me that my only absolute duty as to political discussion, was to forward the great ends of liberty, and to exclude nothing but what had a tendency to promote servile, sordid, and corrupt principles. As to the *means* of attaining these ends, I thought that considerable latitude should be indulged, and that

unless the excesses were very great and revolting, every man of talent should be allowed to take his own way of recommending them.[50]

The core of Jeffrey's own political philosophy can be found in his essays on electoral and economic reform. In the first number of the *Edinburgh Review*, in an essay on Mounier's *De l'influence attribuée aux philosophes . . . sur la révolution de France* (1801), Jeffrey advised British readers to 'begin to study the moral of that great tragedy'.[51] The tragedy was the French Revolution; the moral was that 'all political power, even the most despotic, rests at last, as was profoundly observed by Hume, upon Opinion'.[52] Hume's observation is contained in his mid-eighteenth-century essay, 'Of the First Principles of Government', and Jeffrey attempted to apply that observation to Britain in the early nineteenth century.[53] Reviewing Gould Francis Leckie's *Essay on the Practice of the British Government* (1812) Jeffrey argued that the power of a sovereign is only the power that a certain faction of his subjects lends him to put his wishes into practice, and the effective check to the power of the sovereign is the refusal of that faction to act as instruments of their sovereign's will. In the early nineteenth century Britain had evolved to the stage in which a large proportion of the population had knowledge of and interest in the conduct of its rulers. Now, in Britain,

> the substantial power of the nation may be said to be vested in the nation at large; or at least in those individuals who can habitually command the good-will and support of the greater part of them; and the ultimate check to the power of the sovereign comes to consist in the general unwillingness of The People to comply with those orders which, if at all united in their resolution, they may securely disobey and resist.[54]

If Britain was to avoid revolution and the fate of France, there must be a mechanism by which the mature opinion of the people could be brought to bear peacefully upon the officers of government. Did the British Parliament, as then constituted, serve as such a mechanism? Gradually Jeffrey came to recognize and then publicly acknowledge that Parliament did not. In a series of articles in the *Review* and in letters to Whig friends in England he argued that the people now possessed more wealth and intelligence than at any former time in British history, 'and therefore they ought to have, and they must have, more political power'.[55] Parliament must recognize their widespread discontent; reforms must be adopted to appease that discontent:

We, in short, are for the monarchy and the aristocracy of England, as the only sure supports of a permanent and regulated freedom; but we do not see how either is now to be preserved, except by surrounding them with the affection of the people. The admirers of arbitrary power, blind to the great lesson which all Europe now holds out to them, have attempted to dispense with this protection; and the demagogues have taken advantage of their folly to excite the people to withdraw it altogether. The friends of the constitution must now bring it back; and must reconcile the people to the old monarchy and the old Parliament of their land, by restraining the prerogative within its legitimate bounds, and by bringing back Parliament to its natural habits of sympathy and concord with its constituents.[56]

The alternative to such a reconciliation would be eventual civil insurrection. Jeffrey reminded his readers of France and 'the most obvious and important lesson in the whole volume of history, that the nation which has recourse to arms for the settlement of its internal affairs, necessarily falls under the iron yoke of a military government in the end, and that nothing but the most evident necessity can justify the lovers of freedom in forcing it from the hands of their governors'.[57] That lesson had been stated in the conclusion of chapter 60 of Hume's *History of England* (1754–62), a chapter that Jeffrey believed to be 'deserving of the most profound meditation', as he believed Hume to be 'the most profound and philosophical of historians'.[58]

John Gibson Lockhart characterized Jeffrey's circle as 'the progeny of the sceptical philosophers of the last age'.[59] That description did not fit all the reviewers, but it was a respectable thumbnail sketch of Jeffrey. Jeffrey had received an eighteenth-century Scottish education – a philosophical education that had introduced him to the major thinkers on moral and mental processes, on aesthetics, on political rights and the evolution of social structures. In the end, Hume proved to be the strongest influence. On basic epistemological and ontological questions, Jeffrey acknowledged the theoretical validity of the more sceptical elements of eighteenth-century Scottish thought. In moral psychology and aesthetics he accepted the more relativistic implications of the Scottish enquiry. In politics his essential pragmatism led him to advocate reforms primarily because public opinion now demanded those reforms, and he believed that public opinion was now the basis of political stability. Although the tone of the *Review* was often magisterial, its editor distrusted all forms of dogmatism. To Francis Horner, one of its co-founders, he remained 'my dear Pyrrhonist'[60] – a critic whose awareness of the fallibility of individual reasoning, including his own, forced him to appeal to 'natural beliefs', 'common impressions of morality' and a consensus of aesthetic response as his standards of conduct and judgement.

Notes

1. Cockburn, i 9.
2. Cockburn, i 10.
3. Cockburn, i 16–17.
4. Cockburn, i 39.
5. Cockburn, ii 23.
6. John Gibson Lockhart, *Memoirs of the Life of Sir Walter Scott* (Boston, 1901), v 244.
7. David Welsh, *Account of the Life and Writings of Thomas Brown* (Edinburgh, 1825), p. 77.
8. Henry Lord Brougham, *The Life and Times of Lord Brougham* (3 vols, Edinburgh, 1871), i 252.
9. Adam Smith, *An Inquiry into the Nature and Causes of the Wealth of Nations, The Glasgow Edition of the Works and Correspondence of Adam Smith*, ed. R. H. Campbell and A. S. Skinner (Oxford: Clarendon Press, 1976), ii 796.
10. 'Pneumatology' – the traditional scholastic term – was used throughout the eighteenth century, although 'science of mind' or 'philosophy of mind' was preferred by those writers who wished to disassociate themselves from the scholastic tradition. 'Psychology' came to be a prominent term in the early nineteenth century. 'Epistemology' was not coined until the mid-nineteenth century, by James Frederick Ferrier of St Andrews.
11. David Hume, 'An Enquiry Concerning Human Understanding', *The Philosophical Works* ed. T. H. Green and T. H. Grose (1882), iv 132.
12. Thomas Reid, *Essays on the Intellectual Powers of Man* (Edinburgh, 1785), p. 555.
13. Ibid., 504.
14. See *Edinburgh Review* 10 (April 1807) 101–2; 42 (August 1825) 417.
15. *Edinburgh Review* 17 (November 1810) 180.
16. Ibid., 172.
17. *Edinburgh Review* 7 (October 1805) 175.
18. *Edinburgh Review* 17 (November 1810) 184. In his *Philosophical Essays* (1810), Stewart responded to Jeffrey's 1804 review of his *Account*. Jeffrey restated and expanded his criticism in the November 1810 review of the *Philosophical Essays*.
19. *Edinburgh Review* 3 (January 1804) 273. Jeffrey was not the first to identify this problem. Hume had acknowledged that the act of observing our mental operations affects what is being observed. Alexander Gerard and Thomas Reid both recognized that mental phenomena are not so easily subjected to experiment as are physical bodies.
20. Francis Hutcheson, *An Inquiry into the Original of Our Ideas of Beauty and Virtue* (2nd edn, London, 1726), pp. 208–9.

21. Henry Home, Lord Kames, *Essays on the Principles of Morality and Natural Religion* (Edinburgh, 1751), p. 63.
22. Thomas Reid, *Essays on the Active Powers of Man* (Edinburgh, 1788), p. 98.
23. Dugald Stewart, *The Philosophy of the Active and Moral Powers of Man* (Edinburgh, 1828).
24. See the quotations from Oswald's rambling *Appeal* in Gavin Ardley's concise *The Common Sense Philosophy of James Oswald* (Aberdeen: Aberdeen University Press, 1980), pp. 11, 16, 57.
25. Thomas Reid, *Essays on the Active Powers of Man* (Edinburgh, 1788), pp. 491–2.
26. See ibid., pp. 22–41, 52–95; Oswald as quoted in Ardley's *Common Sense Philosophy of James Oswald*, pp. 31, 87; James Beattie, *Elements of Moral Science* (1790–3), i 373–403; Stewart, *Philosophy of the Active and Moral Powers of Man*, 209–22, 268–324.
27. *Edinburgh Review* 10 (April 1807) 197. See Sydney Smith's letter to Jeffrey, April or May 1804, in which he mimics Jeffrey's Humean analysis of the moral sentiments; Nowell Smith i 95–6.
28. *Edinburgh Review* 7 (January 1806) 416; 10 (April 1807) 89; 4 (April 1804) 12; see also *Edinburgh Review* 13 (January 1809) 349–50.
29. *Edinburgh Review* 10 (April 1807) 197.
30. *Edinburgh Review* 4 (April 1804) 11.
31. *Edinburgh Review* 7 (January 1806) 418.
32. Hutcheson, *Enquiry* 177.
33. William Duff, *An Essay on Original Genius* (London, 1767), p. 254.
34. Hugh Blair, *Lectures on Rhetoric and Belles Lettres* (2 vols, London, 1783), i 37.
35. Kames, *Elements of Criticism* (6th edn, Edinburgh, 1785), i 13.
36. Alexander Gerard, *An Essay on Taste* (2nd edn, Edinburgh, 1764), p. 181.
37. Ibid., 191.
38. Kames, *Elements of Criticism* i 6, ii 488.
39. See Treatise I ('Concerning Beauty, Order, Harmony, Design') of Hutcheson's *Inquiry into the Original of Our Ideas of Beauty and Virtue*. Hutcheson distinguished what he called *original* or *absolute* beauty (the idea of uniformity amidst variety), from *comparative* or *relative* beauty (the idea of just imitation), a distinction subsequently adopted by Kames in his *Elements*.
40. 'Dissertation Exhibiting a General View of the Progress of Metaphysical, Ethical, and Political Philosophy', *The Works of Dugald Stewart* (Cambridge, 1829), vi 65.
41. See Archibald Alison, *Essays on the Nature and Principles of Taste* (New York, 1844), pp. vii–xvi, 19–113.
42. See the section of Jeffrey's Oxford essay on beauty, quoted Cockburn, i 39.
43. See *Edinburgh Review* 3 (January 1804) 277. Jeffrey probably took his associationism from Hume and Adam Smith rather than from Hartley.
44. *Edinburgh Review* 18 (May 1811) 40, 43, 44. This review, in revised form, was the article on 'Beauty' that Jeffrey contributed to the Supplement of the 1824 edition of the *Encyclopaedia Britannica*. It was published subsequently in the 1841 edition of the *Encyclopaedia* and included in Jeffrey's *Contributions*. In revising this review Jeffrey criticized more closely Alison's claim that the free play of associative imagination is the essence of aesthetic response.
45. It was not, however, the only standard he used. Most eighteenth-century Scottish aestheticians had agreed that art is an important force of moral

instruction, operating more often through our sympathetic emotions than through our reason's grasp of moral principles. In the Preface to his collected *Contributions* Jeffrey asked to be remembered for having made 'the moral tendencies of the works under consideration a leading subject of discussion'. For Jeffrey's criticisms of Byron, Burns, Campbell, Rogers and the Lake Poets on *moral* grounds, see *Edinburgh Review* 27 (December 1816) 281, 36 (February 1822) 438, 13 (January 1809) 253, 14 (April 1809) 1–2, 31 (March 1819) 325–52, 1 (October 1802) 64.

46. Jeffrey reviewed Millar's works in *Edinburgh Review* 3 (October 1803) 154–81 and 9 (October 1806) 83–92.

47. Alexander Carlyle, *Autobiography of Dr Alexander Carlyle of Inveresk, 1722–1805* ed. John Hill Burton (London, 1910), p. 156.

48. *Edinburgh Review* 135 (April 1872) 207.

49. James Mackintosh in the Preface to Stewart's *Philosophy of the Active and Moral Powers of Man.*

50. Cockburn, ii 151–2.

51. *Edinburgh Review* 1 (October 1802) 17.

52. *Edinburgh Review* 30 (September 1818) 283.

53. There are echoes of Hume's *Essays, Moral and Political* (1741–2) throughout Jeffrey.

54. *Edinburgh Review* 20 (November 1812) 327.

55. *Edinburgh Review* 15 (January 1810) 520.

56. Ibid., 520–1.

57. *Edinburgh Review* 6 (April 1805) 140–1. See also *Edinburgh Review* 11 (October 1807) 133 and 30 (September 1818) 308.

58. *Edinburgh Review* 6 (April 1805) 142. For Jeffrey on the strengths and weaknesses of Hume's *History*, see *Edinburgh Review* 40 (March 1824) 92–146.

59. J. G. Lockhart, *Peter's Letters to His Kinsfolk* (2nd edn, Edinburgh, 1819), ii 128. This was in fact the first edition. The pretence that it was a second was one of Lockhart's and Blackwood's many literary hoaxes.

60. *Memoirs and Correspondence of Francis Horner, MP* ed. Leonard Horner (Boston, 1853), ii 272.

2
The *Edinburgh Review* and the Representation of Scotland

Fiona Stafford

When Sydney Smith came to publish his collected *Works* in 1839, he recalled his days as a private tutor in Scotland in the tumultuous period which had seen the beginnings of both the nineteenth century and the *Edinburgh Review*:

> The principles of the French Revolution were then fully afloat, and it is impossible to conceive a more violent, and agitated state of society. Among the first persons with whom I became acquainted were Lord Jeffrey, Lord Murray (late Lord Advocate for Scotland), and Lord Brougham; all of them maintaining opinions upon political subjects a little too liberal for the dynasty of Dundas, then exercising supreme power over the northern division of the island.
>
> One day we happened to meet in the eighth or ninth story or flat in Buccleugh-place, the elevated residence of the then Mr. Jeffrey. I proposed that we should set up a Review; this was acceded to with acclamation. I was appointed Editor, and remained long enough in Edinburgh to edit the first number of the Edinburgh Review. The motto I proposed for the Review was,
>
> > 'Tenui musam meditamur avena.'
> > 'We cultivate literature upon a little oatmeal.'
>
> But this was too near the truth to be admitted, and so we took our present grave motto from *Publius Syrus*, of whom none of us had, I am sure, ever read a single line; and so began what has since turned out to be a very important and able journal.[1]

Smith's inclusion of his own suggestion for a motto for the new periodical rather than the well-known quotation that actually adorned the title-page of each volume of the *Edinburgh Review* ('judex damnatur cum nocens absolvitur' – 'The judge stands condemned when the guilty is acquitted') initially seems little more than a typical example of his desire to be seen as a wit. When Henry Crabb Robinson met him in 1836, for example, he noted somewhat caustically that Sydney Smith's manner was 'that of a person who knows that a joke is expected'.[2] In his own brief account of the embryonic *Edinburgh Review*, Smith certainly emerges as the more light-hearted member of a heavyweight team, who plumped instead for the 'grave' maxim of Publius Syrus. What appears to be merely an entertaining anecdote may nevertheless point to some of the complicated and even contradictory aspects of the new periodical, which set itself up as both severe judge of contemporary publications and a quarterly event designed for the entertainment of a wide audience.

For although Francis Jeffrey, who took over editorship of the *Edinburgh Review* in 1803, claimed that its purpose was primarily 'to go deeply into *the Principles*' and to take 'large and Original views of all the important questions', he also admitted to the importance of 'enjoyment' and recognized the need to amuse and interest his readership.[3] From its very foundation, however, the relationships between serious philosophical enquiry and entertainment, and between educating and attracting a wide audience, were problematic. Smith himself, though initially amenable to Jeffrey's request that he curb his 'excessive levity', subsequently came to warn that although Edinburgh might be 'a very grave place', in London the complaints had become 'loud and universal of the extreme dulness and *lengthiness* of the *Edinburgh Review*'.[4] Such observations perhaps reveal the same kind of irritation that made Smith condemn the 'envious pedant' whose reaction to anything humorous was to 'comfort himself that it must be superficial',[5] but they nevertheless convey a point that Jeffrey could not safely ignore. The inclusion of 'levity' was a serious issue for a periodical whose very survival depended on its ability to continue attracting readers and, therefore, sales. However much Jeffrey might wish to present the *Edinburgh* as a grand judge, Smith was well aware that the verdict of its audience was ultimately critical: 'almost anybody of the sensible men who write for the Review would have written a much wiser, and more profound article than I have done upon the Game Laws; but I am quite certain nobody would obtain more readers for his essay upon such a subject'.[6] His later inclusion in the collected *Works* of the amusing motto rejected by the grave men of the North is thus indicative not so much of an anecdotal mind-set, as of a longstanding difference between the major contributors to the *Edinburgh Review* – a difference which Smith consistently presents in terms of national character.

Smith's advice to Jeffrey may have been couched in an appropriately ironic tone ('I am a very ignorant, frivolous, half-inch person'), but beneath the self-deprecatory remarks lay a hard-hitting defence of his own vital contribution to the periodical: 'Too much I admit would not do of my style; but the proportion in which it exists enlivens the Review if you appeal to the whole public, and not to the 8 or 10 grave Scotchmen with whom you live.'[7] In other words, high-mindedness and erudition might appeal to a small intellectual circle in Edinburgh, but such an audience was distinctly limited and hardly enough to keep the journal alive, let alone at the forefront of British culture. Since the *Edinburgh* always prided itself on its commitment to liberal causes and its ability to stimulate debate, the image of a readership dwindling down to '8 or 10 grave Scotchmen' was peculiarly damning. In such a context the adjective 'grave', which seems so readily associated with Jeffrey and his fellow Scottish intellectuals, also acquires a certain dark irony.

As the only Englishman among the group of young men who founded the periodical, Smith's perception of the *Edinburgh Review* as distinctively Scottish in character is perhaps not surprising. More difficult to establish is just what being Scottish suggested at the turn of the nineteenth century, when both developments in Europe and the momentous reconfiguration of British/Irish relations combined to render national identity an uncertain but vitally important issue. Smith's adaptation of a motto from Virgil's first Eclogue, 'tenui musam meditamur avena', which loses its accustomed pastoral connotations in his witty translation, 'We cultivate literature upon a little oatmeal', plays on well-established associations between oats and Scots.[8] This was the prejudice satirized by Smollett in *Humphry Clinker* when Matthew Bramble's servants are told in Newcastle that they will find nothing to eat in Scotland 'but *oat-meal* and *sheep's heads*', and which remained indelibly inscribed in British minds by Samuel Johnson's dictionary definition of oats as the grain 'which in England is fed to horses'.[9] Indeed, the rejected motto ironically anticipates Byron's later depiction of the *Edinburgh Reviewers* as an 'oat-fed phalanx', descending from the north to attack unsuspecting English bards.[10] The oat-eating Scots frequently emerge in the period as a hardy, undernourished but often rather menacing band, whom the English encounter at their peril.

Since his fellow contributors were close friends, however, it is clear that Smith's anecdote is affectionate and intended to amuse rather than offend. The comment that it was 'too near the truth to be admitted' also suggests that it was inspired not by any general stereotyping of the

Scots as poor, ill-fed and canny, but by the immediate personal circumstances of those assembled. As he was subsequently to tell Crabb Robinson, the *Edinburgh Review*, unlike the later *British and Foreign Review*, which depended on a wealthy patron, was founded not by 'Dives' but by '*lazzaroni*'.[11] The original contributors may have been brilliant, well educated and energetic, but they were also very short of money. Both Sydney Smith and Francis Jeffrey had recently married and were struggling to support themselves and their wives, who were already expecting their first babies. Their personal difficulties were further aggravated, however, by the contemporary political situation. In the wake of the French Revolution, circumstances in Scotland had been particularly trying for those who, like Francis Jeffrey or Henry Brougham, espoused opinions 'a little too liberal for the dynasty of Dundas'. As Jeffrey battled to establish himself as a lawyer, he admitted to feeling unmanageable 'emotions of despondency and ambition', and began contemplating a career at the English bar, or even a post in India.[12] Similar discontent was expressed by Brougham, who despite having been called to the Scottish bar in 1800, saw no future in Edinburgh in the current climate: 'I am either tossed about and harassed by a thousand perplexities, or sink into a deceitful and dangerous calm. In short, I am completely discontented, as I have long been, with all prospects in this place, and I much fear that I shall find it impossible to make the exchange I so much desire.'[13]

The situation for young barristers committed to liberal views at the turn of the century was bleak. As John Clive argues in his study of the *Edinburgh Review*, the Scottish bar was 'predominantly Tory', and as a result young Whigs such as Jeffrey and Brougham 'lounged year after year', underemployed and frustrated by their virtual exclusion from the influential profession for which they had trained.[14] Living on 'oatmeal' was thus a matter of principle, rather than any sign of inadequacy or social inferiority. Far from indicating a general anti-Scots prejudice, Smith's Virgilian tag encompasses a high-minded austerity and commitment to the truth, the light-hearted and self-mocking tone, as so often, acting as a mask for more serious concerns. Indeed, the combination of poverty and principles was oddly beneficial to the *Edinburgh Review* for, as Brougham observed in a letter to his friend James Loch, study was 'cheaper than dissipation'.[15] The absence of a proper professional outlet meant that Brougham possessed not only a surplus of intellectual energy and political opinion, but also time to channel his excess into essays. A new periodical, sympathetic to liberal views, could act as a conduit into the public domain, enabling Brougham, Jeffrey and others similarly frustrated to let their ideas flow freely. If they were not able to practise their eloquence in court, then they would perhaps manage to exert some influence as the self-appointed judges of contemporary printed opinion.

The sense of an urgent need for liberal voices to find a public platform is clear in Sydney Smith's account of the *Edinburgh Review*'s foundation:

> The Catholics were not emancipated – the Corporation and Test Acts were unrepealed – the Game Laws were horribly oppressive – Steel Traps and Spring Guns were set all over the Country – Prisoners tried for their Lives could have no Counsel – Lord Eldon and the Court of Chancery pressed heavily upon mankind – Libel was punished by the most cruel and vindictive imprisonments – the principles of Political Economy were little understood – the law of Debt and of Conspiracy were upon the worst possible footing – the enormous wickedness of the Slave Trade was tolerated – a thousand evils were in existence, which the talents of good and able men have since lessened or removed.[16]

These were the 'evils' that the Edinburgh Reviewers, with their remarkably active pens, were committed to fighting. In such a context, a plain diet of oatmeal may be seen as a metaphor for sound common sense and principles uncorrupted by luxury or personal advancement. And in this light, Smith's emphasis on attracting readers may reflect a concern not so much with profit margins, as with the widest possible audience whose opinions might be influenced for the better.

Sydney Smith's picture of the sorry state of the nation in the opening decade of the nineteenth century is vivid enough, but it is still worth focusing in a little more detail on the momentous events of 1801–2 in order to understand the context of the *Edinburgh Review* and, in particular, its Scottish dimension, more fully. For despite Clive's persuasive argument that the journal's existence depended largely on the professional abyss confronting the principal contributors, it is helpful to bear in mind the peculiar mood of 1802, which in some ways represented a moment of possibility after years of war with France. The previous year had seen the startling resignations of William Pitt and his Scottish ally, the immensely powerful Henry Dundas, which, as Brougham recalled, produced astonishment and profound anxiety in Scotland:

> a Ministry without Pitt, nay without Dundas, and an opposition leaning towards its support. Those who are old enough to remember

that dark interval may recollect how the public mind in Scotland was subdued with awe, and how men awaited in trembling the uncertain event, as all things quail during that solemn pause that precedes an earthquake.[17]

In a letter of 11 April 1801, another of James Loch's correspondents, Andrew Clephane, had expressed just such sentiments: 'We are all at a stand here, not knowing where to look for a glimpse of light; all is darkness.' However, his letter continues with a more optimistic note: 'I really think we have made a pretty business of it at last, and that we shall have some other hands at the helm.'[18] By the following year, some were already looking forward to a better future as the pause in hostilities enabled the government to turn for a moment to internal issues. Walter Scott, for example, commented in January 1802 that there 'never was a period in the history of this country apparently more favourable to the improvement of its laws than that in which we are now placed'.[19] Although the controversial Peace of Amiens, signed in March 1802, did little to defuse the threat of Napoleon who marched into Switzerland that summer, it did at least create a moment in which the mood of the country was very different from the years preceding. 1802 was a year of intense discussion, as people from all parts of the political and social spectrum reacted to the news of peace, the possibility of renewed warfare, the rise of Napoleon, the successive invasions of Switzerland, the consequences of the French Revolution, the power of the monarchy and the government, and the uncertainty of the future.

Bound up with the vigorous political debates was a new sense of Britain, predominantly forged (to use Linda Colley's term) through the war with France, but now wrought into an unfamiliar form by the Union with Ireland. For the downfall of Pitt and Dundas had been a direct consequence of the momentous Act which was passed in August 1800 and came into effect in the following January. The period of deep uncertainty, but also possibility, which preceded the inaugural issue of the *Edinburgh Review* was profoundly connected with the creation of the United Kingdom. It is thus a fascinating context through which to approach the content and even the form of the new journal, and especially the question of its Scottish identity, for while the frequent inclusion of reviews of Scottish books may seem to represent little more than a natural interest in local authors and subjects, the immediate post-Union context imbues these editorial choices with a wider significance. Effectively, the selective policy pioneered by Jeffrey, which highlighted certain publications and ignored others entirely, together with the journal's title, placed Edinburgh at the centre of British intellectual consciousness, just at a time when the Union with Ireland might have knocked Scotland into the margins.

While it would be mistaken to suggest that the *Edinburgh Review* was driven primarily by any narrowly nationalistic considerations, it nevertheless demonstrates a pervasive fascination with questions of nationhood, regional variation, land use, and the culture and political institutions of different countries. The very first volume, for example, included reviews of Mounier's *De l'Influence attribué aux Philosophes, aux Franc-Maçons, et aux Illuminés, sur la Revolution de France; Asiatic Researches; The Journal of Frederick Horneman's Travels;* Joseph Acerbi's *Travels through Sweden;* G. A. Olivier's *Travels in the Ottoman Empire, Egypt, and Persia;* George Baldwin's *Political Reflections relative to Egypt;* Alexander Mackenzie's *Voyages from Montreal . . . to the Frozen and Pacific Oceans;* together with discussions of subjects closer to home such as Alexander Irvine's *An Inquiry into the causes and effects of Emigration from the Highlands, and Western Islands of Scotland* or Alexander Christison's *The General Diffusion of Knowledge, one great Cause of the Prosperity of North Britain.* These may well have been chosen because they struck the editors as the most important publications of the year, but for readers the different reviews constituted a new whole. The overall effect is of direct, and broadly Whiggish comment on the contemporary political situation juxtaposed with the other kinds of reflection that emerge through implicit comparisons between British and foreign affairs, and through the discussion of new poetry or scientific discovery. The preoccupation with different places at home and abroad serves to accentuate national differences but, at the same time, the pervasive sense of current instabilities works to undermine any notion of permanent national entities. The very nature of nations thus seems under investigation through the juxtapositions of the different essays, which take the reader around the globe, and backwards and forwards through time.

The prevailing international uncertainties meant that demand for intelligent analysis of contemporary events was running especially high. The *Edinburgh* demonstrated in the first issue that it would not hesitate to offer views on political issues, as Smith waded in to attack Bowles's *Reflections at the Conclusion of the War* and Brougham gave readers the benefits of his research on the West Indies in an analysis of *The Crisis of the Sugar Colonies*, which had been escalating 'since the cessation of hostilities in Europe'.[20] The periodical form meant that it was possible to respond quickly to current affairs, in the knowledge that even if political developments took an unexpected turn on the very day of publication, it would only be three months until further comment could be offered. More substantial and wide-ranging than a pamphlet or newspaper, less absolute and time-consuming than a book, the periodical provided a medium for intelligent, well-informed but infinitely fluid discussion – and thus seemed the perfect form to respond to the uncertain times in which it appeared. An additional advantage of the magazine format was the presence of historical and cultural perspectives which could be introduced through reviews of a wide variety of contemporary publications. If the *Edinburgh Review* was able to respond rapidly to the changing political climate, it could also reach back to earlier times, or remind readers of future developments not wholly determined by war and politics.

The immediate success of the *Edinburgh* indicates that the journal fulfilled an important need. Its capacity to appeal to a wider social sphere in Scotland than in England (where, according to Brougham, 'the gentlemen alone' read it[21]) also suggests that either the need was felt more strongly in the north, or that the new journal was somehow especially suited to Scottish tastes. This distinction might help to explain Sydney Smith's sense of his own difference from the other contributors and perennial anxieties about the decline of a London readership. In view of Benedict Anderson's well-known thesis on the importance of print culture to the development of national consciousness, it is also tempting to see the *Edinburgh Review* as an expression of an emerging sense of national community, at once reflecting and contributing to the imaginings of the Scottish people. For if Anderson is correct in regarding the novel and the newspaper as the forms which in late eighteenth-century Europe provided 'the technical means for "re-presenting" the kind of imagined community that is the nation', then the periodical must also have had an important role to play.[22] Like the novel and the newspaper, the periodical creates a sense of shared experience among thousands of readers who do not know each other, but yet understand the same language and have a common interest in certain public events. The effect of quarterly publication, too, even more than the daily 'ceremony' analysed by Anderson, increases the sense of occasion which, being significant for many, increases the feeling of community among silent readers. Since the *Edinburgh Review* was also designed to stimulate debate through its vigorous reviewing style, its audience was not generally content with silent imaginings, but was frequently provoked into active discussion with fellow readers.

Timothy Brennan has engaged with Anderson in his own discussion of the rise of European nationalism, observing that it was 'the *novel* that historically accompanied the rise of nations by objectifying the "one, yet many" of national life, and by mimicking the structure of the nation, a clearly bordered jumble of languages and styles'.[23] The novel, when viewed in this way, is seen emerging in a period when traditional modes of thought and structures of power have declined, taking with them the old genre of the epic. In place of timeless myths of origin comes the parodic 'hotch-potch' of the novel, with its variety of registers and internalized generic mixtures. Whether old ways of thinking collapsed entirely at the end of the eighteenth century is a matter for debate, but it is certainly possible to see the combined influences of the Enlightenment, scientific advance, and political revolution in America and France as causing fundamental damage to traditional conceptions of the world. In Scotland, too, the history of internal division and warfare, the loss of Parliament, together with the dismantling of the older myths of monarchy, meant that new literary forms were needed to represent the new society.[24] Both Macpherson's *Ossian* and the novels of Scott, Galt and Hogg might fruitfully be considered in terms of a 'national longing for form', but it was perhaps the periodical that was best able to offer expression to the diverse and developing nature of the nation. And while it could be argued in the case of the *Edinburgh Review* that the firm editorial hand restricted the range represented, it is also possible to see Jeffrey's influence as a crucial binding force, introducing a sense of coherence and preventing fragmentation and chaos.

Like the new United Kingdom, the *Edinburgh Review* was varied, heterogeneous, constantly changing in attitude and focus, and yet undeniably a single entity. Within the familiar blue and buff covers lay a great variety of style and subject matter, but the basic form was sufficiently flexible to allow internal difference without any danger of wholesale collapse. Each article was carefully constructed and, if not written by Jeffrey, often carefully edited and positioned in relation to the other pieces, so that each volume had a distinctive character, created from juxtaposition and variety. The forum for exploring questions of nationhood and identity was thus able to play a significant role in the creation of a new sense of Britain, and especially of Scotland's place within the newly united islands.

To suggest that Jeffrey and his fellow contributors were consciously creating a periodical for the new Britain would be to invest their efforts with an anachronistic awareness of theoretical relationships between texts and contexts. However, it is not unreasonable to consider the general significance of the Act of Union for the *Edinburgh Review*, and its treatment of Scottish material. The Union had, after all, come into effect only after extensive debate about the various advantages and disadvantages for all interested parties, which inevitably brought to the fore questions of national identity and difference. In Scotland, the issue prompted Henry Dundas's only extensive statement on Anglo-Scottish relations, as he approached the possibility of Union with Ireland through direct reference to the debates over the 1707 Union between England and Scotland.[25] Dundas's speech alluded specifically to Lord Belhaven's well-known anxieties about the Treaty of Union, and although this was largely a rhetorical ploy to demonstrate the benefits that Scotland had enjoyed since 1707, it also had the effect of raising the old questions of Scotland's relationship with England and her continuing role within Britain.

The *Edinburgh Review* was in broad support of the Union with Ireland, as is made plain in reviews of Belsham's *History of Britain* or Gordon's *A History of Ireland*,[26] but the questions raised in the debates surrounding the 1800 settlement had focused attention on the presence of the different countries within the larger political entity. For Jeffrey, in particular, Scotland was of crucial importance. Unlike Smith, Horner and Brougham, who left Edinburgh in the first decade of the nineteenth century and sent their contributions from London, Jeffrey continued to be based in Scotland's capital city and to include numerous reviews of Scottish publications. His attachment to Scotland was deep and seems to have become painfully conscious during the brief but unhappy period he spent as an undergraduate in Oxford some ten years before the foundation of the *Edinburgh Review*. His misery is abundantly evident in the letters he wrote to his sister shortly after arriving at the Queen's College,

> On Wednesday morning my father, John, and Napier departed for Buxton, and left me here alone and melancholy in a strange land.... I felt as if I were exposed to starve upon a desert island; as if the hour of my death were at hand, and an age of torture ready to follow it. I came to dinner at the common hall – got a little acquainted with one or two of the students, and kept in their company, for I was afraid of solitude till I retired to sleep. Why must I dream that I am always in Edinburgh. The unpacking of my trunk rendered me nearly mad. I cannot yet bear to look into any of my writings. I have not now one glimpse of my accustomed genius nor fancy. O! my dear, retired, adored little window; I swear I would forfeit all hopes and pretensions, to be restored once more to it, and to you, could I do it with the honour and applause of others.[27]

Jeffrey's homesickness did not abate, and months later, he was still yearning for 'Scotland – Scotland!' He returned to Edinburgh with relief in July 1792, but his experience of life in England had a lasting effect. As he acknowledged at the time, 'I am as much, nay more, a Scotchman than I was while an inhabitant of Scotland. My opinions, ideas, prejudices, and systems are all Scotch.'[28]

For Jeffrey the question of personal identity was bound up with his sense of national belonging. It is not surprising, then, to find that as the relationship between England and Scotland became a subject of public debate and general conversation, he should have maintained a powerful sense of being 'a Scotchman'. The periodical that was to become so closely associated with him advertised its provenance in its title, and continued to feature essays relating to the Northern parts of Britain. Indeed, Jeffrey periodically drew attention to his editorial practice, as for example in an 1823 review of 'Secondary Scotch Novels'. The essay on recent fiction by Galt and Wilson opens with a defence against the charge frequently levelled against the *Edinburgh Review* of 'partiality to the writers of our own country'. With characteristic sophistication, Jeffrey parries accusations of national prejudice while taking the opportunity to write a long and enthusiastic review of recent Scottish novels, on the grounds that they had 'attracted, and very deservedly, a large share of attention in every part of the empire – issuing from the press, successively for four or five years, in this very city, and under our eyes, and not hitherto honoured by us with any indication of our being conscious of their existence'.[29] He thus draws attention to Scottish writing and the Edinburgh publishing trade, even while arguing that his admiration is objective and not a consequence of local bias.

Jeffrey's pride in works popular enough to command attention 'in every part of the empire' reveals his sense of Scottish importance, but it is a value that seems proved by the attitude of readers in other countries. Although Galt's distinctively Scottish subject matter is at the forefront of Jeffrey's review, the novels are not seen as works for a Scottish audience alone, but as objects of admiration for 'many distant eyes'.[30] National success seems to require an international arena and hence Jeffrey's commitment to Scotland is by no means inconsistent with an enthusiasm for the United Kingdom and her expanding Empire. Paul Langford has observed in connection with the development of 'Britishness' in the eighteenth century, 'numerous Scots took advantage of a formula which left them national self-respect while participating in the commercial and professional possibilities of an empire whose metropolis was London, not Edinburgh'.[31] With the revival of the debates over

Union in 1800, however, it once again became crucial for Scots to regard 1707 in the words of Colin Kidd, as 'a treaty between sovereign equals, and not the reabsorption within an English pan-Britannic imperium of a wayward vassal-nation'.[32] When Dundas addressed the issue of the Union, he argued, as Michael Fry points out, for both 'a Scotland for the Scots' *and* 'a United Kingdom and an Empire fully opened up to them'.[33] So too the *Edinburgh Review*, though differing in so many points from the Tory administration, can be seen to promote Scottish interests and to emphasize Scottish capabilities, while still welcoming a larger sphere of influence and opportunity.

The awareness of alternative cultures that marks the *Edinburgh Review* from its first issue often informs Jeffrey's approach to Scottish material. For not only is the journal characterized by its fascination with different countries, but even the reviews of Scottish literature reveal a comparative and sociological approach. The first volume, for example, included a substantial review of Scott's *Minstrelsy of the Scottish Border* in which the traditional lifestyle of those living in the Borders is compared to that of a 'Tartarian or Arabian tribe'.[34] Again Jeffrey achieves a skilful balance between an obvious personal interest in Scottish subjects and his desire to project an air of editorial detachment and metropolitan sophistication (we 'can scarcely persuade ourselves that this country contained, within these two centuries, so exact a prototype of the Bedouin character'[35]). Scott's collection of traditional ballads offers vivid insight into life in the Borders, but Jeffrey is at pains to emphasize that this is only one element in the rich alloy that is Scotland. The outlaws, cattle-stealers and romantic heroines who haunt Scott's pages belong to an earlier age and a distinct region, and so despite 'the strength of sentiment and energy of expression' on display, the Border ballads constitute only a small part of the national literature. Indeed, Jeffrey's concern about Scott's vigorous promotion of Border culture emerges in a later, and also largely favourable, review of the highly successful *The Lay of the Last Minstrel*:

> we really cannot so far sympathise with the local partialities of the author, as to feel any glow of patriotism or ancient virtue in hearing of the *Todrig* or *Johnston* clans, or of *Elliots, Armstrongs,* and *Tinlinns;* still less can we relish the introduction of *Black John of Athelstane, Whitslade the Hawk, Arthur-fire-the-braes, Red Roland Forster,* or any other of those worthies who
>
> > 'Sought the beeves that made their broth,
> > In Scotland and in England both,'

into a poem which has any pretentions to seriousness or dignity. The antient metrical romance might have admitted these homely personalities; but the present age will not endure them; and Mr Scott must either sacrifice his Border prejudices, or offend all his readers in the other parts of the empire.[36]

In comments such as this, it is difficult to decide whether Jeffrey is demonstrating a certain metropolitan prejudice against the provincial, or rather grappling to reconcile his natural attraction towards the essentially Scottish with conflicting ideals of universality and international acclaim. Given his well-known attack on Wordsworth for retreating into rural seclusion rather than choosing to live, as 'all the greater poets lived ... in the full current of society',[37] it might be assumed that Jeffrey is upbraiding Scott for being too parochial. However, when he turned his attention to Burns it was to announce that poetry had found 'almost all her favourites among the recluse and uninstructed' and that Burns's creativity had been fostered by his 'humble retirement, where he had no reputation to lose'.[38] The criticism of Scott in the review of the *Lay* thus seems connected not so much with the locale as with a narrowness of outlook and an attachment to outmoded values which will not be shared by the modern reading public. Burns, on the other hand, though born and bred in rural Ayrshire, had produced poetry of 'simple and unpretending tenderness' that could be transmitted to 'all future generations'.[39] For Jeffrey, the value of Scottish poetry needed to be proved beyond its immediate currency, either by 'distant eyes' or 'future generations'.

If Scott's roots in the Borders nourished strengths and occasional weaknesses in his poetry, they were also vital to his stance as a critic. Jeffrey's identification of Scott with the Borders is less explicit, though still apparent in the review he commissioned from the poet in the same volume that carried the review of the *Lay of the Last Minstrel*. For as Scott brought his own knowledge and eloquence to bear on two important new works relating to Macpherson's *Ossian*, he revealed a sense of distance from these other 'Scottish' publications. Henry Mackenzie's *Report of the Committee of the Highland Society, appointed to inquire into the Nature and Authenticity of the Poems of Ossian* and Malcolm Laing's edition of *The Poems of Ossian* both represented the fruit of many years of investigation into the authenticity, or otherwise, of Macpherson's translations of Gaelic Ossianic poetry. In his selection of the two publications for an extensive review, and in commissioning such an able writer for the task, Jeffrey was reminding the public of the high-profile controversy which had divided opinion so deeply north and south of the Border half a century before. Scott's review seems to emphasize the end of hostilities, as he states that 'this celebrated controversy seems now to be finally at issue', but within a matter of sentences he displays an awareness of the old divisions within Scotland, as well as his own difference from the parties under discussion: 'Although, by mingling in the approaching storm, we run the risk of a chance-blow from a Highland claymore, or an Orcadian battle-axe, our duty to the public impels us within the reach of these antient and formidable weapons.'[40] Not content with emphasizing the differences between the members of the Highland Society and Malcolm Laing, who came from Orkney, Scott continues his discussion with a succession of references to 'Celtic song', 'ancient Lowland authors' and the various visitations of the Romans, Vikings and Dr Johnson. There is little sense here of a monolithic, unified 'Scotland', but the very history of division and turmoil seems excitingly fraught with imaginative possibility. Even as he acknowledges the long history of internal conflict, Scott concludes that despite the evidence of Macpherson's somewhat creative handling of traditional materials, 'our national vanity may be equally flattered by the fact that a remote, and almost a barbarous corner of Scotland, produced, in the 18th century, a bard, capable not only of making an enthusiastic impression on every mind susceptible of poetical beauty, but of giving a new tone to poetry throughout Europe.'[41]

While by no means attempting to play down the differences that characterize 'Scotland', Scott still celebrates the power of a Scottish text to reach an international audience. As in Jeffrey's reviews, the measure of value seems determined at least in part by societies outside the British Isles. A true understanding of what it means to be Scottish – or indeed British – thus seems to require an awareness not only of internal diversity but also of other tastes and cultures, while Scottish achievement is ratified by readers in Europe and the Empire. By choosing a reviewer who was at once Scottish but at the same time distanced from the authors of the texts under discussion, Jeffrey could promote Scottish culture in an apparently objective, and therefore more powerful way. The *Edinburgh Review*'s championing of Scottish ability thus seemed not so much the admiration that arises from an ignorance of alternatives, but rather a judgement of true worth based on informed comparisons.

Both the national pride displayed in essays such as Scott's review of the *Ossian* controversy and the simultaneous acknowledgement of internal division reflects the *Review*'s contribution to the new idea of Britain. Scott's sense in 1805 of a moment when old controversies had ceased, but when a new consensus was marked by deep-rooted regional and lineal differences may have been articulated in response to the two volumes he was reviewing; nevertheless the tone accords well with the national situation. The new United Kingdom was created from diverse elements – and yet this very diversity, however unhappy in the past, could now be presented as a strength, uniting Britons against the world.

The issue of *Ossian* was particularly interesting in the wake of the Union since it symbolized a past in which Scotland and Ireland had been closely linked, whatever the subsequent history of conflict. As Scott observed: 'The similarity of language and manners, together with the constant intercourse betwixt the Scottish Highlanders and the Irish, rendered the transmission of popular pieces of poetry from one nation to the other, a very simple and common event.'[42] This emphasis on the common heritage follows immediately from the previous review in which Belsham's *History of Britain* is said to conclude with the political Union of 1800, a development 'approved . . . by all thinking men in England'.[43] For readers who moved straight from one review to the next, the *Poems of Ossian* provided a strong reminder of the old ties between the islands, and hence perhaps a means of legitimating the recent Union. Scott's review made it clear that Scottish, Irish and English allegiances had frequently been reconfigured over the centuries and hence the apparently new Union might be seen in some ways as a re-Union, at least as far as the most northern and western parts of Britain were concerned. It also emphasized the crucial role of culture to the unity of a nation – an attitude at once endorsed and embodied by the new journal in which it appeared.

The serial form of the *Edinburgh Review* facilitated such mental links between apparently unconnected publications, creating points implicitly by the contrasts and juxtapositions which began to lodge in the minds of its readers. The effect of reading Scott's review in its original company, next to Napier's discussion of the *History of Britain*, is quite different from reading it in isolation as a statement on Macpherson's *Ossian*. In order to understand the *Edinburgh*'s contribution to the way in which its readers imagined their community, it is thus important to see the articles in their original contexts, rather than in the reordered volumes published by the individual contributors later in the century (even though these compilations have their own interest). For it is as much the variety and internal contradiction that seems to express the evolving sense of the nation as any consistent attitude from any single contributor. Even Jeffrey's essays, though distinctive in style, were by no means uncritically nationalistic, as his unease over Scott's 'local partialities' or his own defensive remarks about carrying a review of 'Secondary Scotch Novels' indicate.

Although the *Edinburgh Review* carried a high number of reviews of Scottish publications, then, they were by no means universally favourable. The third volume, for example, includes a devastating article on John Cririe's *Scottish Scenery; or, Sketches in Verse, descriptive of Scenes chiefly in the Highlands of Scotland*, which warns that the volume, though beautifully produced, is not 'so well calculated for reading; and...that most of those who take it up with such an intention, will very speedily lay it down again'.[44] The piece proceeds with a characteristic display of quotation and excoriation, until the unfortunate poem has been reduced to strings of placenames and trite expressions. As with the later review of Galt, Jeffrey gives precious space to Scottish material, but avoids any charge of local prejudice through an overtly unsympathetic response.

Indeed, the most vigorous critical assaults often seem to have been directed at those closest to home. Sir John Sinclair suffered a broadside attack on his essays, while Stewart's *Account of William Robertson* was dismissed with similarly caustic comments.[45] The Scottish elements of Byron's *Hours of Idleness* attracted the derision of Brougham who criticized the young poet for producing Ossianic translations 'pretty nearly as stupid and tiresome as Macpherson's' and for failing to discover during his boasted youth in the Highlands that a '*pibroch* is not a bagpipe, any more than duet means fiddle'.[46] Even the notorious attack on Wordsworth's *Excursion* seems to have derived some of its animus from the inclusion of Scottish characters. Jeffrey's sardonic summary of Wordsworth's Pedlar ('He was born, we are happy to find in Scotland – among the hills of Athol; and his mother, after his father's death, married the parish schoolmaster – so that he was taught his letters betimes') adopts a matter-of-fact tone designed to suggest his own superior knowledge of Scottish rural life, thus setting up the rest of the narrative for the relentless attack on its inflated descriptions, and 'absurd and fantastic' choices of plan and character.[47] Although the entire poem is discussed in some detail, it is the figure of the Pedlar that seems to irritate Jeffrey most:

> Did Mr Wordsworth really imagine, that his favourite doctrines were likely to gain any thing in point of effect or authority by being put into the mouth of a person accustomed to higgle about tapes, or brass sleeve-buttons?...A man who went about selling flannel and pocket-handkerchiefs in this lofty diction, would soon frighten away all his customers.[48]

The objection to *The Excursion*'s improbable representation of the Scottish rustic reads almost as a sequel to Jeffrey's earlier review of Cromek's *Reliques of Robert Burns*, which had concluded with praise for Burns's ability to copy 'the spoken language of passion and affection, with infinitely more fidelity' than Wordsworth and his fellows in the Lake School.[49] Whereas Wordsworth claimed to admire the simplicity of low and rustic life, in Jeffrey's eyes it was Burns who, having grown up in such a situation, could actually embody the ideals of simplicity and passion in his poetry:

> Let them contrast their own fantastical personages of hysterical schoolmasters and sententious leechgatherers, with the authentic rustics of Burns's Cotter's Saturday Night, and his inimitable songs; and reflect on the different reception which these personifications have met with from the public. Though they will not be reclaimed from their puny affectations by the example of their learned predecessors, they may, perhaps, submit to be admonished by a self-taught and illiterate poet, who drew from Nature far more directly than they can do, and produced something so much liker the admired copies of the masters whom they have abjured.[50]

The attack on Wordsworth here is in turn a development from Jeffrey's original onslaught in the very first number of the *Edinburgh Review*, when Southey's *Thalaba* had provided the platform for a startling denunciation of the linguistic principles and 'low-bred heroes' of *Lyrical Ballads*.[51] Both were, of course, issues of some sensitivity for a critic who had inherited from the Edinburgh philosophers of the previous generation an esteem for originality and a certain self-consciousness about provincial modes of speech.[52] To have Wordsworth assuming rustic language in the name of originality was thus doubly irksome, since it revealed one of the fundamental tensions in Enlightenment aesthetics, which simultaneously celebrated the spontaneous 'fire' of the untaught genius while deploring the unrefined speech of many contemporary Scots. Jeffrey's own comments on Burns are riven with this kind of contradiction – and hence, perhaps, his desire to repudiate Wordsworth's poetic principles while lionizing Burns for the more accurate representations of nature that came from first-hand knowledge.

Given Jeffrey's ongoing campaign against Wordsworth's 'low-bred heroes', the appearance of idealized figures in *The Excursion* who were not only 'low' but also Scottish may have seemed almost deliberately provocative. Jeffrey's review certainly demonstrates a degree of irritation and, not content with devoting the first thirty pages of the volume to a largely negative discussion of Wordsworth, he reiterates many of the points indirectly in the concluding review of recent work by James Hogg and William Tennant. Both of these poets had, like Burns, grown up in unassuming homes in rural Scotland, but neither produced verse remotely resembling the language of Wordsworth's Pedlar. Jeffrey was once again exploiting the miscellaneous format of the *Edinburgh Review* to strengthen points and implant further ideas through juxtaposition. The reader who began the November number with *The Excursion* and ended with *The Queen's Wake* and *Anster Fair* might well be left feeling that where the English poet was recycling old ideas at ever greater length, Scotland had now sent up two more rising stars whose work displayed the very qualities which Wordsworth consistently admired and persistently failed to demonstrate.

Jeffrey explicitly eschewed the notion of local bias in his pages, adopting a strategy similar to that used some years later in two consecutive reviews on Hogg's *The Queen's Wake* and Tennant's *Anster Fair*. He begins by emphasizing that Hogg's poem has been in print for some time without attracting his notice ('There can be no better proof, we think, of our superiority to all sorts of national prejudice or partiality'[53]); by the end of the 1814 review such protestations had begun to sound a little hollow. For after detailed discussion of the two poems and their authors' situations, Jeffrey concludes with remarks that do not entirely accord with the earlier claim to objectivity:

> Perhaps we have detained our English readers too long with our two tuneful countrymen. They have neither of them, we confess, the pathos or simplicity of Burns, or the energy and splendour of Scott; but they appear to us to be persons of promise; and, at all events, to be singly worth a whole cageful of ordinary songsters from the colleges and cities of the south.[54]

Such unconcealed glee may have pleased some readers north of the Border, but was unlikely to win much support further south. At moments such as this, the determination to prove Scotland's importance in the United Kingdom seems as likely to provoke irritation, or even ridicule, as respect, while the *Edinburgh*'s commitment to variety and regional difference verges on a more monolithic separatism. Whether the receding threat from France made the notion of unity among the diverse parts of the islands seem less crucial by 1814 is perhaps a topic for future consideration, but it is noticeable that Jeffrey's promotion of

Scotland, though conceived within a United Britain, could at times sound nationalistic and essentially exclusive.

Contemporary readers were certainly conscious of the Scottish dimensions of the *Edinburgh Review*. Coleridge's response is characteristic: the journal, he commented to Crabb Robinson, was 'a concentration of all the smartness of all Scotland'.[55] 'Smartness' is nevertheless a somewhat loaded term, as shown by Crabb Robinson's subsequent observation that the *Edinburgh Review* was written with 'great smartness, but without any poetical sense whatever'.[56] The remark relates specifically to Jeffrey's review of Southey's *The Curse of Kehama*, but may well have been influenced by Byron's recent and popular attack in *English Bards and Scotch Reviewers*. In the satire composed in response to what he assumed was Jeffrey's review of *Hours of Idleness*, Byron made much of the Edinburgh critic's cleverness and his Scottishness:

> Then prosper JEFFREY! pertest of the train!
> Whom Scotland pampers with her fiery grain!
> Whatever blessing waits a genuine Scot,
> In double portion swells thy glorious lot,
> For thee, Edina culls her evening sweets,
> And showers their odours on thy candid sheets,
> Whose Hue and Fragrance to thy work adhere,
> This scents its pages, and that gilds its rear,
> Lo! blushing Itch, coy nymph, enamoured grown,
> Forsakes the rest, and cleaves to thee alone,
> And, too unjust to other Pictish men,
> Enjoys thy person, and inspires thy pen![57]

Byron revels in Edinburgh's reputation for poor sanitation in order to make Jeffrey central to his quasi-Popean vision – thus implying publicly, as Wordsworth exclaimed in private, that the modern Aristarch was 'the greatest Dunce in this island'.[58] The division between English poets and Scottish critics also plays on an old anxiety about the absence of literary talent north of the Border, which Byron highlights in one of his irreverent notes to the poem: 'I could not say Caledonia's Genius, it being well known there is no Genius to be found from Clackmannan to Caithness'.[59] Byron's satire, with its lengthy comments on contemporary literature, suggests that while criticism is something easily accomplished by an English bard, Jeffrey and his fellow journalists are capable only of turning out prose at 'ten sterling pounds per sheet'.[60] Jeffrey's Scottish identity is thus associated with a lack of genius, taste or compassion, and an overabundance of pride, clubbishness and grubby, commercial interest. Even as Jeffrey fought to dispel some of the traditional caricatures of his nation, his own polemical approach seemed to provoke new versions of the old stereotypes. And since Byron's poem had reached its fifth edition by 1811, the influence of those condemned by the Edinburgh judges was not to be underestimated.

Scottish law still remained distinct from England and so provided a fruitful source of imagery for Byron's satire. Among the many jibes at Jeffrey is the reference to him as a 'Self-constituted Judge of Poesy'.[61] The notion of Jeffrey as a judge, which enabled Byron to pun on the dreaded Judge Jeffreys, was particularly appropriate in view of the 'grave' motto chosen for the *Edinburgh Review* – 'judex damnatur cum nocens absolvitur'. The reviewers, as trained lawyers, also tended to employ legal imagery in their assessments of contemporary poetry, as both Byron and Wordsworth had found to their cost. Byron's description of the 'self-constituted Judge' is indeed very similar to Wordsworth's reference to Jeffrey as 'a man, self-elected into the office of a public judge of the literature and life of his contemporaries', which appeared in one of his carefully considered retaliations against Jeffrey, *A Letter to a Friend of Robert Burns*.[62] It was Edward Copleston, a Fellow of Oriel College, Oxford, who had spelled out the implications of the judicial metaphor most plainly, however, when he composed his own retort to the *Edinburgh Review* in 1807. As he took issue with the idea advanced so energetically by Jeffrey and his fellow contributors that 'a Reviewer acts in a judicial capacity', Copleston stated clearly that

> there is no analogy between the two cases. A Judge is promoted to that office by the authority of the state; a Reviewer by his own. The former is independent of controul, and may therefore freely follow the dictates of his own conscience: the latter depends for his very bread upon the breath of public opinion: the great law of self preservation therefore points out to him a different line of action.[63]

Copleston's point that the only law for the reviewer was the rule of 'what will sell' made Jeffrey's elevated stance seem little more than a rhetorical ploy to impress readers, while all the time the real motivation was economic. If Sydney Smith was warning his editor against an excessive seriousness congenial only to '8 or 10 grave Scotchmen', less sympathetic readers saw him cashing in on the public under an assumed mantle of high-minded authority.

The notion that such accusations derived from old prejudices about the canniness of the Scottish people is nevertheless checked by the discovery that one of the most hard-hitting attacks on Jeffrey's journal came from a fellow countryman and sometime contributor. For when the *Westminster Review* was launched in 1824, it carried a lengthy analysis of the *Edinburgh Review* by James Mill, which reiterated the charge of commercial motivation and emphasised a general toadying attitude: 'To render men wiser or better is but a secondary concern: to please the public taste is the first.'[64] For Mill, the desire to increase the readership was epitomized by the *Edinburgh Review*'s enthusiasm for English culture: 'the *Edinburgh Review* is written for Englishmen: Shakespeare is the idol of Englishmen: Shakespeare, therefore, must be praised, and for the more complete satisfaction of his admirers, all his merits must be exaggerated, and all his demerits must be sunk'.[65] If Jeffrey was worrying about accusations of local bias in his literary reviews, he must have been startled by Mill's pronouncement that his journal pandered to a rather different set of national prejudices: 'English and excellent it employs as synonymous terms.'[66]

The ironies of Mill's assault on the *Edinburgh Review*'s anglophilia need hardly be pointed out, but the article in the *Westminster* demonstrates the range of reactions provoked by the Scottish journal. Where Byron had perceived an 'oat-fed phalanx' harrying unsuspecting southern bards, Mill found an excessive enthusiasm for all things English. The very diversity of the *Edinburgh Review*, which Jeffrey skilfully exploited for so many purposes, resulted inevitably in a variety of responses. While it is difficult to reconstruct details of the imaginative experience of earlier generations – or, more specifically, to ascertain which reviews were enjoyed by different readers and in what order they were read – the numerous comments in journals and letters together with the more substantial, published replies to Jeffrey give an indication of the notice attracted by the *Edinburgh Review*.

Despite the varied criticisms of the reviewers, there can be no doubt that their work was taken seriously by a large number of readers. If the young lawyers had felt frustrated by their obscurity and lack of prospects at the turn of the century, within a decade they had the satisfaction of seeing their views stimulating debate throughout the country. No longer was there any danger of Edinburgh disappearing into provincial oblivion when such a lively, controversial journal was issuing forth so regularly. Just as the Scottish capital had been widely perceived as a centre of philosophical power in the previous century, when David Hume, William Robertson, Adam Smith, Hugh Blair,

William Cullen and Adam Ferguson had congregated in the clubs and lecture halls, so too the Edinburgh of Francis Jeffrey became associated with intellectual brilliance and debate. The New Town, conceived in the 1750s, had now developed to make Edinburgh one of the finest cities in Europe, while its cultural edifices, raised on the firm foundations of Enlightenment thought, attracted admiration from around the world.[67]

It was the very 'smartness' of the *Edinburgh Review* that made its victims turn critic, alarmed by the extensive influence of its judgements. As Copleston observed in a later essay written to defend the University of Oxford against the *Edinburgh Review*, 'It is one of the ablest of our literary journals; and, with the power of doing much good, seems to delight (shall I say it?) in doing evil.'[68] What spurred Copleston into print was his awareness not only of the *Review*'s cleverness but also of its popularity. Its undesirable – and, in Copleston's eyes, inaccurate – ideas were likely to spread at a horrifying rate unless firm efforts were made to keep them in check. Similar anxieties seem to have driven Wordsworth to compose his *Essay Supplementary to the Preface* of 1815, in an attempt to defend himself from the 'very senseless outcry' raised against his poetry by his 'most active and persevering Adversaries'.[69] As Wordsworth argued that 'every Author, as far as he is great and at the same time *original*, has had the task of *creating* the taste by which he is to be enjoyed', he was deeply conscious of the way in which his own task had been rendered more difficult by Jeffrey's unsympathetic and far-reaching series of reviews.[70]

Jeffrey's intelligence and influence, though deplored by many of his more prominent readers, ensured that the perception of Scotland in the early nineteenth century was by no means confined to 'oat-meal and sheep's heads'. Instead, readers north and south of the Border were dazzled by the cleverness and erudition of the reviewers, while being drawn into intellectual debate by the internal contradictions and diversity. The choices of books under discussion transported readers to the different regions of Scotland, to the rest of Britain, to Europe and the more distant parts of the world, enabling multiple reflection on the wide range of issues that were raised *en route*. As Britain united with Ireland, and consciousness of the world beyond these islands grew, Scottish voices did not seem threatened with silent obscurity, but rather to welcome the vast stage before them. And although not all members of their audience might applaud the contents of Jeffrey's journal, there seems to have been little doubt about the respect commanded by its intellectual quality and interest. If all the smartness of all Scotland was concentrated in its pages, no one could safely ignore the *Edinburgh Review*.

Notes

1. *Sydney Smith*, i pp. iii–iv. See also Alan Bell, *Sydney Smith* (Oxford: Clarendon Press, 1980), 35–42.
2. 16 May 1836; see Morley, ii 493.
3. *Contributions*, i p. ix.
4. Smith to Jeffrey, August 1802; 7 August 1819; Nowell Smith, i 72, 331–2.
5. *Edinburgh Review* 16 (April 1810) 186.
6. Smith to Jeffrey, 7 August 1819, Nowell Smith, i 332.
7. Ibid.
8. Virgil, *Eclogue* i 2: 'silvestrum tenui musam meditaris avena'.
9. Tobias Smollett, *The Expedition of Humphry Clinker*, ed. O. M. Brack (3 vols in 1, Athens, GA: University of Georgia Press, 1990), ii 306; Samuel Johnson, *A Dictionary of the English Language* (1755), 'oats'. The *OED*, under 'oats. 1a' records Eliza Acton's 1857 note: 'In the south of England oats are not employed for bread, but only for feeding horses'.
10. *English Bards and Scotch Reviewers*, 508.
11. Morley, ii 493. The reference is to Luke 16: 20–5.
12. Francis to John Jeffrey, 2 March 1800; Cockburn, i 104.
13. Brougham to Loch, 20 August 1802, Atkinson and Jackson, i 344.
14. John Clive, *Scotch Reviewers: The Edinburgh Review, 1802–1815* (London: Faber and Faber, 1957), p. 27. Leslie Mitchell has discussed the Whiggish inclination of the Edinburgh Reviewers in 'The *Edinburgh Review* and the Lake Poets 1802–1810', *Essays Presented to C. M. Bowra* (London: The Alden Press, 1970), pp. 24–38.
15. Brougham to Loch, 20 August 1802, Atkinson and Jackson, i 345.
16. *Sydney Smith*, i p. vi.
17. Henry Brougham, *Historical Sketches of Statesmen in the Time of George III* (London, 1839), p. 231, cited in Michael Fry, *The Dundas Despotism* (Edinburgh: Edinburgh University Press, 1992), p. 242.
18. Clephane to Loch, 14 March 1802, Atkinson and Jackson, i 306.
19. Scott to Lady Anne Hamilton, 17 January 1802, Grierson, i 127.
20. *Edinburgh Review* 1 (October 1802) 216. See also Brougham to Loch, 20 August 1802, Atkinson and Jackson, i 345.
21. Brougham to Loch, 12 December 1803; ibid., ii 103.
22. Benedict Anderson, *Imagined Communities*, rev. edn (London: Verso, 1991), p. 25.
23. Timothy Brennan, 'The National Longing for Form', *Nation and Narration* ed. Homi K. Bhabha (London: Routledge, 1990), pp. 44–70, 49.
24. On the sceptical dismantling of monarchical myths in Scotland, see Colin Kidd, *Subverting Scotland's Past: Scottish Whig Historians and the Creation of an Anglo-British Identity, 1689–c.1830* (Cambridge: Cambridge University Press, 1993). And on the effects of the 1707 Union, David Daiches, *The Paradox of Scottish Culture* (London: Oxford University Press, 1964); K. Simpson, *The Protean Scot: The Crisis of Identity in Eighteenth-Century Scottish Literature* (Aberdeen: Aberdeen University Press, 1988); Leith Davis, *Acts of Union: Scotland*

and the Literary Negotiation of the British Nation 1707–1830* (Stanford: Stanford University Press, 1999).

25. Michael Fry, *The Dundas Despotism* (Edinburgh: Edinburgh University Press, 1992), p. 236.
26. *Edinburgh Review* 6 (July 1805) 422; 10 (April 1807) 116–24.
27. Jeffrey to his sister, Mary Napier, 19 October 1791, Cockburn, i 36–7.
28. Ibid., i 46.
29. *Edinburgh Review* 39 (October 1823) 159.
30. *Edinburgh Review* 39 (October 1823) 162.
31. Paul Langford, *Englishness Identified: Manners and Character 1650–1850* (Oxford: Clarendon Press, 2000), p. 13.
32. Colin Kidd, *British Identities before Nationalism* (Cambridge: Cambridge University Press, 1999), p. 133.
33. Michael Fry, *The Dundas Despotism* (Edinburgh: Edinburgh University Press, 1992), pp. 236–7.
34. *Edinburgh Review* 1 (January 1803) 398.
35. Ibid.
36. *Edinburgh Review* 6 (April 1805) 18.
37. *Edinburgh Review* 24 (November 1814) 3.
38. *Edinburgh Review* 13 (January 1809) 251.
39. *Edinburgh Review* 13 (January 1809) 263.
40. *Edinburgh Review* 6 (July 1805) 429.
41. *Edinburgh Review* 6 (July 1805) 462.
42. *Edinburgh Review* 6 (July 1805) 430.
43. *Edinburgh Review* 6 (July 1805) 422.
44. *Edinburgh Review* 3 (January 1804) 328–9.
45. *Edinburgh Review* 2 (April 1803) 206–10; 233.
46. *Edinburgh Review* 11 (January 1808) 288.
47. *Edinburgh Review* 24 (November 1814) 1–30.
48. *Edinburgh Review* 24 (November 1814) 30.
49. *Edinburgh Review* 13 (January 1809) 276.
50. Ibid.
51. *Edinburgh Review* 1 (October 1802) 67.
52. Essays on Genius had been published by William Duff and Alexander Gerard (1767, 1771). For a discussion of the problems attending the spoken language of Scotland, see David Craig, *Scottish Literature and the Scottish People 1680–1830* (London: Chatto and Windus, 1961); Robert Crawford, *Devolving English Literature* (Oxford: Clarendon Press, 1992). Jeffrey was said to have lost his own 'broad Scots' at Oxford, Cockburn, i 46–8.
53. *Edinburgh Review* 24 (November 1814) 158.
54. *Edinburgh Review* 24 (November 1814) 182.
55. Morley, i 28. But see also Coleridge's letter to Southey of 12 March 1803 which describes the second number of the *Edinburgh Review* as 'despicable – the hum-drum of pert attorneys' Clerks, very pert & yet prolix & dull as a superannuated Judge' (Griggs, ii 936).
56. 14 March 1811, Morley, i 26.
57. *English Bards and Scotch Reviewers*, 528–39.
58. Wordsworth to Gillies, 14 February 1815, *MY*, ii 197. For interesting discussion of Wordsworth's relationship with Jeffrey, see Mitchell, 'The Edinburgh

Review and the Lake Poets'; Owen and Smyser, iii 56–60; Stephen Gill, *William Wordsworth: A Life* (Oxford: Clarendon Press, 1989), pp. 224–5, 266–70, 301–12; Duncan Wu, *Wordsworth's Reading 1800–1815* (Cambridge: Cambridge University Press, 1996), pp. 116–19.

59. McGann and Weller, i 409. For Byron's Scottish ancestry and sense of national identity see Leslie Marchand, *Byron: A Biography* (3 vols, London: John Murray, 1957); Angus Calder (ed.) *Byron and Scotland: Radical or Dandy?* (Edinburgh: Edinburgh University Press, 1989).

60. *English Bards and Scotch Reviewers* 70.

61. *English Bards and Scotch Reviewers* 62.

62. Wordsworth, *A Letter to a Friend of Robert Burns* (1816); Owen and Smyser, iii 127. For examples of legal language in the *Edinburgh Review*, see the reviews of Wordsworth's *Poems in Two Volumes* and Byron's *Hours of Idleness* (*Edinburgh Review* 11 (October 1807) 214–31; *Edinburgh Review* 11 (January 1808) 285–9).

63. Edward Copleston, *Advice to a Young Reviewer with a Specimen of the Art* (Oxford, 1807), pp. 3–4.

64. James Mill (continued by John Stuart Mill), 'Periodical Literature: Edinburgh Review', *Westminster Review* 1 (April 1824) 536. For discussion of Mill's essay and other contemporary reactions, see Joanne Shattock, *Politics and Reviewers: The Edinburgh and the Quarterly in the Early Victorian Age* (Leicester: Leicester University Press, 1989), pp. 104–24.

65. *Westminster Review* 1 (April 1824) 521. Mill seems concerned with the *Edinburgh's* anti-Gallic prejudice, rather than any neglect of Scottish merit. On the contribution of periodical literature to the developing sense of 'Englishness' in the nineteenth century, see Stefan Collini's wide-ranging analysis, in *Public Moralists: Political Thought and Intellectual Life in Britain 1850–1930* (Oxford: Clarendon Press, 1991).

66. *Westminster Review* 1 (1824) 535.

67. The title *Edinburgh Review* had originally been chosen for the short-lived critical journal founded by Alexander Wedderburn and Adam Smith, with contributions from Hume, Blair and Jardine in 1759. Philip Flynn has examined Jeffrey's debts to, and differences from, the thinkers of the Scottish Enlightenment in *Francis Jeffrey* (1978). The classic account of the late eighteenth-century transformation of Edinburgh is A. J. Youngson, *The Making of Classical Edinburgh* (Edinburgh: Edinburgh University Press, 1966), which includes details of the National Monument on Calton Hill, whose construction was supported by Jeffrey, (pp. 159–60).

68. Copleston, *A Reply to the Calumnies of the Edinburgh Review against Oxford, containing an account of the studies pursued in that University* (Oxford, 1810), p. 4.

69. Owen and Smyser, iii 62. Wordsworth seems to have been particularly dismayed by Jeffrey's tenacity; he represented him as 'this persevering Aristarch' in *A Letter to a Friend of Robert Burns* (Owen and Smyser, iii 127).

70. *Essay, Supplementary to the Preface*, Owen and Smyser iii 80. The observation echoes Coleridge's preface to his *Poems on Various Subjects*, which Wordsworth had quoted in a letter to Lady Beaumont, 21 May 1807 (*MY*, i 150).

3

A 'great theatre of outrage and disorder': Figuring Ireland in the *Edinburgh Review*, 1802–29

Timothy Webb

In November 1812 the *Edinburgh Review* printed a long and carefully argued assessment by James Mackintosh of Edward Wakefield's *Account of Ireland, Statistical and Political*.[1] At an early stage in his review Mackintosh reminded his readers that they had reached 'a moment when that country is the great hinge, on which the whole of our domestic policy turns, and when the speedy as well as general prevalence of right opinions concerning it may materially affect the safety of the Empire'.[2] The rest of his account leaves no doubt that Mackintosh was sympathetically inclined to the claims of the Irish and especially of the Catholics whose practical exclusion from many professions and most positions of note amounted to a 'helotism . . . which either breaks [the Catholic's] spirit or excites his rage'.[3] Mackintosh's analysis also makes it clear that the results of this alienation and strongly registered sense of exclusion were unfortunate, not only because of their implications for the large number of people involved but because of their threat to the cohesiveness of the Union and of the British Empire itself; what was involved included the 'sense of degradation, as well as that of insecurity'.[4]

Contributors to the *Edinburgh Review* had been concerned with the Irish question, and particularly with the increasingly pressing issue of Catholic Emancipation, since shortly after the periodical had been founded in 1802. Even the quickest glance at the contents would suggest the continuity of this concern which was repeatedly discussed, often at length, until the granting of Catholic Emancipation in 1829, after which the Irish question partly changed shape and focus, but continued to exercise the minds of politicians and administrators. Responses were predominantly, if not even exclusively, favourable to the concession of Catholic claims, yet as Mackintosh's account clearly demonstrates, the claims of natural justice were usually coupled with the demands of expediency. Most reviewers were agreed that there was an undeniable if uncomfortably close link between Ireland and England, and failure to acknowledge this and recognize its implications might produce catastrophic results. Mackintosh's article is dated November 1812 and was, presumably, written slightly earlier, at a time when the status of Ireland had an unusually potent currency because of the official recognition of the insanity of George III and the accession of the Prince Regent to power through the passing of the Regency Act (first enacted on 5 February 1811 and confirmed by Act of Parliament on 11 February 1812). One direct result was to focus attention on Ireland. Among the more obvious consequences were Coleridge's series of articles for the *Courier* in May, August and September 1811; Byron's speech in the House of Lords in March 1812; Shelley's *Address to the Irish People* (1812), his *Proposals for an Association of Philanthropists* (1812), and his attempt to intervene directly in Irish politics by visiting Dublin, making a speech at a public meeting and exercising his influence by personal example. There was also Leigh Hunt's 'The Prince on St Patrick's Day', a leading article for *The Examiner* on 22 March 1812 which, by his own later admission, was motivated by his concern for the Irish and his disappointment that the recently empowered Prince Regent had not lived up to his promise (or his promises), and which eventually led to the imprisonment of Hunt himself and his brother John for seditious libel.

Of these four significant writers, Coleridge was the least susceptible to the force of Catholic claims since he was much influenced by fears of religious massacre and remembered recent episodes such as the rising of 1798 with troubled anxiety; he was resistant to arguments in favour of Catholic Emancipation but, with whatever reservations, the other three thought differently. Like Mackintosh, but with a variety of emphasis, they recognized an important conjunction in the development of Irish history and international relations which demanded that something should be done.

Unlike other writers in the *Edinburgh*, Mackintosh did not dwell on the possibility that a disaffected Ireland might be exposed to the risk of invasion by Napoleon – such fears were triggered for some (not least for Coleridge and his brother-in-law Robert Southey) by memories of 1796 and 1798 and the abortive insurrection of Robert Emmet in 1803, and also by a larger suspicion of Napoleon's intentions and his ability to take advantage of English (or perhaps British) discomfort. Yet his use of the phrase 'the great hinge' (compare Coleridge's descriptions of Ireland as 'the Achilles' heel of our Empire'[5] and the earlier 'that vulnerable heel of the British Achilles'[6]) underlines his understanding that Ireland should not be regarded as an unknown and alien territory which required no exercise of responsibility by those English administrators who were responsible for its welfare. For example, he reprinted a brutal anecdote from Wakefield (also retold by James Mill) which involved an Englishman ('a gentleman of some rank') at Carlow races in June 1809 striking an Irishman ('a poor man...[who] was standing in his way') across his face with his whip:

> *But what astonished me more even than the deed, and what shows the difference between English and Irish feeling was, that not a murmur was heard nor hand raised in disapprobation;* but the surrounding spectators dispersed running different ways, like slaves terrified at the rod of their despot.[7]

'I never felt so proud of being an Englishman',[8] commented Wakefield, only to be reprimanded by Mackintosh (who was himself Scottish in origin but was giving voice to an affronted sense of universal human dignity): 'The pride of Mr Wakefield ought to have been converted into an opposite feeling, if he had recollected that laws imposed by an English colony, and now supported by English influence, were the true source of the shocking outrage, and still more shocking patience which he had indignantly witnessed.'[9] Mackintosh was unequivocal in his allocation of blame: 'Ireland, we must say, is not the country where an Englishman is best entitled to be proud of the name.'[10] James Mill, who repeated the anecdote in more concentrated form the following year, did not take issue with Wakefield but commented curtly: 'A fact like this is one of a family. It demonstrates habit. It is decisive.'[11] Where Mackintosh had repeated the story primarily to illustrate the 'feelings entertained by the higher classes of a people to the lower'[12] (even if the episode also carries more ominous resonances), Mill presents it in a context in which 'the barbarity with which the poor are treated will hardly admit of aggravation',[13] and prefaces it with another extract, this time from the travels of Arthur Young.

Undoubtedly, the period immediately before and after the official establishment of a Regency allowed for an extensive and explicit review of the Irish situation. Yet Mackintosh's powerful contribution can be seen not simply as an expression of its own moment in time, but as part of a succession of reviews, or articles, which focused on Irish matters throughout this period with a variety of emphasis and concentration, but with a remarkably unified sense both of the nature of the threat and of the urgency of the situation. Slightly earlier, the warnings were just as fierce, if not fiercer. In July 1807, for example, Sydney Smith was quite apocalyptic. Diagnosing symptoms of downright madness and utter stupidity, he urged the importance of speedy remedial action since that might deliver the English from 'that destruction which is ready to burst upon them' and 'there would be still some chance of saving England from the general wreck of empires'.[14] This language and imagery seems to imply that England is in danger of suffering from the curse which punishes the careless exercise of imperial power. In October Francis Jeffrey recorded that there was 'a great and tremendous evil' and 'a giant hazard':

> We live in a most melancholy and momentous crisis of every thing that relates to the public; nor is it possible for any rational being to take into computation the resources, the ambition and animosity of the enemy, without feeling that there is room for great apprehension as to the result of this arduous contest. We may be successfully invaded by a foreign power, and our whole boasted and cherished system of government, religion, and commerce, may be overwhelmed in an instant. This is the great and tremendous evil, within the peril of which we now stand.[15]

Expediency alone demanded a speedy settlement, at whatever cost and with no theological considerations or reservations: 'With the merit or demerit of the Catholics in such schemes of rebellion, we have at present no concern.'[16] If this involved negotiating with those who were otherwise unacceptable or 'uncivilized', this was a price which must be paid: 'We must make treaties with Algiers, and capitulations with rebels and pirates.'[17] In October of the following year Smith repeated his earlier warning in slightly different terms: 'we conceive it to be by no means improbable, that the country may be, ere long, placed in a situation where its safety or ruin will depend upon its conduct towards the Catholics.'[18] Elsewhere in the same article he speaks of 'the folly and horror of such a code' [the Penal Laws], 'this grand effort of obstinate folly' and 'such a disgraceful spectacle of ingratitude and injustice'.[19] Here it is clear that Smith is not exercised by abstract apocalyptic anxieties, but is specifically troubled that an alienated Catholic population will collaborate with Napoleon and the French.

A similar point is made in 1809 by Malthus, who is less effusively and indignantly sympathetic than Smith, but who reminds his readers that there is a daily risk of losing Ireland and that Napoleon constitutes a threat that must be acknowledged and negated. Looking anxiously towards Spain, he recognizes an awkward and threatening comparison:

> Are we not even, by repeated insults and disappointments, taking the most effectual means to alienate, disgust, and irritate a people who will soon have the same offers made to them from the same quarter? The blaze of hope and of joy which lately illumined the horizon of Spain, is now sunk into a few feeble gleams; the impending effort of Austria seems to be but the prelude to her final extinction; and what shall then prevent the ruthless victor from turning his conquering arms towards the west? We own that we should see with dread even a very small French army in Ireland ... [20]

Strict justice and good policy both suggest that the Catholics should have all they ask for: 'There is one, and one only way, of rendering all the offers and efforts of Bonaparte powerless. The time is short; but it may yet be sufficient. Before the conquering legions of France return from the Danube, let us, by a great and generous act, prepare the hearts of the Irish for their reception.'[21] In 1809 another article (conjecturally attributed to Smith) again acknowledges 'the precarious foundation on which our empire rests'.[22] The situation is dangerous: 'Ireland is distant, – smarting under the destruction of its separate empire, of a different religion, and exposed to the intrigues of France.'[23] In such extreme circumstances, prompt and even apparently gratuitous concessions are necessary:

> Ireland increases rapidly in strength – rapidly, we fear, in disaffection, and in the desire of separation. The Catholic strength and wealth, it must be remembered, increases eight-fold in proportion to that of the Protestants. The time for petitioning may soon end, as it did with America; and the time for demanding begins.

He openly admits: 'To conciliate Ireland, scarcely any price is too great.'[24] In November 1810 Jeffrey continues to insist on the danger constituted by government's reluctance to conciliate the Catholics: 'It is now equally needless to aggravate, and impossible to disguise, the tremendous peril in which Ireland will be placed, if Bonaparte should ultimately succeed in obtaining possession of the Southern Peninsula.'[25] He emphasizes the part which the wind might play in any such transfer of power since, according to his argument, the 'very winds which would best serve for their [i.e. the French] passage, would blow all our fleets from any station where they could be intercepted'; such anxieties might help to explain, by anticipation, his choice of language earlier in the paragraph, where he fears that priests and 'ambitious and enterprizing individuals of every description ... would all be driven into the service of the invader, if they were driven there at all, by the pressure of Catholic disabilities.'[26]

In November 1812 Mackintosh followed Jeffrey's reasoning when he reminded his readers that for sixteen years, apparently, the security of Ireland had been dependent on the winds; it was now imperative that no further delay was allowed: 'While Napoleon is employed in Russia, such a reinforcement [the 20,000 troops needed to secure Ireland] might enable Lord Wellington to drive the French beyond the Pyrenees. A delay of Catholic emancipation for six months may therefore be decisive of the fate of Spain.'[27] Mackintosh was acutely aware that even the immediate enactment of Catholic Emancipation could not absolve the English from the inevitable consequences of history, but he also insisted on the importance of swift action:

> Much of the immediate benefit of Catholic emancipation must depend on its manner, and on the motives from which it shall seem to issue. To be well done – to inspire confidence – to deserve gratitude – it must be done with the alacrity of men eager to begin the reparation of long injustice. But such alacrity is impatient of all delay. Delay is a proof of a reluctant and sullen submission to necessity, which can neither deserve nor command the thanks of any people.[28]

In the year after Mackintosh's review, James Mill claimed that there was not a more instructive page in the history of mankind than a record of what had happened in Ireland if interpreted in the appropriate spirit.[29] In spite of his appearance of generalized objectivity, he too approached the problem not simply as an impartial historian or an abstract analyst. The condition of Ireland represented 'to the empire at large, not a support, but a burthen; and not merely a burthen, but a terror – the source of her fears and her danger.'[30]

In spite of such warnings, in spite of the eventual defeat and banishment of Napoleon, little seemed to change and similar guilt and anxieties were experienced much later. In reviewing the life of Curran in May 1820, Francis Jeffrey notes that there are many traits 'that make one blush for the degradation, and shudder at the government of that magnificent country.'[31] He is unsparing in his admission that a 'feeble and infatuated ministry...looked with helpless consternation at the giant spectre they had contributed to raise'[32] (a Gothic imagining, perhaps with intimations of Frankenstein's monster) and admits that Irish history provides 'the most appalling, and most instructive part of our domestic history'.[33] The record of oppression and the causes of violence in 'that unhappy country', which he describes as 'a great theatre of outrage and disorder', deliver 'a loud memento to England'.[34]

Even in 1825, four years after the death of Napoleon, Ireland still seemed to represent a serious threat. In the course of a long, detailed and carefully argued contribution in which he reviewed five articles,[35] J. R. McCulloch (or Henry Parnell) acknowledged the flagrant and shameful abuses in the system[36] and the 'deep-rooted and cordial hatred of the English name and nation in the minds of the vast majority of the Irish people'.[37] The consequences were bleak and required swift remedy: 'the first foreign standard that is erected on the Irish soil will be the signal for a rising *en masse*, of a whole population impatient of oppression and burning for revenge!...Nor do we think that it is possible to point out another instance in the history of the world, of a people so completely estranged from their rulers, and so thoroughly ripe for rebellion.'[38] Emancipation was urgently needed and its prompt enactment was fraught with vital implications for the political health of England: 'It depends entirely on our future conduct, whether Ireland is to be rendered our best friend and ally, or our most dangerous and mortal foe.'[39] According to this reading, the future prosperity of the Union itself and of both countries involved must rely on a more enlightened government strategy. In March 1827 Sydney Smith was still warning that 'the danger of losing Ireland by insurrection and invasion, which may happen in six months, is utterly overlooked, and forgotten.'[40] But if a foreign influence were properly established in Ireland, 'how many hours would the Irish Church, how many months would the English Church, live after such an event?'[41]

Any survey of the *Edinburgh Review* during this period would reveal how its readers were familiarized with the situation of contemporary Ireland and how they were encouraged to address themselves responsibly and in an appropriately unprejudiced spirit to the resolution of its problems. Irish matters were first explicitly and extensively introduced in Alexander Murray's review of Vallancey's *Prospectus for an Irish Dictionary* in April 1803 followed by Sydney Smith's brilliant and indicative response to the Edgeworths' *Essay on Irish Bulls* in July of the same year. Over the succeeding years reviews included the following: Plowden's *History of Ireland* (?James Loch, October 1804); *Transactions of the Royal Irish Academy* (January 1805); Carr's *Stranger in Ireland* (Richard Lovell Edgeworth and Maria Edgeworth, April 1807); Gordon's *History of Ireland* (Macvey Napier, April 1807); Parnell's *Historical Apology for Irish Catholics* (Sydney Smith, July 1807); Pamphlets on the Catholic Question (Francis Jeffrey, October 1807); Newenham and others on the State of Ireland (Thomas Robert Malthus, July 1808); Parnell's *History of Irish Popery Laws* (Sydney Smith, October 1808); Dr Milner...on the Catholics of Ireland (Sydney Smith, April 1809); Newenham on the State of Ireland (Thomas Robert Malthus, April 1809); Catholic Question (Francis Jeffrey, November 1810); Lord Clarendon on Catholics (Peter Elmsley, February 1812); Wakefield's Ireland (James Mackintosh, November 1812); State of Ireland (James Mill, July 1813); Toleration of Catholics (?Francis Jeffrey, February 1816); Catholic Question (Henry Brougham, December 1816); Irish Affairs (November 1817); Catholics of Ireland (unidentified author, December 1818); Irish Distillery Laws (Andrew Rutherfurd, March 1819); Ireland (Sydney Smith, November 1820); Ireland (J.R.McCulloch or Henry Parnell, June 1822); Ireland (J. R. McCulloch or Henry Parnell, January 1825); Recent History of the Catholic Question (unidentified author, April 1825); Absenteeism (J. R. McCulloch, November 1825); Catholic Emancipation (partly about Ireland; Henry Parnell, November 1825); Education of the Irish Poor (Thomas Spring-Rice, November 1825); Civil Affairs of Ireland (Henry Parnell, February 1826); The Catholic Question (Sydney Smith, March 1827); O'Driscol's *History of Ireland* (Francis Jeffrey, October 1827); The Last of the Catholic Question (partly about Ireland; William Empson, March 1829); Sadler on Ireland (J. R. McCulloch, June 1829). Other reviews were concerned with issues which included an Irish dimension, either explicitly or by implication: for example, Tithes, Toleration and Catholic Emancipation. As this long list indicates, regular readers of the *Edinburgh* would have been well versed in Irish history and particularly in the disabilities of Irish Catholics (a subject on which Sydney Smith, one of the founding members of the *Edinburgh* whose amusingly pointed *Peter Plymley's Letters* appeared incrementally in 1807–8, expressed himself with fierce and indignant wit). Jeffrey's lengthy account of four pamphlets on the Catholic question was itself published as a pamphlet. The regularity, intensity and range of the *Edinburgh's* focus, and its emphasis on humane and well-informed understanding, distinguishes it from the *Quarterly Review* whose Irish coverage during these crucial years was much less extensive and less generous in attitude. It is fitting that the reign of Jeffrey as editor, which began in 1802, should have concluded in 1829, the year in which Catholic Emancipation was finally conceded.

This catalogue suggests that the *Edinburgh* was most concerned, justifiably perhaps, with political and legislative matters. Yet the coverage indicates that it was also alert to other manifestations: it carries reviews of biographical studies of Dermody (Francis Jeffrey, April 1806); James Barry (Richard Payne Knight, August 1810); Lord Charlemont (Francis Jeffrey, November 1811); John Philpot Curran (Francis Jeffrey, May 1820); Richard Lovell Edgeworth (Francis Jeffrey, August 1820); and Richard Brinsley Sheridan (Francis Jeffrey, December 1826). The Irishness of some of these figures is scarcely noticed; others such as Charlemont and Curran are of interest both because of their connections with crucial episodes in Irish history and because they seem to embody characteristics which are more than merely personal. This certainly applies to the reviews of speeches by Curran (Francis Jeffrey, October 1808), Charles Phillips (unidentified reviewer, November 1817) and Henry Grattan (Henry Brougham, February 1823), and the survey of Irish oratory (unidentified reviewer, October 1815). Charles Maturin's *Melmoth the Wanderer* was severely criticized (possibly Francis Jeffrey, July 1821) for exhibiting a 'peculiar tendency' to the 'gaudy and ornate style' which was common among Irish writers, a 'national peculiarity'[42] which had damaged even Thomas Moore.

Moore himself was sometimes reviewed as a poet of 'that Green Isle of the West' (Jeffrey's phrase) but more often his Irishness as a poet was ignored (John Eyre, July 1803; Francis Jeffrey, July 1806; Francis Jeffrey, November 1817). The *Edinburgh* ignored *Irish Melodies* and, although he reviewed *Lalla Rookh*, Jeffrey never mentioned the fact that parts of it (notably *The Fire-Worshippers*) referred to contemporary Irish politics in a conveniently coded way. By contrast, Moore's work as a prose writer produced much more focused and admiring reactions. The seemingly uncharacteristic *Memoirs of Captain Rock, the Celebrated Irish Chieftain* caused Sydney Smith to rehearse the injustices of British rule and to remark that 'old England' had behaved badly towards Ireland by indulging in 'a steady baseness, uniform brutality, and unrelenting oppression.'[43] Celebrating his *Life of Sheridan* in December 1826 Jeffrey admitted that Moore's full range had not yet been recognized: 'Mr Moore has been hitherto most known for the least valuable perhaps of his talents.'[44]

In keeping with this diagnosis, it was Moore (who also wrote on the French novel) who had produced a particularly suggestive review of a number of Irish novels earlier in the year in which he predicted, with an eye towards commerce and imaginative possibilities, 'At present Ireland bids fair to be the great mart of fiction'.[45] (In turn, this prediction was followed by T. H. Lister's review in January 1831 of novels descriptive of Irish life,[46] an example which, strictly speaking, falls just outside the range of this survey but which is suggestive of a new direction.)

Moore writes of the awakening of the Irish novel; neither he nor the *Edinburgh* (at least officially) seems to have taken much notice of the efforts of Sydney Owenson (usually known as Lady Morgan). Only two books of hers are accorded a full review in this period. One is *The Life and Times of Salvator Rosa*, which was noticed at length in July 1824 by William Hazlitt who admitted that he was not 'among [her] devoted admirers' but objected to the 'unjust...disgusting and disgraceful' abuse to which she had been subjected by the Tory journals.[47] The other is *Absenteeism* (1825) which provoked a scrupulous treatment of the subject by J. R. McCulloch, which attends to the issue but scarcely mentions the author.[48] The one novelist who seems to be exempt from this kind of neglect or misunderstanding is Maria Edgeworth, who was a favourite subject with the *Edinburgh* and particularly with Jeffrey himself. In addition to the *Essay on Irish Bulls* which Sydney Smith consistently and deliberately attributes to 'Mr Edgeworth' ('in spite of the mixture of sexes'), though on the last page he refers to 'Edgeworth & Co.' and 'The Firm', her work was noticed in July 1804, April 1806, July 1809, July 1812, January 1814 and August 1817 (all of these reviews were by Jeffrey, except possibly that in January 1814).

Unmistakeably, Jeffrey had a great admiration and affection for Maria Edgeworth, which can be traced through most of these reviews. For example, he celebrates 'the cottage scene at Clonbrony' in *The Absentee* (1812): it 'has made us almost equally in love with the Irish, and with the writer who has painted them with such truth, pathos, and simplicity.'[49] He (or perhaps another unidentified reviewer) praises 'her *manly* understanding' in *Patronage* (1814), her 'inimitable talent for pourtraying her poor countrymen' and her recognition of the connection between dancing, revolution and national feelings.[50]

The effect of her fiction is marked in a sentence which is lightly ironical, but which also suggests a particular affinity between the Irish writer and the Scottish reviewer from which mere English readers are disqualified by poverty of temperament: 'the calmer spirits of the South can hardly yet comprehend the exhilarating effect which her reappearance uniformly produces upon the saturnine complexion of their Northern Reviewers.'[51] Jeffrey regularly alludes to what he regards as her moral objectives: 'the duties of a *Moral Teacher* are always uppermost in her thoughts.'[52] At times, he concedes, she can be too obviously didactic or can too rigidly reject 'everything that does not teach a safe and practical moral lesson.'[53] Consequently, her characters are too stiff: 'Except in the case of her Irish rustics, she has hardly ever ascribed any burst of natural passion, or any impulse of reckless generosity to her characters.'[54] Yet, whatever her limitations as a creator of fictions, she exhibits 'an affectionate love of Ireland, and a concern for her happiness, which cannot be for ever unfruitful.'[55] This apparently moderate and genial patriotism influences the reviewer in turn, who admits to 'the love we bear to the fair writer's country, and her pictures of its natives'.[56]

This comfortable and comforting chain of 'love' might cause one to suspect that Jeffrey is at least partly conditioned by an emotional response which he may consider appropriate to the writer's gender. Certainly, the apparently easy and benevolent tone contrasts with the troubled and painfully conscientious considerations of his long pieces on Irish religion and politics. But perhaps it is also worth recalling what Jeffrey had written in an early review of July 1804 in which he had celebrated the virtues of *Popular Tales* in terms which might appear extravagant:

> This is an attempt, we think, somewhat superior in genius, as well as utility, to the laudable exertions of Mr Thomas Paine to bring disaffection and infidelity within the comprehension of the common people, or the charitable endeavours of Messrs Wirdsworth [*sic*] & Co. to accommodate them with an appropriate vein of poetry. Both these were superfluities which they might have done very tolerably without; but Miss Edgeworth has undertaken to improve, as well as to amuse them, and to bring them back from an admiration of pernicious absurdities, to a relish for the images of those things which must make the happiness of their actual existence. In this view, she rather deserves to be compared to those patriotic worthies who first ventured, after the revival of letters, to write in their native language, and to interest their countrymen in stories of their home manufacture . . .[57]

The tone of the later reviews is never as sharp as this nor so willing to detect challenging virtues in Maria Edgeworth's writing. Yet this early piece (which appeared only a year after Smith's review of *Essay on Irish Bulls*) seems to claim both that the achievement of these apparently modest *Tales* was in its own way a literary experiment which might be compared to *Lyrical Ballads* and that it was a genuinely patriotic contribution to the literature of nation.

The unique and peculiar status of Ireland was regularly enforced or illustrated by analogy or comparison. The wretchedness of many of its inhabitants was frequently attested in this way. In 1812, for example,

James Mackintosh introduces a quotation from Wakefield in which the condition of the average Irishman is compared unfavourably to that of the Russian peasant.[58] The next year James Mill discusses Turkish despotism where the 'lower orders' are 'subject to the caprice and insolence of power'; such power is confined to the 'instruments of government'; 'but where an aristocracy of wealth has a power over the people [as in Ireland], distinct from the laws, the lower orders have an oppressor at every door.'[59] Starkly and without qualification he concludes: 'In no country, however, in Europe, scarcely excepting even Russia, where they are slaves, is the people so completely degraded, as in Ireland.'[60] 'Helotism', the term employed by Wakefield, is used on a number of occasions by other writers to indicate the serfdom of the average Irishman; for example (see p. 58), Mackintosh writes: 'The helotism of the Catholic, which either breaks his spirit or excites his rage, in either case equally unnerves his arm, and devotes his fields to barrenness.'[61] The word signifies bondage or serfdom but for classically educated readers, it may well have raised uncomfortable images of ancient Sparta. In spite of some measures which were intended to effect improvements, the situation was just as serious in 1825: 'We question whether the law either of Morocco or Algiers, sanctions any more flagrant and shameful abuse.'[62] The same writer (perhaps J. R. McCulloch or Henry Parnell) cites a passage from Bell in which he draws analogies with the relations between the Grand Seignior and the Janissaries (that is, with the feudal practices of the Ottoman Empire).[63]

What all these comparisons have in common is reference to a despotic system connected with an imperial power from which most readers would automatically recoil. What is even more common, surprisingly perhaps, is the clear and recurrent suggestion that there are unfortunate but unmistakeable parallels between the English practice of political control in Ireland and the slave trade which was regularly debated in Parliament and discussed in the pages of journals like the *Edinburgh Review*. In October 1807 Jeffrey had addressed the 'incapacities' of Irish Catholics and had concluded that, when they were excluded from 'the privileges and liberties of Englishmen', their condition was at least acknowledged and dignified by voting rights; when these too were removed, 'nothing remained to two thirds of the inhabitants of Ireland, by which they could be distinguished from slaves or aliens', even in their own country.[64] Writing in November 1812 Mackintosh referred critically to that 'body of gentlemen who believed themselves to be the disciples of Locke, men of polished manners and elegant accomplishments'.[65] Whatever their wider virtues, they too were involved in an unjust system: 'But towards the Catholics they inherited all the scorn, the hatred, and the alarm of a lord towards subdued slaves.'[66] This relationship is specifically invoked again by James Mill when he quotes a passage from Arthur Young: 'Landlords of consequence have assured me, that many of these cotters would think themselves honoured by having their wives or daughters sent for to the bed of their master; a mark of slavery that proves the oppression under which such people must live. Nay, I have heard anecdotes of the lives of people being made free with, without any apprehension of the justice of a jury.'[67] One of Young's editors later charged him with naïve credulity since Irish sexual practices could never have consented to such a *droit de seigneur*; yet the important fact here is that Young seems to have credited such stories and Mill, in turn, quotes his comment in his own review. James Mackintosh set out the charge with forceful clarity:

> The exclusion of the Catholics from the privileges of the constitution is a fact of a very peculiar nature, and extremely different from those precautions which have been adopted in other countries by predominant sects, to secure their monopoly of profit and power. It is not to be discussed solely on the general principles of religious liberty. It was not directed against a sect – it was directed against a nation. It was the proscription of a people, under the name of a religion. It was first pronounced by a conquering colony against a conquered nation. It long preceded that religious distinction which is now its outward sign.[68]

According to his interpretation, this exclusion constituted nothing less than a form of slavery: 'When the most cautious and temperate of our classical writers, such as Addison and Blackstone, called the people of France by the name of slaves, they thought the term sufficiently just, as signifying exclusion from the blessings of a free constitution. Emancipation from such a slavery is now the demand of Ireland.'[69] This insistence on the appropriateness of the term 'slavery' is enforced by the comparison which Mackintosh introduces on the same page while reviewing the record of British rule in Ireland and specifically the political and psychological aftermath of the 'total conquests' by Cromwell and King William, 'the utter expulsion of the ancient lords of the soil' and the revolt of 1641: these events left 'a mixture of contempt and hatred in the minds of the governing faction, and of hatred and fear in those of the governed, scarcely to be paralleled in any other region of the globe, unless perhaps in a West India island, immediately after the suppression of a revolt of slaves.'[70]

Mackintosh continued to explore the effects of this state of mind and the evil consequences of the Penal Laws, 'a new code of persecution' which operated in an otherwise 'fortunate age' of toleration when even 'Hungarians and Muscovites were suffered to worship God as they thought best.'[71] These laws were 'felt in every relation of human life' and their effect on 'the national character, was more mischievous than their direct action.'[72] Mackintosh's culminating description interprets these effects in terms of the operation of political power and the deep traces of a colonial system; more damagingly still, and even more shockingly, he suggests that the kind of discrimination which excluded Catholics is directly comparable to the working of a colour bar:

> It is the outward and visible sign of the evil spirit. It is like the operation of colour in those climates where importance and power are determined by complexion, and where the slightest tinge of the degraded colour excludes a man from the privileged caste as effectually as the sablest hue. If the remaining disabilities were in themselves less important than they are, they would still be hideous scars left by painful and disgraceful wounds. They constitute a principle of hostile distinction between a conquered and an enslaved race. They are the badges of six hundred years tyranny in the one, and the brand of six hundred years slavery in the other.[73]

Mackintosh was unusually direct and persuasive, yet one can detect in his account elements which can be found in other writers. These include the attempt to suggest the barely credible by way of comparison ('scarcely to be paralleled in any other region of the globe';[74] compare 'the barbarity with which the poor are treated will hardly admit of aggravation'[75]); the badges of tyranny (compare 'that impatience for the removal of their remaining badges of inferiority'[76] and 'the badge of the triumph of England over Ireland – of Protestantism over Catholicism – and . . . the seal of his own degradation'[77]); the reference to a 'privileged caste' (compare '*five-sixths* of the people as an inferior and degraded *caste*'[78]); and the specific invocation of colour and the slave trade. James Mill, for example, who is now better known as the historian of British India, quotes Kirby Trimmer: 'I am convinced that the African hut possesses comfort and cleanliness beyond what the generality of the inhabitants in the Irish cabin know.'[79] Mill, who had a particular interest in the operation of systems, also cites the observant and curious Arthur Young who had noticed punishments 'which seemed calculated for the meridian of Barbary.'[80] The 'meridian of Barbary' is, of course,

a geographical location, but it also hovers close to the condition of barbarism which most thoughtful analysts and readers associated with Ireland;
in the same review, Mill himself had diagnosed 'a state of barbarity'.

The connection is suggested more directly by Sydney Smith who
contributed several particularly effective pieces on the history and condition of unemancipated Ireland. In 1820 Smith reflected on the fact that
Ireland still was, as Mill had put it, 'stationary in wretchedness':[81] 'Public talk and clamour may do something for the poor Irish, as it did for
the slaves in the West Indies'.[82] In 1824 he remarked tartly: 'They
debarred the Irish even from the pleasure of running away, and fixed
them to the soil, like Negroes'.[83] As early as 1807 he had recognized that
only an appropriate act of the analogical imagination would provide an
orientating sense of how the Irish could not be judged by the normal
standards of civilized society: 'In speaking of the Irish about the reign of
Elizabeth, or James the First, we must not draw our comparisons from
England, but from New Zealand; they were not civilized men, but
savages; and, if we reason about their conduct, we must reason of them
as savages.'[84] The period in question was the late sixteenth and early
seventeenth centuries, yet much that Smith says elsewhere about the
wretched condition of the contemporary Irish suggests that they too
could still be defined as savages. As Macvey Napier had put it earlier in
the same year: 'It is painful to reflect, that the acts and deeds of a
barbarous system, have too often found countenance in kindred
proceedings of more enlightened times.'[85]

These apparently unlikely points of comparison were introduced, of
course, not to suggest that there was anything exotic either in Irish
history or in the state of contemporary Ireland but to bring home to the
well-meaning reader that the state of the 'sister island' was still start-
lingly primitive and that those who, directly or indirectly, contributed
to its administration and government had a responsibility to introduce
improvements. The reaction of the comfortable reader or the average
Englishman is frequently invoked or anticipated. So, for example, when
James Mill devotes his attention to the episode at Carlow races, his
quotation from Arthur Young clearly distinguishes between, on the one
hand, the unlimited power of the landlord in an Irish setting and the
anxiety of the Irish spectators to protect themselves and, on the other,
the opposition of an imaginary Englishman who knows his own rights:
'Knocking down is spoken of in the country in a manner that makes an
Englishman stare.'[86] Sydney Smith declares that 'It is impossible to live
in Ireland, without perceiving the various points in which it is inferior
in civilization.'[87] Such a recognition is far from comforting since, in

Smith's view: 'With such a climate, such a soil, and such a people, the inferiority of Ireland to the rest of Europe is directly chargeable to the long wickedness of the English Government.'[88] Yet even an acknowledgement of this 'wickedness' could lead to a guilt which was smugly comfortable. Smith works against the possibility of so passive a condemnation of English policy by insisting on a comparison with contemporary England which requires imaginative projection: 'The whole is a scene of idleness, laziness, and poverty, of which it is impossible, in this active and enterprising country, to form the most distant conception.'[89]

Earlier in the same year, reviewing a biography of John Philpot Curran, Francis Jeffrey had introduced a complicated anecdote which involved a nobleman striking an elderly priest, who was legally represented by the young Curran with the consequence that 'he was blamed and pitied by all his prudent friends for his romantic and Quixotic rashness.'[90] Jeffrey's first comment can be compared to Mackintosh's account of the damaging psychological effects of the Penal Laws: 'These facts speak volumes as to the utter perversion of moral feeling that is produced by unjust laws, and the habits to which they give rise.'[91] He continues by suggesting that this 'perversion' manifests itself in painful and puzzling contradictions: 'No nation is so brave or so generous as the Irish, – and yet an Irish nobleman could be guilty of the brutality of striking an aged priest, without derogating from his dignity or honour: – No body of men could be more intrepid or gallant than the leaders of the Irish bar; and yet it was thought too daring and presumptuous for any of them to assist the sufferer in obtaining redress for an outrage like this.'[92] Jeffrey defines this episode as a phenomenon which is recognizably Irish: 'In England, those things are inconceivable.'[93] Yet, like Smith, he does not pass such a judgement in order to exempt English (or Scottish) readers and to insulate them in a complacent superiority. His effort is, characteristically, to make his readers conceive, and understand, behaviour which they might otherwise dismiss as inexplicably foreign.

A particular point of concern with the reviewers is that the operation of the legal system in Ireland is often very different from what might be expected in England. Sydney Smith rehearsed more than once the provisions of the Penal Laws and was unequivocal in his condemnation of a code 'which reflects indelible disgrace upon the English character, and explains but too clearly the cause of that hatred in which the English name has been so long held in Ireland.'[94] Reviewers were often at pains to explain the systems of tithing and absenteeism, the role of the assistant-barrister and the practices of Irish courts. James Mill acknowledged that English law does not really work in an Irish setting where the contexts are so widely different.[95] At best, these variations could be interpreted as a failure of administrative imagination; at worst, they might signal an anomaly with revolutionary potential. Sydney Smith also considered the operation of the law through comparative spectacles: 'And if this is true in England, it is much more strikingly true in Ireland, where it is extremely difficult to obtain verdicts for breaches of covenant in leases.'[96] Earlier in 1820 guided by the lawyer's instinct for impartiality which he often brought to bear on such matters, Francis Jeffrey drew attention to the implications and effects of such damaging inconsistencies. Discussing the fact that in Ireland a man might be convicted of treason through the evidence of a single witness, he declared with unambiguous indignation: 'nothing can be more revolting than such an anomaly in the constitutional law of united kingdoms.'[97] For Jeffrey the Union certainly did not imply equality of practice in legislative and judicial concerns; as another writer (perhaps J. R. McCulloch or Henry Parnell) expressed it in 1825: 'There is at this moment no such thing as a real union between England and Ireland.'[98]

This serious concern with the practices of the law and its larger implications for an understanding of the Irish question is characteristic both of Jeffrey himself (who later became Lord Advocate) and of many others who wrote for the *Edinburgh Review*. Yet, if one way of illustrating the uniqueness of Ireland was to compare its legal system with that of England, the reviewers also had quietly confident recourse to the Scottish example. Not surprisingly, the periodical's public affiliation not only liberated them from any simplistically patriotic allegiance to the English way of doing things but also allowed them to suggest that the Scottish experience pointed towards solutions which were fairer, more thoughtful and, ultimately, more effective. So, for example, in October 1807 Jeffrey is threateningly explicit about the exclusions and disabilities suffered by Irish Catholics which he contrasts with the positive effects achieved by adopting a constructive approach to the Scottish Presbyterians, which was at once more enlightened and more expedient. Any observer of the 'loyalty, tranquillity, and security' of contemporary Scotland should think back to the period 'when the prevailing religion was discountenanced'; he should ask himself 'in what condition he conceives it would have stood at this moment, if the establishment of Episcopacy had been upheld in that country by the same means that Protestantism has been upheld in Ireland, and if Presbyterians had been subjected to all the disqualifications, and exposed to all the insults and injuries, which are now the lot of the Catholics in the neighbouring island?'[99] Had the Scottish solution not been followed,

Is there any one who does not see, that, instead of a pattern of loyalty, and a nursery for our soldiers and sailors, it would have been a centre of sedition and discontent, and required the controul of more forces than it now supplies; – that, instead of adding to the strength of the empire, it would have been a source of weakness and apprehension; and would have been, in one word, like Ireland, the seat of rebellion, and the point of attack for every power with which we were at enmity?[100]

In 1809 it was Malthus who looked to Scotland for an example of what might be affected by the creation of an established church. Sixteen years later the comparison was still potent and its consequences could be interpreted through the everyday appearance of the Scottish landscape. The virtues of Scotland were, at least partly, the products of a system which was more equitable and less divisive: 'they are seen in the extensive farms and improved estates, in the flourishing condition of agriculture, in the increasing wealth of the farmers, and in the comfort, happiness, and moderate numbers of the peasantry of Scotland!'[101]

These idealized images of a happily regulated society could be set against the description of an Ireland bitterly divided against itself by the thoughtless continuation of a system of church establishment and especially of tithes (an abuse much criticized by contributors to the *Edinburgh*): 'I have beheld at night houses in flames, and for a moment supposed myself in a country exposed to the ravages of war, and suffering from the incursions of an enemy.' These are the words of Edward Wakefield but they were quoted in 1825 by a reviewer (perhaps McCulloch) who set this disturbing evocation of a country reduced to the hostilities of a civil war against the supposed tranquillity of the Scottish model.[102]

Some contributors, at least, recognized here another anomaly: if Ireland had attracted the same administrative attention as Scotland, such catastrophes need not have occurred and the deep-seated animosity between 'the vast majority of the Irish people' and 'the English name and nation' might have been avoided. As late as October 1827 Jeffrey is still insisting on the comparison. He tells his readers: 'The prevailing religion of the people was proscribed and persecuted [in Scotland] with a ferocity greater than has ever been systematically exercised, even in Ireland.'[103] Now, thanks to sensible government policies, 'There are no local oppressions, no national animosities.' Ireland's miseries are to be ascribed largely to the delay in achieving the Union and to its 'ultimate incompleteness'.[104]

There seems to have been a recurrent recognition that Ireland and Scotland had much in common, but that they had also become strikingly and instructively different. A review of John Carr's *The Stranger in Ireland* in April 1807 presents the contrast in the form of slightly pompous instructive advice and indicates, rightly, the importance of education: 'We hope that it will not be thought to arise from national partiality, if we advert to the state of education in our own country, and if we say that Ireland may look with advantage to North Britain, for an example of the success which rewards the labour and expense bestowed on national instruction.'[105] This review has been attributed hestitantly to Richard Lovell Edgeworth, or jointly to him and his daughter Maria, yet such an attribution must account for what appears to be a pride in the effects of Scottishness. Whether this nationality is a fictional assumption or not, the article insists on the virtues of a Scottish approach which is carefully distinguished from the Irish. Noting what it regards as an excessive effusiveness in Carr, it expresses its distaste by a slightly awkward criticism which draws on received notions of Scottish thrift: 'Far be it from us to censure the generous overflowings of gratitude: but we must own, that our author has, on some occasions, startled our Scottish notions of economy, by the profuseness of his remuneration for trifling civilities.'[106]

Carr was English but, according to this account, he seems to have captured, or been captured by, a rhetorical generosity which was expressive of nation: the critique implies that style gives voice to something which is not merely personal but is informed by a deeper cultural life. If this antipathy was actually articulated by a writer (or writers) who was (or were) Irish, the irony would be sweet; whatever the truth, the point of the criticism is based on an antithesis between 'Irish' and 'Scottish' values which effects a suggestive comparison.

Behind many of these accounts, implicitly and sometimes explicitly, can be found certain assumptions about the Irish character and the nature of Irish identity. Apparently, Maria Edgeworth was prized by Jeffrey partly because of her 'affectionate love of Ireland' and 'her pictures of its natives.'[107] The Irish, it seemed, were 'known to be highly susceptible of gratitude and affection' (Malthus, April 1809); impetuous (Jeffrey, November 1811); 'susceptible in the highest degree of sudden and ardent feelings, and not more lukewarm in their affection than in their resentment' (Mackintosh, November 1812); partakers in 'the lively temperament of the whole nation' (Moore, February 1826). In May 1820 Jeffrey pronounced: 'No nation is so brave or so generous as the Irish'. In the same year Smith characterized them as 'light-minded', with their own deficiencies and limitations, but also inescapably the victims of English misgovernment. In the course of his survey of Irish history and contemporary Ireland, he assessed the people in a way

which gave expression to his admiration but which partly balanced this
by enumerating their weaknesses:

> The Irish character contributes something to retard the improvements
> of that country. The Irishman has many good qualities: He is brave,
> witty, generous, eloquent, hospitable, and open-hearted; but he is
> vain, ostentatious, extravagant, and fond of display – light in
> counsel – deficient in perseverance – without skill in private or pub-
> lic economy – an enjoyer, not an acquirer – one who despises the
> slow and patient virtues – who wants the superstructure without the
> foundation – the result without the previous operation – the oak
> without the acorn and the three hundred years of expectation. The
> Irish are irascible, prone to debt, and to fight, and very impatient of
> the restraints of law. Such a people are not likely to keep their eyes
> steadily upon the main chance, like the Scotch or the Dutch.[108]

The question of national identity and its relation to the modes of
expression becomes much clearer in other contexts. Sydney Smith's
review of the *Essay on Irish Bulls* remains unconvinced by the claims for
a distinctively Irish imagination advanced in that seminal work
although he provides a notable definition of the mental operations
involved in the bull and concludes by commending the book's 'lively
feeling of compassion ... for the distresses of the wild, kind-hearted,
blundering poor of Ireland.'[109] More generally, the *Edinburgh* seems to
focus on rather different social groupings, even if some of its definitions
might be applied to Smith's 'blundering poor'. There are detailed
reviews of collections of speeches by Phillips and Curran in which the
reviewers (Jeffrey in particular) concentrate on the phenomenon of
'Irish eloquence' with more exactitude and precision than they sometimes bring to more obviously 'literary' texts. In October 1808 Jeffrey
offers a useful definition:

> There is something very peculiar, and very well worth attending to,
> in the character of Irish eloquence. More vehement, and figured and
> poetical than any that is now attempted in this country, it aims
> almost always at dazzling the imagination, or enflaming the passions
> at least, as much as at enlightening the understanding. On almost
> every subject, it aspires at being pathetic or magnificent; and, while
> it adorns what is grand, or kindles what is interesting with the rays of
> its genius, is apt to involve in the redundant veil of its imagery, what
> is either too low or too simple to become such a drapery. Being the

natural language of fearless genius and impassioned feeling, it will not always be found to express judicious sentiments or correct reasoning; but will generally lead to lofty principles, and glimpses of great theory. It is sometimes coarse, and frequently noisy and redundant; but it has usually strength in its coarseness; and, for the most part, fancy if not reason in its extravagance. Though the design and the drawing may frequently be faulty, the colouring is always brilliant, and the expression, for the most part, original and powerful.[110]

In Jeffrey's view this style had been 'defiled' and had degenerated. The case of Curran provided a vivid example of how even its virtues may become dangerous both to the individual and to the larger national discourse which it may influence and corrupt. Milton, Bacon and Jeremy Taylor did not allow themselves such rhetorical self-indulgence:

There is fancy and figure enough certainly in their compositions; but there is no intoxication of the fancy, and no rioting and revelling among figures – no ungoverned and ungovernable impulse – no fond dalliance with metaphors – no mad and headlong pursuit of brilliant images and passionate expressions – no lingering among tropes and melodies – no giddy bandying of antitheses and allusions – no craving, in short, for perpetual glitter, and panting after effect, till both speaker and hearer are lost in the splendid confusion, and the argument evaporates in the heat which was meant to enforce it.[111]

One unidentified reviewer, possibly Jeffrey, was particularly resistant to such characteristics, which he identified as symptomatic of a certain kind of Irishness, and which he detected in Maturin's *Melmoth the Wanderer*:

Their genius runs riot in the wantonness of its own uncontrolled exuberance; – their imagination, disdaining the restraint of judgment, imparts to their literature the characteristics of a nation in one of the earlier stages of civilization and refinement. The florid imagery, gorgeous diction, and Oriental hyperboles, which possess a sort of wild propriety in the vehement sallies of Antar the Bedoween chieftain of the twelfth century, become cold extravagance and floundering fustian in the mouth of a barrister of the present age; and we question whether any but a native of the sister island would have ventured upon the experiment of their adoption.[112]

The surprising reference to 'a barrister of the present age' reveals clearly that, in the judgement of the reviewer, the shortcomings of Maturin were also those of contemporary Irish lawyers such as Phillips and Curran. This 'splendid vice' was identified by other reviewers including Thomas Moore (himself one of Jeffrey's targets) who diagnosed in February 1826 'that superfinery of phrase and thought, to which the Irish...are but too much addicted'.[113] In a suggestive formulation, Moore claimed that there was 'a continual phosphorescent sparkling of wit and humour going on'.[114] The image reminds one of Jeffrey's reviews of Moore's own poetry and suggests that, here as elsewhere, the process of definition went forward by way of antithesis and comparison. The Irish, the argument went, were much like the English and could be appropriately instructed or, if necessary, tamed and conciliated; and yet, as these responses suggest, they could also be charmingly, if sometimes frighteningly and unmanageably, different.

Notes

1. *Edinburgh Review* 20 (November 1812) 346–69.
2. Ibid., 347.
3. Ibid., 352.
4. Ibid.
5. CC *Essays*, ii 280.
6. CC *Friend*, i 311.
7. *Edinburgh Review* 20 (November 1812) 354.
8. Ibid.
9. Ibid., 354–5.
10. Ibid., 355.
11. *Edinburgh Review* 21 (July 1813) 355.
12. *Edinburgh Review* 20 (November 1812) 354.
13. *Edinburgh Review* 21 (July 1813) 354.
14. *Edinburgh Review* 10 (July 1807) 299, 305.
15. *Edinburgh Review* 11 (October 1807) 132.
16. Ibid., 134.
17. Ibid., 135.
18. *Edinburgh Review* 13 (October 1808) 77.
19. Ibid., 82.
20. *Edinburgh Review* 14 (April 1809) 169.
21. Ibid.
22. Ibid., 64.
23. Ibid., 63.
24. Ibid., 64.
25. *Edinburgh Review* 17 (November 1810) 3.
26. Ibid.
27. *Edinburgh Review* 20 (November 1812) 366.

28. Ibid.
29. *Edinburgh Review* 21 (July 1813) 341.
30. Ibid., 343.
31. *Edinburgh Review* 33 (May 1820) 267.
32. Ibid., 271.
33. Ibid., 277.
34. Ibid., 269, 282, 269.
35. *Edinburgh Review* 41 (January 1825) 356–410.
36. Ibid., 394.
37. Ibid., 356–7.
38. Ibid., 358.
39. Ibid., 410.
40. *Edinburgh Review* 45 (March 1827) 427.
41. Ibid.
42. *Edinburgh Review* 35 (July 1821) 355–6.
43. *Edinburgh Review* 41 (October 1824) 143.
44. *Edinburgh Review* 45 (December 1826) 1.
45. *Edinburgh Review* 43 (February 1826) 359.
46. *Edinburgh Review* 52 (January 1831) 410–31.
47. *Edinburgh Review* 40 (July 1824) 316.
48. *Edinburgh Review* 43 (November 1825) 54–76.
49. *Edinburgh Review* 20 (July 1812) 119.
50. *Edinburgh Review* 22 (January 1814) 417, 422, 434.
51. Ibid., 416.
52. *Edinburgh Review* 28 (August 1817) 391.
53. Ibid., 395.
54. Ibid., 394.
55. Ibid., 396.
56. Ibid., 398.
57. *Edinburgh Review* 4 (July 1804) 330.
58. *Edinburgh Review* 20 (November 1812) 349.
59. *Edinburgh Review* 21 (July 1813) 353.
60. Ibid., 354.
61. *Edinburgh Review* 20 (November 1812) 352.
62. *Edinburgh Review* 41 (January 1825) 394.
63. Ibid., 368.
64. *Edinburgh Review* 11 (October 1807) 119–20.
65. *Edinburgh Review* 20 (November 1812) 364.
66. Ibid.
67. *Edinburgh Review* 21 (July 1813) 354.
68. *Edinburgh Review* 20 (November 1812) 363.
69. Ibid.
70. Ibid.
71. Ibid.
72. Ibid., 365.
73. Ibid.
74. Ibid., 363.
75. *Edinburgh Review* 21 (July 1813) 354.
76. *Edinburgh Review* 11 (October 1807) 125.

77. *Edinburgh Review* 41 (January 1825) 361.
78. Ibid., 357.
79. *Edinburgh Review* 21 (July 1813) 355.
80. Ibid., 357.
81. Ibid., 364.
82. *Edinburgh Review* 34 (November 1820) 336.
83. *Edinburgh Review* 41 (October 1824) 144.
84. *Edinburgh Review* 10 (July 1807) 301.
85. *Edinburgh Review* 10 (April 1807) 119.
86. *Edinburgh Review* 21 (July 1813) 354.
87. *Edinburgh Review* 34 (November 1820) 333–4.
88. Ibid., 334.
89. Ibid., 335.
90. *Edinburgh Review* 33 (May 1820) 267.
91. Ibid.
92. Ibid., 267–8.
93. Ibid., 268.
94. *Edinburgh Review* 13 (October 1808) 81.
95. *Edinburgh Review* 21 (July 1813) 359–60.
96. *Edinburgh Review* 34 (November 1820) 328.
97. *Edinburgh Review* 33 (May 1820) 280.
98. *Edinburgh Review* 41 (January 1825) 365.
99. *Edinburgh Review* 11 (October 1807) 131.
100. Ibid.
101. *Edinburgh Review* 41 (January 1825) 398.
102. Ibid., 378.
103. *Edinburgh Review* 46 (October 1827) 436.
104. Ibid., 436–7.
105. *Edinburgh Review* 10 (April 1807) 55.
106. Ibid., 47.
107. *Edinburgh Review* 28 (August 1817) 396, 398.
108. *Edinburgh Review* 34 (November 1820) 335.
109. *Edinburgh Review* 2 (July 1803) 402.
110. *Edinburgh Review* 13 (October 1808) 136.
111. *Edinburgh Review* 33 (May 1820) 297.
112. *Edinburgh Review* 35 (July 1821) 356.
113. *Edinburgh Review* 43 (February 1826) 369.
114. Ibid., 359.

4
Prejudiced Knowledge: Travel Literature in the *Edinburgh Review*

Massimiliano Demata

I

From its first issue of October 1802, the *Edinburgh Review* provided its readers with a broad spectrum of material – discussions of the slave trade and the importance of the colonies, reviews of sermons, law and political economy, poetry and prose fiction, and even mineralogy and optics. Although Francis Jeffrey is now mainly associated with poetry, Francis Horner with political economy and Henry Brougham with education and politics, the *Edinburgh*'s main writers exercised their critical talents on disparate subjects. One genre favoured by virtually all of the *Edinburgh* contributors was travel literature. Under Jeffrey's editorship, the journal devoted an extraordinary number of articles to it, and the implications of this have until now gone unnoticed.

One explanation for this may be found in the Enlightenment roots of the journal: Hume, Smith, Ferguson, Kames and Monboddo had drawn on travel books and considered them an adjunct to philosophy. Similarly, Jeffrey and his reviewers expected them to support the study of human nature by providing readers with information about foreign people and places. The *Edinburgh* therefore laid emphasis on the methods adopted by travellers to gain knowledge of the countries visited as well as the literary strategies by which such knowledge was presented to readers.

Given the large number of reviews of travel literature, and the variety of themes analysed in them, I am compelled to focus on the *Edinburgh*'s coverage during its first five years, as it was during that period that the critical features of the genre were mapped. Furthermore, the period 1802–7 was dominated by the Napoleonic Wars, when travel literature represented the only available 'window' to a world which, due to difficulties in travelling, British readers could know only from a distance. It is hardly surprising that the genre, and the *Edinburgh* itself, became a forum for discussion of the relationships – cultural, political, social – between Britain and the wider world. This period also witnessed the continuing development of the British empire, and travel books provided the *Edinburgh* reviewers with the opportunity of discussing foreign policy issues; central in this respect are some of the articles which the *Edinburgh* devoted to the Ottoman Empire and the role of British imperialism in the emerging Eastern Question.

II

The *Edinburgh*'s selectiveness in the choice of works reviewed was notorious and has been recognized as one of its innovations. The Advertisement to the first number states that it was the reviewers' intention 'to confine their notice, in a great degree, to works that either have attained, or deserve, a certain portion of celebrity'.[1] Although Jeffrey would adhere to this criterion for the most part, his coverage of travel books would be wider. In an early review of William Hunter's *Travels in the Year 1792 through France, Turkey, and Hungary, to Vienna,* Brougham spelt out the policy of the *Edinburgh* on this point:

> We are of opinion, that books of travels deserve a greater degree of attention, in proportion to their merits, than other works of more ordinary and easier composition; and we have, therefore, during the course of our undertaking, been disposed to relax in their favour that strict rule of selection, which has been our guide in some other branches of literature.[2]

Brougham goes on to express frustration at what he considers the poor standard of the majority of contemporary travel books – 'Unhappily, we have hitherto found very little room for bestowing any further marks of admiration on the writings in question.' All the same, the *Edinburgh* remained true to Brougham's determined statement in favour of travel writing from the first volume onwards. Of the 29 essays published in October 1802, five were devoted to travel books: *Voyage dans les Départemens de la France,* Guillaume Antoine Olivier's *Travels in the Ottoman Empire, Egypt, and Persia,* Friedrich Conrad Hornemann's *Journal from Cairo to Mourzouk,* Alexander Mackenzie's *Voyages from Montreal, on the River St. Laurence, through the Continent of North America,* and Giuseppe Acerbi's *Travels through Sweden, Finland, and Lapland, to the North Cape.*

Almost the whole world was covered by these works. Two other essays on works not strictly classed as travel literature – the sixth volume of *Asiatic Researches* and George Baldwin's *Political Reflections relative to Egypt* – indicate the degree of interest that the *Edinburgh* took in works that discussed distant parts of the world, especially when they concerned potential colonial acquisitions.[3]

Each number of the journal from 1802 to 1807 featured at least one article on travel literature (sometimes they contained as many as four), and from 1805 to 1807 travel books were lead reviews in at least one of the four issued annually.[4] After 1807, the average number of the articles in each volume dwindled from 18–20 to 14–15; then it dropped to ten as contributions grew longer. But travel-writing was always given priority, and by 1815 only seven out of a total of 48 numbers did not contain at least one such article.[5]

In their emphasis on the contribution of the genre to the expansion of knowledge of geographical, cultural and social contexts, Jeffrey, Brougham, Horner and Smith followed the methodology of the Scottish Enlightenment. Scottish thinkers differed widely in some respects but were united in believing that, whatever conclusion they came to, it should emerge out of an inductive method whereby data gathered through observation led to theories and 'systems' – never vice versa. In his Preface to the *Essays and Observations, Physical and Literary, Read before a Philosophical Society in Edinburgh* (1754), Hume states: 'at worst, our collections will be a species of magazine, in which facts and observations, the sole means of true induction, will be deposited for the purposes of philosophy.'[6] The collection of such data is a necessary first step for any inquiry into the nature of man. It is a wide-ranging approach by which general principles could be drawn from the comparative study of phenomena and data collected by empirical means. As Hume noted in *A Treatise of Human Nature* (1759–60), the risk of blindly accepting 'theories' without foundation in fact is that of falling into 'unphilosophical probability', which is

> deriv'd from general rules, which we rashly form to ourselves, and which are the source of what we properly call PREJUDICE. An *Irishman* cannot have wit, and a Frenchman cannot have solidity; for which reason, tho' the conversation of the former in any instance be visibly very agreeable, and of the latter very judicious, we have entertain'd such a prejudice against them, that they must be dunces or fops in spite of sense and reason. Human nature is very subject to errors of this kind; and perhaps this nation as much as any other.[7]

It is significant that, by way of presenting an example of 'prejudice' (one of the most typical 'errors' of 'human nature'), Hume mentions the relationship between the English and other nations, and those generalizing and commonplace assumptions unverified by facts. Clearly 'prejudice' is an obstacle to the attainment of knowledge as it generates false notions of other peoples and cultures. On this basis, Scottish philosophers viewed travel literature as founded on true, 'unprejudiced' facts – the only ones on which a valid philosophical system could be founded. The works of those philosophers were based on the study of man's gradual evolution from primitive forms of society (some of which could be observed in remote parts of the world) to more advanced ones. Such 'gradualistic' and comparative methods aimed to define what Gladys Bryson has called an 'essentially natural and predictable progress'.[8] This approach was typical of Scottish culture, as Robert Crawford has noted: 'eighteenth-century Scottish writing is filled with comparisons of cultures at various stages of development, and with speculations about how societies "improve".'[9]

In their studies of 'physical anthropology',[10] Lords Kames and Monboddo were more interested in human biology than in social behaviour and institutions, but still found it necessary to refer to travel literature. Their researches, derived from discussions about the theories of Buffon and Linnaeus, led them to consult numerous accounts of travellers in remote parts. Their use of these sources led to divergent conclusions: Monboddo was alert to proofs that would demonstrate the uniform nature of man in all conditions whereas Kames argued that races were different – not least the native North Americans who, he claimed, comprised a lower order of being. Kames's *Sketches of the History of Man* (1774) necessarily drew on travel books as it demanded precise and reliable accounts of communities outside Europe.[11] His reflections on the various races living in, and adapting themselves to, different climates relied on information provided by travel literature. In Book II, chapter 3 of his *Of the Origin and Progress of Language* (1773–92) Monboddo produced 'Examples from antient and modern history of Men living in the Brutish State, without Arts or Civility', based on accounts by such classical and contemporary travellers as Diodorus Siculus ('a traveller as well as an historian'), Leo Africanus, Garcilasso de la Vega and Keoping.[12] Monboddo's study of human anatomy, and his researches into the 'men with tails' and orangutans, depended on reports of those who had visited Africa and South America.

Adam Ferguson found travel literature useful in the study of man's social, political and economic development. In his *Essay on the History of Civil Society* (1767) he attempted to establish the basic uniformity of man's social nature – a uniformity adapted to different ages and places. The evolution of society from rude to barbarous, and eventually civilized, was a process which, Ferguson assumed, could be studied. In order to do this he turned to history and travel books, finding proof for the idea that man was naturally a social animal in 'the earliest and the latest accounts collected from every quarter of the earth'.[13] Works on 'savage' populations from all over the world, including those by Charlevoix,[14] gave Ferguson hints as to the state of man prior to modern civilization, on his progress and place in contemporary society. The materials in Part Two of the *Essay*, 'Of the History of Rude Nations', derive entirely from travel books – for instance, his analysis of property:

> If mankind, in any instance, continue the article of property on the footing we have now represented, we may easily credit what is farther reported by travellers, that they admit of no distinctions of rank or condition; and that they have in fact no degree of subordination different from the distribution of function, which follows the differences of age, talents, and dispositions.[15]

The use made of travel literature by Ferguson, Kames and Monboddo in their research was only the most visible indication of its importance; it also played an important role in forming the Scottish teaching system and was an essential part of the curriculum at the University of Edinburgh.[16] The holdings of the Physiological Library of the University, founded in 1724 by Robert Steuart, Professor of Natural Philosophy, and used by the young Hume during the session of 1724–5, included the textbooks used in Steuart's classes, and 'it was to contain the best Editions of Books, both ancient and modern' on various scientific subjects including volumes 'Of Navigation, Geography, and Voyages'.[17] Adam Smith often discussed the works of Charlevoix and Lafitau in his lectures on jurisprudence at Glasgow in 1762–3,[18] and nearly three decades later John Millar, Professor of Civil Law at Glasgow, made use of travel books in lectures on jurisprudence and politics which Jeffrey attended.[19]

The *Edinburgh*'s idea of literary style in books of travel was influenced by Hugh Blair and the ensuing debate on the purity and clarity of English. The interdisciplinary and empirical method used by Scottish thinkers required a clear and straightforward idiom that would give wide diffusion to their ideas. Even the language used in the debating societies of Edinburgh and Glasgow (some of which had *Edinburgh* reviewers among their members) had to take into account their varied social composition, and required a universally understandable style.[20] In his *Lectures on Rhetoric and Belles Lettres* (1783) Hugh Blair discusses 'philosophical writing' in a way that Jeffrey and Brougham would make their own:

> As the professed object of Philosophy is to convey instruction, and as they who study it are supposed to do so for instruction, not for entertainment, the Style, the form, and dress, of such Writings, are less material objects. They are objects, however, that must not be wholly neglected. He who attempts to instruct mankind, without studying, at the same time, to engage their attention, and to interest them in his subject by his manner of exhibiting it, is not likely to prove successful. The same truths, delivered in a dry and cold manner, or with a proper measure of elegance and beauty, will make very different impressions on the minds of men.[21]

Blair's emphasis on clarity is echoed in reviews on travel literature published by the *Edinburgh*. Besides providing its readers with a reliable picture of a people or geographical area, travel literature was expected to do so in a clear and enjoyable language.

III

In early issues of the *Edinburgh*, reviews of travel literature fell mainly to its four founders: Jeffrey, Brougham, Smith and, to a lesser extent, Horner. Brougham was particularly prolific: of the 78 reviews of travel books published between 1802 and 1815, 30 were his. Jeffrey's preference for travel literature was a mark of his early criticism. He wrote up to nine reviews of travel books in the first 17 issues: four on works by John Barrow, two on works about Scotland, and one each on Mackenzie's *Voyages in North America*, Vivant Denon's *Voyage dans la Basse et la Haute Egypte*, and Holcroft's *Travels*. His high regard for the genre is indicated by the fact that during this period his nine articles on travel literature formed a large share of the total number – 55–60 – he contributed to the *Edinburgh*.

After October 1806 Jeffrey's interest in reviewing travel books waned. Other writers – mostly Brougham, and, more sporadically, Smith, John Allen and Macvey Napier – took them on, leaving him free to concentrate on literary criticism, politics and editorial duties. Despite the amount of thought and energy he had put into travel at that early period, Jeffrey included only four such articles in the volume of collected essays he published in 1844, in the closing 'Miscellaneous' section, all written after 1822. It would be wrong to be misled by this into thinking that, to him, travel literature was little more than a temporary infatuation.

Jeffrey famously told Scott that 'The Review, in short, has but two legs to stand on. Literature no doubt is one of them: But its *Right leg* is Politics.'[22] Crucially, travel reviews provided Jeffrey and his staff with opportunities to discuss *both* politics and literature. His thoughts on the popularity gained by the *Edinburgh* are linked to the moralizing function of criticism:

> If I might be permitted farther to state, in what particular department, and generally, on account of what, I should most wish to claim a share of those merits, I should certainly say, that it was by having constantly endeavoured to combine Ethical precepts with Literary Criticism, and earnestly sought to impress my readers with a sense, both of the close connection between sound Intellectual attainments and the higher elements of Duty and Enjoyment; and of the just and ultimate subordination of the former to the latter.... [I have] neglected no opportunity, in reviews of Poems and Novels as well as of graver productions, of elucidating the true constituents of human happiness and virtue: and combating those besetting prejudices and errors of opinion which appear so often to withhold men from the path of their duty – or to array them in foolish and fatal hostility to each other.[23]

The *Edinburgh*'s criticism is dominated by the idea that travel books should enlarge the knowledge of man in the most disparate geographical, social and cultural conditions. Accordingly, Jeffrey emphasizes the need for travel writers to avoid 'prejudices and errors of opinion' so as to attain the two principles of 'Duty' and 'Enjoyment'. By revealing new aspects of human nature, travellers would contribute to man's moral and social improvement. What the *Edinburgh* expected from travel literature is consistent with the use Ferguson had made of it: human social nature could only be learned through solid evidence; travel literature must in turn follow an empirical approach which should avoid preconceived and unproven notions and instead lead to the truth.

A central issue addressed by Jeffrey in his travel reviews is the research method used by travellers and, as a consequence, their reliability. His attitude is often prescriptive as he outlines those principles – literary and, from the traveller's point of view, practical – which travel writers should follow in order to legitimize their accounts. The writings of John Barrow, a favourite target,[24] provided Jeffrey with his best opportunities to discuss the nature and function of travel literature. In the first of these reviews he laments one of the main defects of many travellers: their ignorance of the language of the countries visited, which inevitably inhibited the gathering of evidence. Prejudice, particularly national prejudice, both derives from, and is a cause of, the imperfect and often biased information obtained by them:

> Till we can travel among them without guards, retinue and attendance; till we can speak their language, and read their books; and, finally, till we can domesticate ourselves with a variety of individuals in different conditions of life, it does not seem likely that we shall ever attain any true notion of their character and genius, or be able to appreciate the place which they ought to occupy in the great scale of nations.[25]

This observation on the Chinese is followed by general reflections on travelling in a foreign country:

> We seldom see foreign nations either fully or fairly; and scarcely ever consider what we do see without prejudice or partiality: novelty is sure either to magnify or diminish the objects with which it is associated, and the spectator of strange manners is almost irresistibly tempted either to despise them for differing from his own, or to admire them as something incomparably superior.[26]

'Prejudice' undermines both the benefits reaped from travelling and the intrinsic value of travel literature because it is a hindrance to obtaining correct and useful information. What Jeffrey calls 'facts' – that is, the products of empirical observation – are necessary to lay 'a broader basis of knowledge and information, before we can erect any solid structure of philosophy'.[27] Indeed, lack of 'prejudice' is the basic parameter according to which travel books are measured: Jeffrey criticizes the structure and the language of Barrow's books on more than one occasion, but acknowledges that he has 'a vein of strong sense and vigilant observation about him' and is 'tolerably free from theory or prejudice'.[28]

Jeffrey occasionally relaxes the utilitarian principles on which his criticism of travel-writers is were based, as when he forgives authors the liberty of relating anecdotes, especially when they describe adventures and dangerous events. Indeed, some of his early reviews resound with an almost adolescent enthusiasm, and regret at not having had the chance to travel outside Britain in his youth. He is aware that for the majority of readers, himself among them, books are the only means of experiencing remote and not-so-remote countries. He is capable of arguing that Mackenzie's *Voyages from Montreal, on the River St Lawrence, through the Continent of North America* 'convey[s] but little information to the geographer, the naturalist, or the statesman', but still offer compelling reading:

> There is something in the idea of traversing a vast and unknown continent, that gives an agreeable expansion to our conceptions; and the imagination is insensibly engaged and inflamed by the spirit of adventure, and the perils and the novelties that are implied in a voyage of discovery. A small band of adventurers, exposed, for months together, in a boat of bark, upon those inhospitable waters, 'which (to use our author's own language) had never before borne any other vessel than the canoe of the savage, and traversing those desarts, where an European had never before presented himself to the eye of its swarthy natives;' exhibit a spectacle that is well calculated to excite our curiosity and attention.[29]

It is easy to discern in this passage the enthusiasm of the young reviewer who, in 1800, saw his prospects of a German tour in the company of his friend Alexander Hamilton dwindle to a less adventurous tour of the Highlands.[30] Jeffrey was fascinated by the emotional reactions of travellers during their adventures, and suggests that readers could experience similar feelings. He had a deep affection for the natural world, which one critic has contrasted with his rational critical dogma.[31]

But such 'romantic' glimpses are rare. More often, the patience of the *Edinburgh* reviewers was tested by the changing function of the genre. During the eighteenth century, 'travel for travel's sake' became widespread, and the literature generated by it came increasingly to neglect scientific purposes and dwell on more personal aspects. The *Edinburgh* often attacked the superficiality of those who published accounts lacking scientific data or indeed any practical utility. Jeffrey's review of Thomas Holcroft's *Travels* is a prime example. Holcroft's mistake, Jeffrey says, was to have applied the style of Sterne's *Sentimental Journey* to a narration of purportedly real events. His explicit aim was 'to delineate the manners of the people among whom he travels; and, by fixing the facts and the philosophy of national character in the most important part of Europe, to enlarge the sphere, and increase the accuracy of our moral observations',[32] but he failed to achieve it because, according to Jeffrey, he did not choose the right facts or objects necessary to his inquiry, or the right literary medium. Holcroft had attempted to assess national character on the basis of incorrect or partial parameters:

> whenever he finds himself disposed to describe a building, a picture, or a dinner he immediately discovers that the manners and characters of a people cannot possibly be better elucidated than by an inquiry into their taste in architecture and the other arts of refined life.[33]

Holcroft's work could not be authoritative or credible because 'To the naturalist – the man of science – the agriculturist – the merchant, or even the admirer of the picturesque, he does not pretend to be capable of affording either information or delight.'[34]

Brougham places the same emphasis on usefulness, by way of attacking 'sentimental' or 'romantic' travel-writers for giving too much attention to trifling episodes. But while he has little tolerance for personal anecdotes and trivial or unimportant events, he still appreciates what he called 'the middle course' – that is, when the traveller 'endeavours to combine a description of the countries which he saw, with the narrative of his own adventures, and the delineation of his feelings'.[35] Brougham censures Carr's *A Northern Summer* because it was full of that 'variety of particulars so little interesting to the generality of mankind';[36] the works of Kotzebue, 'who, true to the character of the literary German, only lives to print', are characterized by 'his perpetual avowal of ignorance in the fine arts, and declamations against what is generally called a cultivated taste in painting and statuary'.[37] Smith also complains about those travellers 'who profess to amuse by anecdotes about waiters and chambermaids'.[38]

Over time Jeffrey may have reviewed less travel literature but he did not lose interest in it. His prescriptive attitude towards it and its practitioners continued to inform the *Edinburgh*'s criticism. There was a shared ideal among the *Edinburgh* reviewers: the aspiration for books that would educate and instruct while at the same time provide an entertaining story. Symptomatic of this was Brougham's application of the Horatian ideal of both teaching and giving pleasure. In opposition to the frivolity of tourists of the day, he proclaims the importance of foreign travels, not only for the traveller's education, but for the cultural advancement of readers. In his review of Hunter's *Travels* he explicitly associates travel with 'the walks of experimental philosophy'. Travellers and scientists face the same difficulties when they decide to produce literary works based on their research; however important their 'discoveries' may be, the difficulty of their subjects should not induce travellers and scientists to neglect the more 'literary' aspects of their undertaking.[39] Brougham thinks that in order for a travel book to be fully appreciated as a source of information, it needs to be an enjoyable read. Following Blair, he argues that the 'ideal' travel book would manage to provide both data and an engaging and entertaining story, in a plain, correct and accessible style.

Edward Daniel Clarke's *Travels in various Countries of Europe, Asia, and Africa*, the publication of which was eagerly awaited at the *Edinburgh*,[40] provided a rare occasion on which Brougham's ideal was realized. Clarke's *Travels* was also a favourite of Byron who, in keeping with his own adherence to the 'real' Orient in *Childe Harold's Pilgrimage* and the Turkish Tales, praised Clarke's correctness of description.[41] Brougham regards Clarke as the perfect example of a traveller who visited both known and unknown countries in the same inquisitive spirit, able to turn his own personal experiences into a useful source of information for his readers: 'he has had the enterprize to encounter both hardships and dangers in the pursuit of useful and interesting knowledge', correct-ing or updating the accounts of his predecessors.[42] Brougham is particu-larly impressed by Clarke's expertise in 'botany and antiquities',[43] and use of a plain and simple style: his book exemplifies the ideal pattern of travel literature, as 'it gives us a plain report of what the author did, saw and heard, and a fair transcript of the impressions which his observa-tions made upon him'.[44]

In some of the *Edinburgh*'s early numbers, the book under review offered a pretext for wider analysis. Typically, the article would incorp-orate a discourse on the author, the genre or topic in question. Smith's article on Joseph Fiévée's *Lettres sur l'Angleterre* is a case in point, his thoughts on the book being subordinate to more general reflections on travel literature. Smith draws a distinction between what the 'mineralo-gical traveller' and the observer of culture and social manners abroad – suggesting that there are two separate areas of interest for travellers, equivalent to natural science and the Science of Man. The 'mineralogical traveller' collects measurable data and is thus less prone to error than the traveller who studies the cultural and social character of a foreign people. The second type of traveller experiences difficulty because of the subject itself – he is 'seduced to distort facts, so as to render them agreeable to his system and his feeling!' Instead, in order to give a valu-able literary rendition of his travels, he must have emancipated his mind from the extensive and powerful dominion of association, must have extinguished the agreeable and deceitful feelings of national vanity, and cultivated that patient humility which builds general inferences only upon the repetition of individual facts.[45]

British travellers are susceptible to these limitations because they 'cannot for years overcome the awkward timidity of their nature'.[46] Writing at a time when impartial judgement on foreign countries is almost impossible, Smith identifies prejudice as one of the main defects of the genre: according to him, travellers abroad suffered from a nationalistic bias. Their inclination to exalt the virtues of their country to the detriment of those visited undermines any objective value that their efforts would otherwise have possessed. This is often the case when the traveller's home country is at war with, or traditionally hostile to, that visited. Prejudice founded on tradition and literature or on earlier accounts leads to blind acceptance of stereotypes. Smith is especially critical of biased research and the use made of it:

> 3rdly. The tendency to found observation on a system, rather than a system upon observation. The fact is, there are very few original eyes and ears. The great mass see and hear as they are directed by others, and bring back from a residence in foreign countries nothing but the vague and customary notions concerning it, which are carried and brought back for half a century, without verification or change.[47]

Smith's emphasis on the generation of a 'system' through the 'repetition of individual facts' defines the traveller's activity as a sort of natural science following the inductive methodology of Scottish philosophers.

Other reviewers are no less emphatic. When reviewing Adams' lacklustre *Letters on Silesia*, Horner complains about 'the absence of almost all those speculations, inferences, and suggestions, which render the pleasures of the traveller an important contribution to the labours of the philosopher and the statesman'.[48] In his article on John Griffiths' *Travels in Europe, Asia Minor, and Arabia*, Napier is even more specific about the function of the genre:

> He who first points out any thing remarkable or characteristic, in the laws, manners, and opinions, even of a barbarous nation, not only adds to our stock of general information, but gives us views of human nature, in situations in which we have not been accustomed to consider it.[49]

IV

Essays on travel literature provided Jeffrey and his reviewers with a forum to discuss British foreign policy. Naturally, the works which attracted the *Edinburgh*'s attention tended to be those dealing with parts of the world where Britain had interests – not least the Ottoman Empire in whose provinces European powers were facing a new political scenario: the Eastern Question.

Towards the end of the eighteenth century, books on the Ottoman Empire were extremely popular. War with France prevented many British travellers from visiting the Continent and therefore from writing travel books. There was a market for works about areas which were relatively safe to visit, and the Ottoman Empire, which remained neutral or Britain-friendly for most of the war, was a favourite option. Books on the Ottoman Empire appealed to the *Edinburgh* reviewers because of the less developed civilization of its rulers and inhabitants. In its numerous articles on travel in the Near East, the *Edinburgh* consistently expressed a low opinion of Ottoman institutions and inhabitants. At the same time it portrayed the Ottoman Empire as occupying a geo-historical space (Greece, Palestine, Egypt) which had been the cradle of modern civilization.

Jeffrey, Brougham, Smith and Hamilton thought the Ottoman Empire was completely removed from European politics and morals. It was a remnant of a feudal past, a crystallized territorial and administrative entity whose manners, politics, religion and language were opposed to those of Europe. They thought there was little chance of modernization, although progress was possible through 'Europeanization', either by military conquest or through gradual improvement brought about by more civilized nations. Most *Edinburgh* articles on the Near East debated the prospects for advancement, and for Britain to expand its sphere of interests in the region. The Scottish comparative approach to man and society thus enabled an assessment of the 'barbarism' of Turks and Greeks, and permeated the *Edinburgh*'s discussions of British foreign policy. Indeed, discussion of the political future of the region was linked to the hope that those under the yoke of the Sultan could somehow rise from the primitive degree of civilization in which they lived.

Of the many *Edinburgh* reviews on the Ottoman Empire, two stand out for their understanding of the nexus between scientific impulse and political practice: Jeffrey's review of Denon's *Voyage dans la Basse et la Haute Egypte*,[50] and Brougham's long essay on Thomas Thornton's *The*

Present State of Turkey.[51] Jeffrey's article can be fully appreciated only in its historical context. Napoleon's invasion of Egypt in 1798 had upset the whole equilibrium between the European powers and put British access to India under threat. Britain's military intervention represented the first step of a deep involvement in Near Eastern affairs. According to Edward Said, the French expedition was not just a military conquest; it was instrumental in Europe's project of knowledge, appropriation and domestication of Egyptian civilization. Napoleon was accompanied by a number of scholars who studied ancient Egyptian remains; their findings were documented in the 23 volumes of *Description de l'Égypte* (1809–28), one of the texts which, according to Said, best exemplifies Orientalism.[52]

For some reviewers, a travel book by a Frenchman about a country which Britain had recently freed from Napoleon's army would have been the opportunity to display national pride. Jeffrey instead stresses the cultural benefits of the French expedition and, in general, of the European presence in Egypt. Aware of the hegemonic implications of Napoleon's Orientalist project, he praises the French occupation because it has enabled Europeans to acquire knowledge of a past civilization:

> At length, however, a civilized nation possessed itself of this wonderful country; a whole college of philosophers was transported to the city of the Ptolemies; a printing-press was established at Cairo; and the scholars of Europe consoled themselves for the violation of the balance of power, by anticipating the sublime discoveries of the Egyptian institute.[53]

In Jeffrey's eyes, cultural benefits prevails over general political considerations, even at the expense of what was seen as the cornerstone of foreign relations – the 'balance of power'. One of the most important results of Napoleon's expedition to Egypt was the establishment (though for only a few years) of an enlightened system of power which eliminated Asiatic tyranny:

> The republican army failed, it is well known, for the generous purpose of redressing grievances; and had nothing farther in view, than the deliverance of the Egyptian innocents from the oppressions of their Mameluke governors.[54]

This passage seems to have escaped the scrutiny of those who would later accuse Jeffrey of Jacobinism for publishing less subversive sentiments.

The escape of the French armament under Nelson's nose is briefly mentioned, but there is no reference to the successful British campaign or to France's final defeat. Jeffrey's vision of Egypt extends beyond the volatile events of wartime and its concomitant nationalism, revealing his understanding of the far-reaching consequences of Napoleon's invasion of Egypt.

Brougham's article on Thomas Thornton's *The Present State of Turkey* came out in July 1807, a turbulent time in Ottoman history and one full of significance for Britain. It was probably written not long after the British fleet under Admiral Duckworth unsuccessfully attempted to threaten Constantinople in support of Russia (Britain's ally and France's enemy) in January and February 1807, and just when news of the deposition of Sultan Selim III by a violent uprising at the end of May reached Britain. The significance of this was not lost on Brougham: it was the first time in history that Britain had sent troops to Constantinople on a hostile footing, at a time when Selim III had introduced a series of European-style reforms of the bureaucratic and military apparatus which seemed the prelude to a wider modernization of a still archaic society.[55]

Thornton's book was a polemical answer to William Eton's *Survey of the Turkish Empire* (1798), a piece of violently anti-Turkish propaganda which advocated the partition of the Ottoman Empire amongst European powers and enjoyed considerable success in Britain, Thomas De Quincey being one of its admirers.[56] Brougham thinks Eton's work offered a misleading account of the Ottomans, 'evidently written under the impression of a political theory'.[57] By contrast, Thornton is 'free from strong prejudices. If he seems to lean a little too much towards the Turks, he fairly states his reasons, and shows that others have exaggerated their defects'.[58] Unlike Thornton, Brougham believes in the barbarism of the Turks and regards them as opposed to European civilization. He claims that Islamic institutions have corrupted the naturally good qualities and customs of Turks, and that 'while a contempt for the enlightened nations which surround them, continues a principle of their religion, we can expect nothing short of a violent change in their government, to promote the cultivation of their abilities.'[59]

Despite such statements, Brougham does not advocate the dissolution of the Ottoman Empire as a way of restoring people's rights; instead he suggests a gradual improvement of the condition of those under Ottoman rule:

> The doctrine, which some advocates of Russia have maintained, that the seizure of Turkey, and the restoration of the Greek empire, would

be an act of strict justice towards the Greeks, and a fair punishment of the Ottomans – is a great deal too absurd to require any discussion. The Turks have the very same right to their dominions, which the Russians themselves have to theirs – or which the descendants of the northern nations have to the greater part of Europe. Nor does it appear, from the best accounts which we have of the Greeks, that their character is such as to promise a more deserving race of subjects to the power that should drive the Turks into Asia. Whatever change it may be deemed adviseable to make in the Ottoman empire, must limit itself to the improvement of all classes of the inhabitants, by the equal preservation of their rights; and the amelioration of their political institutions.[60]

Free of neoclassical reverie, Brougham avoids the vindication of Greek independence based on remembrances of her past – something that was about to become political and cultural currency. Brougham is also thinking in Fergusonian terms. He ascribes the backward state of the subjects of the Porte to Islamic misrule – or, as he puts it, 'the despotic and purely warlike structure of their government' and 'the intolerant bigotry of their religion'.[61] The Ottoman Empire is indeed 'barbarous', and its development has been hampered by the brutal and warlike nature of its social structure. The help of European powers is necessary for the Ottomans to emerge from this primitive state. While any 'amelioration' should occur within the Empire itself, the 'external' example of European civilization is necessary for the Turks to become a modern nation.[62]

The *Edinburgh*'s condemnation of 'prejudice', by which most British travel-writers seemed to be affected, derived from both Jeffrey's adherence to enlightenment principles, and his repudiation of the sense of (national) superiority that British travellers displayed when abroad. No useful or 'real' knowledge could be reaped by travellers and their readers unless their agenda avoided prejudice and was directed by a purely scientific spirit. The nationalism of some travel-writers would naturally distort their impression of the countries they visited. Jeffrey and his reviewers acknowledged that a book of travel should not be only a repository of information and a part of the Science of Man, but also a literary form in its own right displaying both scientific rigour and narrative appeal. They believed that travellers should analyse the geographical, historical and cultural phenomena they encountered with unprejudiced eyes, rejecting 'sentimentalism' and the distorting rhetoric of nationalism. Travel literature on the Ottoman Empire posed a real challenge for the *Edinburgh*, as it offered a field of enquiry which was by its very nature prone to prejudice.

Notes

1. Advertisement, *Edinburgh Review* 1 (October 1802), n.p. On the originality and initial impact of the *Edinburgh* see Cockburn i 131–7, and John Clive, *Scotch Reviewers: The Edinburgh Review, 1802–1815* (London: Faber and Faber, 1957), pp. 31–41.
2. *Edinburgh Review* 7 (April 1804) 207. Cf. *Edinburgh Review* 21 (October 1807) 88, and *Edinburgh Review* 33 (April 1808) 212–13.
3. The importance of the genre is indicated by the fact that poetry totalled three articles (Southey's *Thalaba*, Mrs Opie's *Poems* and Pratt's *Bread*), natural sciences four, while only the extensive presence of economics, politics and social sciences could be said to balance the overwhelming presence of travel literature and other works on the East.
4. The volume for January 1805 opens with Jeffrey's 29-page essay on Barrow's *Travels in China*, the one for October 1806 with Jeffrey's essay on Barrow's *Voyage in Cochinchina*, and that of July 1807 with that of Brougham on Thomas Thornton's *Present State of Turkey*.
5. In January 1808 and 1809, April 1810, February 1811, July 1812, November 1814 and June 1815.
6. Preface, *Essays and Observations, Physical and Literary. Read before a Society in Edinburgh, and published by them*, vol. 1 (Edinburgh, 1754), p. vi. In 1783 the Philosophical Society would in turn lay the basis for the Royal Society of Edinburgh. For a fuller view of the eclectic intellectual approach of the Philosophical Society see Davis D. McElroy, *Scotland's Age of Improvement: A Survey of Eighteenth-Century Literary Clubs and Societies* (Washington: Washington State University Press, 1969), pp. 27–30, and Flynn, 21–2.
7. David Hume, *A Treatise of Human Nature*, ed. L. A. Selby-Bigge (Oxford: Clarendon Press, 1978), pp. 146–7.
8. Gladys Bryson, *Man and Society: The Scottish Inquiry of the Eighteenth Century* (Princeton: Princeton University Press, 1945), p. 42.
9. Robert Crawford, *Devolving English Literature* (Oxford: Clarendon Press, 1992), p. 16.
10. The definition is given by Robert Wokler, 'Apes and Races in the Scottish Enlightenment: Monboddo and Kames on the Nature of Man', *Philosophy and Science in the Scottish Enlightenment* ed. Peter Jones (Edinburgh: John Donald, 1988), p. 162.
11. When he was preparing his *Sketches*, Kames wrote to William Creech, his publisher, and asked him for a number of travel books. See Ian Simpson Ross, *Lord Kames and the Scotland of His Day* (Oxford: Clarendon Press, 1972), pp. 333–5.
12. James Burnet, Lord Monboddo, *Of the Origin and Progress of Language*, vol. 1 (Edinburgh, 1773–92), pp. 217–39.
13. Adam Ferguson, *An Essay on the History of Civil Society*, ed. Fania Oz-Salzberger (Cambridge: Cambridge University Press, 1995), p. 9. Cf. Bryson, 47–8.

14. Pierre François Xavier de Charlevoix (1682–1761), a Jesuit missionary and traveller to North America, is mainly famous for his *Histoire et description générale de la Nouvelle France* (1744), but also wrote works on Japan and Paraguay. He was a favourite among Scottish philosophers. In *History of the Reign of Charles V* (1769), William Robertson used Charlevoix as well as Lafitau's *Moeurs des Sauvages Ameriquains comparées aux moeurs des premiers temps* (1724). See Ronald L. Meek, *Social Science and the Ignoble Savage* (Cambridge: Cambridge University Press, 1976), pp. 57–64, 120–2, 139.

15. Ferguson, 83.

16. On the academic excellence of the University of Edinburgh throughout the eighteenth century, see Nicholas Hans, *New Trends in Education in the Eighteenth Century* (London: Routledge & Kegan Paul, 1951), pp. 24–36, and D. B. Horn, *A Short History of the University of Edinburgh 1556–1889* (Edinburgh: Edinburgh University Press, 1967), pp. 62–71.

17. Cited in Michael Barfoot, 'Hume and the Culture of Science in the Early Eighteenth Century', *Studies in the Philosophy of the Scottish Enlightenment* ed. M. A. Stewart (Oxford: Clarendon Press, 1990), p. 155.

18. Meek, 120–2.

19. Flynn, 29–30.

20. See Flynn, 21–4.

21. Hugh Blair, *Lectures on Rhetoric and Belles Lettres* (2 vols., London and Edinburgh, 1783), pp. 290–1.

22. *Contributions*, p. xvii. On the general political bias of literary criticism of the early nineteenth century see Walter Graham, *English Literary Periodicals* (New York: Thomas Nelson & Sons, 1930), pp. 227–55.

23. *Contributions*, p. x.

24. Jeffrey reviewed *Voyage in China* (*Edinburgh Review* 10 (January 1805)), and *Voyage in Cochinchina* (*Edinburgh Review* 17 (October 1806)). The articles on Barrow's *Travels into the Interior of Southern Africa* (*Edinburgh Review* 8 (July 1804)) and *Account of a Journey in Africa* (*Edinburgh Review* 16 (July 1806)) are likely to have been written by Jeffrey as well. In a letter to Horner, Jeffrey expressed his 'profound contempt for the Chinese' and admitted his indecision as to the real value of Barrow's *Travels in China* (Cockburn, ii 93).

25. *Edinburgh Review* 10 (January 1805) 260.

26. Ibid.

27. Ibid., 261.

28. *Edinburgh Review* 17 (October 1806) 2.

29. *Edinburgh Review* 1 (October 1802) 141.

30. See Cockburn, i 115–16. The idea of leaving the country altogether surfaced at least twice in Jeffrey's life. In 1801, his prospects of advancement at the Scottish bar looked dim and he toyed with the idea of relocating to India. In 1803, he refused the offer of a Professorship of moral and political science at the New College of Calcutta. See Cockburn, i 116–17, 152–3; ii 50–1.

31. J. Raymond Derby, 'The Paradox of Francis Jeffrey: Reason Versus Sensibility', *Modern Language Quarterly* 7 (1946) 489–500.

32. *Edinburgh Review* 7 (April 1804) 84.

33. Ibid., 84–5.

34. Ibid., 85.

35. *Edinburgh Review* 1 (October 1802) 163. See also *Edinburgh Review* 7 (July 1804) 420.
36. *Edinburgh Review* 12 (July 1805) 395. Carr's work is nevertheless praised by Brougham for its entertaining contents and scant pretension.
37. *Edinburgh Review* 14 (January 1806) 456; *Edinburgh Review* 9 (October 1804) 82.
38. *Edinburgh Review* 5 (October 1803) 154. See also *Edinburgh Review* 6 (January 1804) 334–5.
39. *Edinburgh Review* 7 (April 1804) 207.
40. See the close of Brougham's (or Sydney Smith's, as the attribution is doubtful) review on Heriot's *Travels in Canada*: 'But why does Dr E. D. Clarke delay to fulfil obligations which he long ago came under to the literary world? If he should cast his eye on these pages, we venture to hope that he may be reminded of his just and lawful debt, and no longer withhold from the public a work, which we are confident will prove one of the most valuable that ever issued from the press' (*Edinburgh Review* 23 (April 1808) 225).
41. Byron expressed his admiration for Clarke's work on a number of occasions. In 1812 Byron congratulated Clarke on the recent publication of the second volume of *Travels*: 'I have retraced some of my old paths adorned by you so beautifully that they afford me double delight. . . . You have awakened all the Gypsy in me, I long to be restless again & wandering' (*BLJ* ii 180–1). In 1813 Byron was full of admiration for Clarke's literary and travelling enterprises: '*You* have been on ye spot – *you* have seen & described more of the East than any of your predecessors – I need not say how ably & successfully – and (excuse the *Bathos*) *you* are one of ye. very few who can pronounce how far my *costume* (to use an affected but expressive word) is correct' (*BLJ*, iii 199).
42. *Edinburgh Review* 32 (August 1810) 336.
43. Ibid.
44. Ibid., 335.
45. *Edinburgh Review* 3 (April 1803) 86.
46. Ibid., 87.
47. Ibid.
48. *Edinburgh Review* 9 (October 1804) 181.
49. *Edinburgh Review* 15 (April 1806) 36.
50. *Edinburgh Review* 2 (January 1803).
51. *Edinburgh Review* 20 (July 1807).
52. Edward W. Said, *Orientalism* (London: Penguin, 1991), pp. 79–87.
53. *Edinburgh Review* 2 (January 1803) 330.
54. Ibid., 332.
55. 'The subject of this work is in an uncommon degree interesting at the present moment; but we are inclined to bestow particular attention upon it, rather from a consideration of the permanent importance of the contents, than because of the temporary attractions which the discussion possesses' (*Edinburgh Review* 20 (July 1807) 249). On Selim's reforms see Stanford J. Shaw, *Between the Old and the New: The Ottoman Empire under Sultan Selim III 1789–1807* (Cambridge, Mass.: Harvard University Press, 1971), and *History of the Ottoman Empire and Modern Turkey. Vol. I. Empire of the Gazis: The Rise and Decline of the Ottoman Empire, 1280–1808* (Cambridge: Cambridge University Press, 1976), pp. 260–6.

56. De Quincey remembered 'the once celebrated work of Mr. William Eton' as 'a book which attracted a great deal of notice about thirty years ago' (review of Thomas Gordon's *History of the Greek Revolution* in *The Collected Writings of Thomas De Quincey*, ed. David Masson (14 vols., Edinburgh, 1890), vii 289, 293).

57. *Edinburgh Review* 20 (July 1807) 250.

58. Ibid., 251.

59. Ibid., 269.

60. Ibid., 270.

61. Ibid., 254.

62. Ibid., 270–1.

5
Walter Scott, Antiquarianism and the Political Discourse of the *Edinburgh Review*, 1802–11

Susan Manning

In Thomas Love Peacock's *Crotchet Castle*, Mr MacQuedy, the Scottish economist whose name is glossed as 'son of a demonstration', attempts to determine the precise age of a supposed Roman Camp on the estate of his antiquarian host Mr Crotchet:

> I must be excused for holding that my proposition, three times six are eighteen, is more intelligible than yours. A worthy friend of mine, who is a sort of amateur in philosophy, criticism, politics, and a wee bit of many things more, says 'Men never begin to study antiquities till they are saturated with civilisation.'[1]

With comic disrespect for his character's pedantic exactitude, the author supplies a footnote: '*Edinburgh Review*, somewhere'.

Perhaps it is evidence of the saturated civility of the early numbers of the *Edinburgh Review* that antiquarian discussion figures prominently in its pages. Between 1802 and 1809, around 20 reviews of broadly antiquarian character and interest appeared, almost half of which were supplied by Walter Scott. This is worth pausing over: in 1802 Scott's literary reputation rested on a handful of translations of German Gothic poetry and tales of terror; he was known to be an obsessional if unmethodical collector of scraps of old balladry, tales and legends. And he was a Tory, implacably opposed to the principles that motivated Francis Jeffrey, Henry Brougham, Sydney Smith and Francis Horner to institute an oppositional voice on liberal principles. But notwithstanding the journal's ostentatiously blue and buff covers, Scott was a valued subscriber and contributor to the early numbers of the *Edinburgh Review*; indeed he and Jeffrey appear to have collaborated in 1806, and again in

1807 on a review of Sir William Forbes's *Life of Beattie*. Scott's own works from *Marmion* onwards were the subject of some of Jeffrey's major essays, amounting to a series of crucial 'position statements' that established the journal's stance on a range of contemporary issues. There is good reason to consider the prevalence of antiquarian discussion in the early numbers of a journal whose editor was deeply antipathetic to most manifestations of antiquarian enthusiasm, and to ask about Scott's role in establishing the pre-eminence of an organ to whose political principles he was known to be opposed.

Scott's prominence as both contributor and subject in the early numbers of the *Edinburgh* was, it appears, directly related to a developing debate with Jeffrey which placed the 'study of antiquities' as the focal issue in determining the cultural politics of the new journal. Why this should have been so is the subject of this essay. The 'Scottish economy' personified by Mr MacQuedy plays a part, as do 'philosophy, criticism, politics, and a wee bit of many things more'. But the crux, as Mr MacQuedy at once astutely and obtusely noted, lies with the question of the 'intelligibility' of antiquities.

By 1802, as weariness at the stalemated war with France and renewed threat of invasion toppled the Dundas regime with that of Pitt, the discourse of antiquarian debate (with the associated lexicon of romance and chivalry) was well developed as a conduit for political antagonism. In the year of the *Edinburgh*'s establishment, the fashion for chivalric revival reached new heights in Britain as construction began on a 'medieval' castle in Kew Gardens. More overt recognition of the political currency of chivalry appeared in the revival of the Order of the Garter in 1805 – a gesture 'well calculated', as a contemporary commentator put it, 'to cherish that chivalrous spirit ... which burned in the breasts of our ancestors', and (at the height of the Napoleonic Wars) 'to fan the flame of loyalty and patriotism'.[2] Chivalry, with its inescapably Burkean overtones in the post-Revolutionary period, may have acted as a kind of political litmus paper, but (like the antiquarian activities to which it owed its revival) it did not reduce to anything as simple as a binary opposition between Tory advocacy and Whig ridicule, or nostalgia *versus* progressivism. Contemporary political affiliations do not in any straightforward way map backwards onto the earlier situation. What we find, at least in the case of the *Edinburgh Review*, is that the word came to operate as something more like a password into a coded discourse, a discursive realm whose implication extended much more deeply into anglophone Scottish self-representation than mere party allegiance (which both Scott and Jeffrey in any case affected to despise). Notwithstanding their ideological differences, Jeffrey and Scott shared an interest in maintaining the stability of the British state; their critiques of antiquarian issues provided a relatively neutral arena in which political and aesthetic differences in relation to preservation and improvement could be canvassed. These debates at once developed their common Scottish Enlightenment inheritance, and extended its range into a theoretical underpinning of contemporary writing.

So what lent antiquarianism this pivotal position in the literary politics of Edinburgh (and the *Edinburgh*) in the first decade of the nineteenth century? To begin with, close connections between politics and the retrieval of antiquities were part of the fabric of post-Union Scottish assimilationism: William Smellie's *Account of the Institution and Progress of the Society of Antiquaries in Scotland* in 1782 had noted that 'till we were happily united to England, not in government only, but in loyalty and affection to a common Sovereign, it was not, perhaps, altogether consistent with political wisdom, to call the attention of the Scots to the antient honours and constitution of their independent monarchy'.[3] Union, that is, was the prior condition for the 'safe' retrieval of a past which survived as fragmented 'remains'. Throughout the eighteenth century, modes of recovery, collection and promulgation associated with antiquarian researches had been politically charged. The evidence of 'British' antiquity was deployed by writers like Lord Kames in response to external threat and to anti-Unionist sentiment (such as that of the Jacobites) from within Britain (*British Antiquities* was published, strategically, in 1746). In eighteenth-century England, mutual enthusiasm for collecting became an important agent of social cohesion as men and women from different class backgrounds and political sympathies participated in retrieving a 'shared past'. This was reflected in widespread collaboration and a rapid institutionalization of antiquarian activities.

However, similar cohesive processes do not appear to have occurred in quite the same way in Scotland, where accumulating the objects of material culture more readily expressed resistance to the political *status quo*. Antiquarianism's uncertain conceptual placing within prevailing Scottish historiographic models, and its primary rationale in the accumulation of material without subordination to system or theory, rendered the implications of the activity ideologically promiscuous and therefore politically suspect.[4] Collection and classification of material – and later verbal – artefacts at once occluded and registered coded political stances; those of a conservative bent readily made a verbal elision between the 'constitution of things' (the self-evidence of objects) and the immutable truths of the British Constitution. In turn, more progressive spirits might express derision of the antiquary's obsession with the minutiae of an irrelevant past, and look to ruins as evidence for advancement away from a barbaric era towards civility and enlightenment.

Antiquarian activities, then, were dialogically spacious, able to accommodate a range of discursive possibilities. By the final quarter of the eighteenth century, the 'ownership' of the large, amorphous field of popular antiquarian studies in Scotland was a bitterly contested political issue between on one hand, the Dundas hegemony which controlled public appointments, the moderate Kirk and the university interest, and on the other, a Whig coalition headed by Henry Erskine (briefly Lord Advocate in 1783) and the Earl of Buchan. The establishment (by Buchan) of the Society of Antiquaries of Scotland in 1780, and the demise of the old Philosophical Society of Edinburgh in 1783, were aspects of a political power struggle that involved most of the city's leading public figures.[5]

Despite these frequently acrimonious internal conflicts, literate Edinburgh society at the beginning of the nineteenth century remained relatively homogeneous; perhaps the crucial common ingredient here was that its members by and large shared an educational background in the late-Enlightenment teaching of the University. The *Edinburgh Review* under Jeffrey's editorship embodies the somewhat anomalous position occupied by the legacy of the Scottish Enlightenment in the cultural climate of a turn-of-the-century Britain preoccupied by the threat of Jacobinical unrest, and whose political agendas were set in Napoleonic Europe. In one sense (like its Enlightened Scots forebears) the *Edinburgh* was conservative – preferring, for example, polished form and polite discourse to experimentation in poetry. But (also like its mentors) it was liberal, Whiggishly inclined in politics, empirically based and speculative in outlook. One of the journal's more daring rhetorical strategies was to mount a critique of Tory stabilizing principles from within an ideological base that was itself premised upon a set of universals which seemed to have been exploded by the French Revolution's violent assertion of *event* over *process*. The representation of antiquarianism in its pages played, I want to argue, a part in this strategy.

To borrow a metaphor from the romances of chivalry which Scott would himself employ to dramatic effect in *Ivanhoe*, the cultural currency of antiquarianism offered a kind of tournament ground for jousting encounters between opposed positions (construed in ideological, class methodological, even religious, terms) which did not threaten – indeed may have reinforced – the meta-context of national unity in which all were perceived to have a stake. But, in addition, it seems that antiquarian disputes were more than a displacement activity or (to change the model slightly) a safe container in which differences too dangerous to enact in direct relation to contemporary conditions might be played out. They functioned also as a kind of crucible or melting-pot in which some of the central formulations of the Scottish Enlightenment 'Science of Man' were forged anew in a post-Revolutionary environment in which the refashioning of universal maxims in the context of particular historical events had become politically, nationally and socially imperative. Antiquarian controversy, which characteristically focused on the uncertain relationship between fragments and wholes, supplied both a context and a vocabulary for such a refashioning.

The key interpreter of the great Scottish Enlightenment philosophers for a later generation was Dugald Stewart, whose philosophical lectures established a discreet vocabulary for political discussion in the considerably restricted discursive environment of the Dundas despotism. Scott, who attended Stewart's moral philosophy classes in Edinburgh between 1788 and 1790, later described the 'striking and impressive eloquence' of a professor who 'riveted the attention of even the most volatile and inattentive student'.[6] Within the moral philosophy curriculum Stewart also lectured on politics, advocating a moderate progressivism in line with the historiographical and sociological principles of Reid, Ferguson and Stewart's contemporary John Millar. In the first volume of his *Elements of the Philosophy of the Human Mind* (1792) based on this course, Stewart indicated that in modern circumstances, the 'progress of human opinion' demanded 'gradual and prudent accommodation of established institutions to . . . varying opinions, manners, and circumstances'; this alone would stem a revolutionary 'rage of innovation'.[7] In the early 1790s – with the threat of 'haughty Gaul's' invasion apparently at hand and declaration of war imminent – 'change', 'progress' and 'gradual and necessary reformations',[8] extracted from the conceptual framework of stadial history which had generated them as part of a lexicon of political quietism, sounded distinctly inflammatory.[9] In a crucial passage Stewart lamented 'The violent revolutions which, at different periods, have convulsed modern Europe', ascribing them, however, *not* to 'a spirit of innovation in sovereigns and statesmen', but rather to a

> bigoted attachment to antiquated forms, and to principles borrowed from less enlightened ages. It is this reverence for abuses which have been sanctioned by time, accompanied with an inattention to the progress of public opinion, which has, in most instances, blinded the rulers of mankind, till government has lost all its efficiency.[10]

This, with his citation of the French perfectibilian *philosophe* Condorcet in the 'Dissertation: Exhibiting the progress of Metaphysical, Ethic, and Political Philosophy Since the Revival of Letters in Europe', had been sufficient (in the volatile atmosphere of 1792) to render Stewart's political loyalties deeply suspect.[11] An unimpeachable character protected the venerable professor against open insult by the Tory Establishment but, according to Henry Cockburn, this shadow lingered beyond the political crisis which had generated it, and complicated Stewart's pedagogical legacy.[12] Though Stewart never repudiated his view that violent revolution was a consequence of blind attachment to antiquity, his later *Biographical Memoir* took pains to moderate the earlier effect of his enthusiasm for Condorcet and Turgot.

While he might be described as in some sense the tutelary spirit of the *Edinburgh*, Stewart's propensity for synthesis and mutual accommodation of the sharper-edged views of his predecessors generated a harmonious vision of gradual institutional and social progress to which a Tory like Scott was readily able to subscribe. The relationship between present and past was (Stewart made clear) construed as a political question as much as it was a historiographical one:

> There are plainly two sets of political reasoners; one of which consider the actual institutions of mankind as the only safe foundation for our conclusions, and think every plan of legislation chimerical, which is not copied from one which has already been realized; while the other apprehend that, in many cases, we may reason safely a priori from the known principles of human nature combined with the particular circumstances of the times. The former are commonly understood as contending for experience in opposition to theory; the latter are accused of trusting to theory unsupported by experience.[13]

Scott's constitutional Toryism clearly inclined to the first camp; the environment of his education and training in the late Edinburgh Enlightenment, and particularly his exposure to the forms of 'conjectural history' practised by Robertson, Hume, Smith and Millar, made him susceptible and sympathetic to the second. The rationale of the first was material and particular; that of the second was primarily speculative and abstracted.

Antiquarianism could be construed as the study of a lost past or as the recovery and reconstitution of a continuous, developing national tradition. Empirical, 'scientific' (in a post-Newtonian sense), antiquaries supplied the 'raw material' of a nation's history, the necessary evidence to substantiate the speculative historiography of the Scottish Enlightenment and give a local habitation and a name to the enlarged abstraction of its theories of societal development. But they also (and the hint of popery was not fortuitous) retrieved and enshrined in their collections the relics of popular culture. Further – in Scott's hands at least – antiquities, the cultural capital of Scotland's past, became a means of generating wealth, the ingredients of a highly successful commercial transaction based on the precepts of Adam Smith.[14] This is where antiquarian activities intersected with another branch of the Science of Man: political economy. Making these antiquities intelligible, 'readable', to an unprecedentedly wide audience, Scott added value simultaneously to Scotland's past and his own estate, so successfully that the two would, in both his own mind and that of his readers, intermittently become confused.

The relation between the economics and the politics of antiquarian romance was particularly acute in the city that might be described as the birthplace of modern political economy. From 1799, Stewart offered a class in Political Economy which took *An Inquiry into the Nature and Causes of the Wealth of Nations* as its core text. Jeffrey, Smith, Horner and Brougham were amongst its enthusiastic adherents; Horner apparently attended three years in succession.[15] A cardinal feature of advanced 'civil society' was its capacity to generate commercial wealth through what Adam Smith described as 'productive labour'.[16] Antiquaries were ridiculed as drudges sifting through the rag-and-bone remains of earlier times; the reshaping of these fragments into structures of continuous existence revalorized the nation's history as a meaningful story with implications either tragic or comic for the present. Given the close links between historiography and political science, a lot might turn on the successful marketing of a particular version of the past. The *Edinburgh* characteristically adopted a stance of ridicule towards antiquarian activities: 'Antiquarian researches are generally excessively insignificant, and form one of the most fatiguing and least amiable species of trifling with which we are acquainted';[17] but it none the less devoted a large amount of space to them.

Reviewing John Millar's *View of the English Government* in 1803, Jeffrey praised the particular shape of its vision of the past:

> While the antiquary pored with childish curiosity over the confused and fantastic ruins that cover the scenes of early story, *he* produced the plan and elevation of the original fabric, and enabled us to trace the connexions of the scattered fragments, and to determine the

primitive form and denomination of all the disfigured masses that lay before us.[18]

'Primitive' is a crucial word here. Antiquaries dig up the decaying material of past lives; enlightened historians construct a theory of progress from the evidence. The *Edinburgh* mocked the antiquary's pedantic perspective-blind labours: discussing Francis Douce's *Illustrations of Shakespeare*, for example, Jeffrey's editorial persona resignedly 'accepts the services of the antiquary and verbal critic', but wearies rapidly of his 'long quotations from contemporary authors, tedious dissertations on old customs, and keen and solemn controversies upon the comparative merit of rival readings or projects of punctuation'. This 'petty sort of antiquarianism',[19] the profession of Scott's Dryasdust in the making, was a favourite target of *Edinburgh* wit; the implication was that such mechanical endeavours added no value to the material they threw up.

This had to be balanced against the ways in which antiquarianism could also be an enlightened and progressive activity. Reviewing George Ellis's *Specimens of the early English Poets*, Scott drew particular attention to its 'preliminary historical sketch of the rise and progress of English poetry and language'.[20] This was antiquarianism as manufacture; its interpretative processes added economic value to the raw material of research. Scott's later comparison of Ellis's and Ritson's classificatory procedures indicated his understanding of their import:

> Mr Ellis's introduction sufficiently illustrates his superior skill as an antiquary, although he has brought forward fewer materials than Mr Ritson, and makes no parade of those which he has acquired: it is evidently because he wished to be an architect, not a mere collector of stones and rubbish. Every thing which he quotes is adapted to fill a place in his system; and thus he avoids the great error of antiquaries, who are too much busied with insulated facts, to present to their readers a connected historical view of the subject under discussion.[21]

Ellis's was a product on whose cultural value Scott and Jeffrey, Tory and Whig, might agree.

In this context, the conventional fun at the expense of pedants performed an additional function in allowing the *Edinburgh* to give space to the antiquaries' preoccupation with national, and local, identity – and therefore to generate its own cultural capital from the raw material under review. It offered, in other words, a means to articulate Scottishness without compromising the journal's enlightened and cosmopolitan stance. Reviewing Elizabeth Hamilton's *The Cottagers of Glenburnie* in July 1808, the *Edinburgh* located its success in a depiction of nationality available only to those familiar with 'our antient and venerable dialect'.[22] Hamilton's success, Jeffrey was clear, lay in her capacity to marry the remnants of a local cultural past to the conditions of the present, and to present the possibility of social renewal. 'A strong current of improvement runs at present through all Scotland,' the review concludes: such works, uniting knowledge of the past to belief in progress, may help to 'effect a reformation' in the condition of the Scots peasantry.[23] The rhetoric of antiquity encouraged expression of sorrow at loss of the old martial and chivalric virtues, within a context of the inevitability of progress. A sense of cultural urgency could be generated from the contemplation of the melancholy remnants of the past.

Viewed in Smithian terms as component fragments of the early stages of a commercial progress, the evidence of antiquity had a part to play in generating the historical 'value' of a nation's story. In late Enlightenment Edinburgh the architect, the political economist and the conjectural historian – and perhaps also the reviewer – seemed briefly to be of imagination all compact: they cooked the books of antiquity to construe an ordered progressive world of commercial exchange. Political economy was a major (and tendentious) plank of the *Edinburgh* enterprise, and an important ingredient in its articulation of a Scottish identity within the British context. 'Though our countrymen have, in general, but little taste for abstract disquisitions,' it declared, *money*, 'the most abstract of all the inquiries connected with political economy, has engaged an extraordinary share of their attention.' A reference to the controversial section of Stewart's *Elements*, on 'Abstraction', gave a clear, if coded signal of the political principles underlying the *Edinburgh*'s advocacy of economic debate, and their relationship to 'conjectural history'. 'The doctrine of money,' wrote the reviewer (James Mill), 'remains as it was left by the great Father of political economy' (that is, Adam Smith).[24] In the repressive climate of the anti-Jacobin period, open discussion of the subject was problematic: 'The great difficulty with which the salutary doctrines of political economy are propagated in this country is . . . a very serious object . . . of regret' – but, therefore (the review implied), they became a particular responsibility of the organ that claimed to be the representative voice of both the nation and of progress.[25] There is something more at stake here: money was the abstract pole of political economy as the 'conjectures' of stadialism were of historiography. In each case, the *Review* maintained, 'value' could be realized only by intersection with the concrete and particular. Enter the material remains recovered by the antiquary.

It seems that in an environment of political interdiction, discussion of the transformative and wealth-generating processes of the manufacture of history served a kind of double turn. Scott's contributions to the *Edinburgh* constituted the other half of a developing debate on the political and aesthetic currency of antiquarianism. His assessment of Mackenzie's *Report of the Committee of the Highland Society . . . into . . . the Authenticity of Ossian* and Malcolm Laing's edition of *The Poems of Ossian* (July 1805), for example, grafted the persona of enlightened stadialist historian onto the romancer of antiquity to offer a carefully balanced view of the controversial poems which conferred emotional and traditionary value on a fragmented past, even as documentary authenticity was denied to its raw vision:

> We do not affirm that their ancestors were incapable of generous or kindly feelings; nor do we insist that their poetry, to be authentic, should be devoid of occasional sublimity, or even elegance. We only say, that the character of all rude poetry, whether in diction or sentiment, is inequality; that bursts of generosity, flowing from the feeling of the moment, and not from the fixed principles acquired in a civilized society, will always be attended by an equally capricious and irregular exertion of the angry passions.[26]

In this view, authenticity and 'inauthenticity' are equally essential outcomes of the antiquarian endeavour; the 'fixed principles' of stadialism are balanced by the disruptive 'capricious' utterances of individual impulse. The alternating succession of antiquarian reviews by Scott and Jeffrey suggest that antiquarian discourse in turn-of-the-century Scotland had the potential to adumbrate more contentious expressions of cultural identity than the fiction of consensual, unifying and unified activity promoted by the English Society of Antiquaries.

Tackling Johnes' edition of Froissart in January 1805, Scott extolled the chivalric ambience of the French historian, 'the high spirit of chivalry imbibed in the courts and castles where he loved to dwell'.[27] Edmund Burke's *Reflections on the Revolution in France* (1790), with its famous vindication of the 'age of chivalry' against the modern world of 'sophisters, œconomists, and calculators', is not far behind this review at many points.[28] Three months after Scott's Froissart review, in the following number of the journal, Jeffrey reviewed *The Lay of the Last Minstrel*, according it the importance of a lengthy lead article. Picking up Scott's 'chivalry' motif, and exposing it to sceptical scrutiny, Jeffrey's account incorporated a clear sense of the political responsibilities of modern-day romance, as well as an appreciation of the alchemical processes of Scott's capacity to transform selectively the dross of the past into a highly marketable commodity:

> We consider this poem as an attempt to transfer the refinements of modern poetry to the matter and the manner of the antient metrical romance. The author, enamoured of the lofty visions of chivalry, and partial to the strains in which they were formerly embodied, seems to have employed all the resources of his genius in endeavouring to recal them to the favour and admiration of the public, and in adapting to the taste of modern readers, a species of poetry which was once the delight of the courtly, but has long ceased to gladden any other eyes than those of the scholar and the antiquary. This is a romance, therefore, composed by a minstrel of the present day; or such a romance as we may suppose would have been written in modern times, if that style of composition had continued to be cultivated, and partaken consequently of the improvements which every branch of literature has received since the time of its desertion.
>
> Upon this supposition, it was evidently Mr Scott's business to retain all that was good, and to reject all that was bad in the models upon which he was to form himself; adding, at the same time, all the interest and the beauty which could possibly be assimilated to the manner and spirit of his original. It was his duty, therefore, to reform the rambling, obscure, and interminable narratives of the ancient romancers, – to moderate their digressions, – to abridge or retrench their unmerciful or needless descriptions, – and to expunge altogether those feeble and prosaic passages, the rude stupidity of which is so apt to excite the derision of a modern reader.[29]

Jeffrey was clear that, as a product for sale, Scott's chivalric narrative assumed a public function and a corresponding social duty. To offer the raw material of antiquity as valuable in itself would have been to abuse the poem's potential purchasers, but the manufacturing processes proper to 'Civil Society' carried their own responsibilities. 'Composition' necessarily involved the private enthusiasms of the author in publicly accountable debate, and Jeffrey was not, without challenge, going to allow Scott to peddle a disjunctive vision of chivalric Toryism for profit. Recognizing that cultural value, as Homi Bhabha has more recently suggested, is produced at the seam between the private and the public, the *Edinburgh Review* tested the ground between the affective pull of antiquity and its economic potential.[30]

So what were the responsibilities involved in creating and marketing a new antique, a kind of souvenir or memento of a lost past, as Jeffrey described Scott doing in his reviews of *The Lay of the Last Minstrel* and *Marmion*? The reviewer, like Mr MacQuedy, was inclined to suspect that Scott's 'partiality for the strains of antiquity, ha[d] imposed a little upon the severity of his judgement';[31] he made clear his own preference for the parts of the poem where Scott had displayed more 'modern' sensibilities, and regretted 'that the author should have wasted, in imitation and antiquarian researches, so much of those powers which seem fully equal to the task of raising him an independent reputation'.[32] *Progress*, the addition of 'value', is the key to Jeffrey's approbation of anything smacking of the antique: he applauded 'the prodigious improvement which the style of the old romance is capable of receiving from a more liberal admixture of pathetic sentiments and gentle affections', and reasserted the principles of aesthetic economy: 'from the improvement of taste, and the cultivation of the finer feelings of the heart, poetry acquires, in a refined age, many new and invaluable elements, which are necessarily unknown in a period of greater simplicity'.[33]

The crux of the matter lay in the issue of *how* modern culture might be manufactured from the dross of time. Replacing a narrative of history and origins with nostalgia for the lost utility of recovered objects and ideas, antiquarians embodied longing for possession of the past, a kind of commodification of sentiment which moved into the public domain as private 'cabinets of curiosities' were reflected in the eclectic cultural repositories of the new national museums.[34] Tourists in the shambles of history, they brought back objects as souvenirs and constructed a cultural narrative around them. The authentication of the past in this way implied a scepticism about the present's claim to confer value through progress. In this frame, antiquarian collections represented what Susan Stewart has described as 'a total aestheticization of use-value', but the currency-change between use value and aesthetic value had inevitable political implications.[35] Historiographically, as Scott was quick and Jeffrey reluctant to grasp, late eighteenth-century antiquarianism occupied the middle ground in a complex dialectic between progress and loss. Empirically based in the collection and preservation of the material evidence of the past, its procedures might simultaneously be directed by the compositional imperatives of conjectural history and the disintegrative impulses of sentiment: Bishop Percy's early ballad collection *Reliques of English Poetry* (1765) was chronologically arranged to display the 'progress' of poetry from primitive expression towards (relatively) reflective refinement, but its long-lasting appeal with its readers derived from the ballads' expressiveness, their manifestation of apparently unmediated emotion 'in the raw'. The form taken in contemporary writing by antiquarianism's preoccupations with the past, its retrieval and incorporation, would, paradoxically, become one of the marks of 'modernity', that separation from the past which disrupted the smooth progress of universalist conjectural history. The world of the collectors was by no means a closed or circumscribed one, and Scott was both their most enthusiastic chronicler and their most astute analyst.

Three numbers of the journal after Jeffrey's review of the *Last Minstrel*, Scott returned to the seductions of chivalry in a review of George Ellis's *Specimens of Early English Metrical Romances* and Joseph Ritson's *English Metrical Romances* (1806), by way of a long digression on the history of antiquarianism itself:

> Warton followed Bishop Percy in his taste for the ancient romance, of which he was an indefatigable student. Whenever he has occasion to mention a tale of chivalry, in his History of Poetry, it seems to operate like a spell, and he feels it impossible to proceed with the more immediate subject of his disquisition, until he has paced through the whole enchanted maze, and introduced his reader into all its labyrinths.[36]

Scott, of course, knew this fascination at first hand. He referred with appreciative recognition to the 'chains of association' that linked Ellis's collection of fragments. In the autobiographical 'Memoirs' written in 1808, he described how, as a young man, 'with a head on fire for chivalry', his first encounter with Percy's *Reliques* had re-awakened the secret 'Delilahs of [his] imagination', now given public currency 'as the subject of sober research, grave commentary, and apt illustration'.[37] The image of the treacherous Delilah undermining the established strength of the masculine public individual, which Scott would revert to in the 'Dedicatory Epistle' to his antiquarian romance *Ivanhoe*, is at once telling and treacherous.[38] Scott's detour from the works under review to Warton turns out, as often, to be highly motivated, as the review reverses Burke's rhetorical exclamation 'the age of chivalry is gone!' into a challenge based in the capacity of antiquarian research to recreate 'the decent drapery of life':[39]

> the age of chivalry, instead of being at an end for ever, may perhaps be on the point of revival. In this point of view, much is gained, and nothing lost by the plan of Mr Ellis.[40]

Enchantment undermined the claims of 'system' to render the past 'intelligible' (to revert to Mr MacQuedy's formula) on principles of progression. It offered instead an emotional intelligibility whose profits, ironically and satisfyingly enough, proved highly material. Jeffrey's objection, which was gradually formulating itself through this alternating sequence of reviews, was that Scott was able to make so much tangible and cultural capital from the manipulation of stadialist theory of production and profit. Revalorizing the fragmentary survivals of the past in a recidivist currency of emotional allegiances, he was, as it were, playing the game of Smithian economy against its own founding principles.[41]

The year 1808 saw a crisis in Scott's relationship with Jeffrey, and with the *Edinburgh,* following the publication of *Marmion.* It was marked on both sides by increasing explicitness in relating antiquarian practice to political principles. The introductory epistles to each of the six Cantos of *Marmion* combined Scott's antiquarian and political interests in slippery ways: the first, addressed to William Stewart Rose, one of the architects of the romance revival, enclosed an internal address to both William Pitt and Charles James Fox (the propriety of which Jeffrey found deeply questionable). This introductory peroration issued a not-very-veiled political challenge to the Whigs, under cover of an indirect appeal to Burke's 'genius', Chivalry:

> While tyrants rul'd, and damsels wept,
> Thy Genius, Chivalry, hath slept:
> There sound the harpings of the North,
> Till he awake and sally forth,
> On venturous quest to prick again ...[42]

The introduction to the fifth Canto, addressed to George Ellis (identified in Scott's footnote as 'The learned editor of the "Specimens of Ancient English Romances"'), keeps the Burkean echoes in play as 'Ten thousand lines of brighter day'[43] gleam in the Edinburgh sky to match, perhaps, the 'ten thousand swords' that Burke had imagined leaping from their scabbards to avenge the insult to the French queen Marie Antoinette.[44] A few lines later, the bard invokes 'Marie of France' and the 'magic art' of Ellis to direct his own labours in reviving 'all the pomp of chivalry'.

Jeffrey's review of *Marmion* in April 1808 took issue with its 'imitations of obsolete extravagance', and declared flatly that 'To write a modern romance of chivalry, seems to be much such a fantasy as to build a modern abbey, or an English pagoda'.[45] Understood within the dynamics of Edinburgh's cultural politics, his reading of Scott's antiquarian reconstructions and their profitable enchantments combined historiographic, political, economic and national objections. Unsurprisingly, he found the poem's historical intrigues, tempered as they were to a much lesser extent than in the *Lay* by a balancing ethos of stadialist progressivism, deeply antipathetic. The broken-up sequence of antiquarian detail was doing a different, less accommodating, kind of political and cultural work here, and Jeffrey did not spare his impatience with 'the insufferable number, and length, and minuteness of those descriptions of antient dresses and manners, and buildings; and ceremonies, and local superstitions; with which the whole poem is overrun'.[46] He complained, too, about the length and number of the poem's antiquarian notes, and attempted to defuse the political charge of Scott's fondness for the 'obsolete extravagance' of chivalry by relegating it to the realms of quixotic fantasy (and, ironically, reclaiming in the process patriotic local ground for a Whig standpoint): 'There is scarcely one trait of true Scottish nationality or patriotism introduced into the whole poem.'[47]

Jeffrey's hostility to the poem's openly unreconstructed antiquarian stances was eloquent and scathing: castigating the 'elaborate pictures extracted by a modern imitator from black-letter books, and coloured, not from life, but from learned theories, or at best from mouldy monkish illuminations, and mutilated fragments of painted glass',[48] the review professed itself enraged by the spectacle of uncooked raw material being passed off as a marketable commodity. Not only did it represent poor commercial value; worse, its disregard for the transformative processes of stadialist historiography implied that the lovingly described remains of a feudal past had value in and of themselves. Contrary to the antiquarian, the mercantilist, as Susan Stewart has put it, 'is not moved by restoration; he is moved by extraction and seriality. He removes the object from context and places it within the play of signifiers that characterize an exchange economy.'[49] Jeffrey, accordingly, censured

all the stupid monkish legends . . . all the various scraps and fragments of antiquarian history and baronial biography, which are scattered profusely through the whole narrative. These we conceive to be put in purely for the sake of displaying the erudition of the author; and poetry, which has no other recommendation, but that the substance of it has been gleaned from rare or obscure books, has, in our estimation, the least of all possible recommendations . . . a taste too evidently unnatural to be long prevalent in the modern world.[50]

This is Jeffrey the advocate of abstraction and general principle, uneasy with the retrograde tendencies of anything that cannot be accommodated to the 'March of Mind'; his sarcastic critique is exercised at great length (it was the lead article of 35 pages in the April 1808 *Review*) in proportion to the seductiveness of the poem's enchanting subversion of the principles of stadialist political economy.[51] Considering it his 'duty to make one strong effort to bring back the great apostle of the heresy to the wholesome creed of his instructors', he threw his own more abrasive rhetoric into the arena to deter 'the herd of rivals and imitators' who were likely to follow Scott's powerful example.[52]

Scott professed to take the criticism lightly: 'I am very glad you like Marmion,' he wrote to Anna Seward,

> it has need of some friends; for Jeffery shewed me yesterday a very sharp review of it; I think as tight a one as he has written since Southey's Madoc. As I don't believe the world ever furnished a critic and an author who were more absolute *poco curantés* about their craft, we dined together, and had a hearty laugh at the revisal of the flagellation.[53]

A month later he wrote reassuringly to Mrs Scott of Harden that 'Jeffrey's flagellation . . . has much more the appearance than the essence of severity', and that the article had 'made an odd sort of compounding between his own character & mine'; but damage had undoubtedly been done, as other letters make clear, to this friendship of political unlikes.[54] The breach between Scott and Jeffrey was waiting to happen when, that October, Jeffrey and Brougham ventured into explicit exposure of Whig principles in a joint article, 'Don Pedro Cevallos on the French Usurpation of Spain'. Taking the occasion of Cevallos's account of the popular Spanish revolt against Napoleon, Jeffrey and Brougham offered an extraordinarily explicit polemic in favour of political change: 'we must state a few observations, sufficiently plain . . . to have damped the romantic hopes even of the English nation.'[55] The important word there is 'romantic' – pertaining to the delusions of romance. This anti-aristocratic and anti-chivalric diatribe against 'base courtiers' and 'crowned or titled intriguers' extolled the 'gallant people' of the middle and lower orders, and championed their cause against the oppressive 'usurpation of Don Pedro Cevallos' as a 'scene of Imperial robbery, royal weakness, and ministerial perfidy'.[56] 'An alteration in the political constitution of the Spanish monarchy', declared the reviewers, was both necessary and inevitable.

Scott was ready for a fight. In the current climate of political fear, this was nothing short of sedition; indeed, the review did not baulk at applying its message directly to the condition of England. The emphatic dwelling on the words *'liberty'*, and *'people'*,[57] and the inflammatory invocation of 'the English reign of terror' could not be ignored, when its proponents openly declared that

> Reforms in the administration of our affairs must be adopted, to prevent more violent changes; and some radical improvements in our constitution, will no longer be viewed with horror; because they will be found essential to the permanence of any reformation in the management of national concerns.[58]

Such political forthrightness moved Dugald Stewart's cautious liberal rhetoric into new territory. Scott was not alone in finding it unacceptable; his immediate cancellation of his subscription to the *Review* was enacted by at least 25 other prominent Edinburgh citizens. Scott, as Jeffrey well knew, was a more dangerous literary-political opponent than most: dissociating himself from the *Edinburgh*, he intensified his efforts to establish a rival Tory organ. (The *Quarterly Review*, with William Gifford as editor, was launched the following year.) Scott's more complete revenge on Jeffrey, however, was to take away with him from the *Edinburgh* debate on antiquarianism a range of possible ways of construing the relationship of continuity and change whose value he would realize in very substantial material terms in the ensuing years.

After 1808, and the departure of Scott from the cohort of contributors, the *Edinburgh* carried fewer reviews of antiquarian collections and fewer articles employing the coded discourse of antiquarianism. Having previously, in the *Marmion* review, chastized Scott for imprisoning his readers in the mouldering and irrelevant realms of bookish antiquity, Jeffrey took some satisfaction in criticizing *The Vision of Don Roderick* (1811) for its inability to make a convincing connection between the past and the modern world of contemporary political affairs; to create, in other words, a history from its accumulated antiquarian detail. He described a work 'substantially divided into two compartments; – the one representing the fabulous or prodigious acts of Don Roderick's own time [the eighth century], – and the other, the recent occurrences which have since signalized the same quarter of the world. Mr Scott . . . is most at home in the first of these fields.'[59] Jeffrey quoted a passage from the poem in which the discourse of antiquity is invoked to upbraid Spanish nobles for their lack of spirit in a just cause –

> And, if the glow of feudal chivalry
>   Beam not, as once, thy nobles' dearest pride,
> Iberia! Oft thy crestless peasantry
>   Have seen the plumed hidalgo quit their side,
> Have seen, yet dauntless stood – 'gainst fortune fought and died –

in order to attach a malicious footnote:

> It is amusing to see how things come round. When we published our review of Don Pedro Cevallos, we were overwhelmed with reproaches for having vilipended the privileged orders of Spain, and said that it was only through the spirit of her commonalty that she could be saved; – and now her nobles are given up by the stoutest champion of nobility in Great Britain! If we will only wait patiently a little longer, we shall all be agreed . . . [60]

By this stage, the *Edinburgh*'s colours declared (and the political climate having moved in the intervening years towards open discussion of change) Jeffrey confidently abandoned the safety of the antiquarian dialogue. The review did not bother to engage with the distancing discourse of the 'glow of feudal chivalry', but moved directly into the terms of the contemporary political arena. Scott's opposition, the article comes very close to saying outright, has become an irrelevance.

In the formative years of the journal, antiquarianism had served the *Edinburgh* as a strategy against certain modes of explicitness; in literary contexts it fostered dialogue between opposed ideological positions that could not be sustained once the contributors moved openly into the arena of current affairs. In the abstract, as I have suggested, the principles of organization and categorization – that is, the syntax – underlying antiquarian collections were all-important: this, rather than the individual elements of which they were composed, constituted their character, and it was here that political import could be encoded, and the fraught relations between general principles of societal advance and enumerated events negotiated.

The naming of accumulated objects whose syntax was obscured allowed for amicable, if partial, communication between those who, had the terms of their discourse been fully articulated, must have been at odds. When this happened with the Cevallos article, Scott had no option but to terminate his part in the dialogue, to take his pots and pans home. And there were a lot of them at home. Scott had turned Abbotsford into a veritable Aladdin's cave of relics, reliques and antiquarian bric-à-brac. The material survival of the past crowded, and still crowds, its walls, tables and showcases in unsyntaxed profusion. Such collections (and Scott was by no means untypical in his enthusiasms here) represented the cultural past of the nation in process of production, accumulated but not yet catalogued, one might say. One of the achievements of his writing on antiquarian subjects would be to indicate the part played by antiquarians in the Enlightenment enterprise itself. Cumulatively, their work inculcated as unavoidable an awareness that 'meanings' generated in the process of cultural retrieval were kaleidoscopic, and 'intelligibility' a function of narrative: another twist of the tale, and the bits and pieces would rearrange themselves into a completely different pattern. 'Authenticity', in these circumstances, was a shifting effect of the light. The pedantic antiquarian personae of his fiction and the elaborate evidential and mock-evidential apparatus erected around the poetry and novels played between these versions of the past: 'official' and subversive, national and popular. As Scott's writing moved into the more spacious realm of the novel, the lessons of the *Edinburgh Review* exchanges developed an altogether more complex dialectic. In *Waverley* and its successors the de-syntactic world of antiquaries (as both narrators and characters) would open into a field of discursive play somewhat akin to the amicable mutual incomprehension practised by Swift's philosophers in the 'school of languages' in the Grand Academy of Lagado, whose scheme 'for entirely abolishing all words whatsoever' was offered as an expedient 'since words are only names for things'.[61]

Empiricism's concern with the relationships of words to things rather than relations between words was implicit in the disintegrative, antisocializing and anti-progressive aspect of antiquarian accumulation. And, as the Humean phase of Scottish Enlightenment thought intimated, scepticism was the dark shadow accompanying the apparent transparency of empirical epistemology. It is scarcely revolutionary to suggest that two tensely balanced affective trajectories, 'improvement' and 'degeneration', later came to energize some of Scott's most important prose: the 'Dedicatory Epistle' to *Ivanhoe*, the opening chapter of *Waverley*, the 1829 'General Preface' to the novels, to name a few examples. But these take on new currency when we see how the association between antiquarianism, economics and politics that generated the Waverley novels derived its unique syntax from the dialectical antagonisms of the early numbers of the *Edinburgh Review*. Scott's writing for the *Edinburgh* increasingly articulated an ambiguous, disordered realm for the anti-quary, in which the irresistible forces of stadialism met the immovable clutter of material survival; celebration and melancholy, confidence and nostalgia, emerged from the alembic in an astonishingly profitable compound. It was from this space that he would imagine the central figure of a novel dealing with antiquaries, the questionable meanings of the fragmentary survival of a material past, speculators in currency, and alarm about Jacobin invasion. The rest, in a manner of speaking, is history.

Notes

1. *Crotchet Castle* (1831), *The Novels of Thomas Love Peacock*, ed. David Garnett (London: Rupert Hart-Davis, 1948), pp. 656, 667.
2. Quoted by Mark Girouard, *The Return to Camelot: Chivalry and the English Gentleman* (New Haven and London: Yale University Press, 1981), p. 24. See also David Duff, *Romance and Revolution: Shelley and the Politics of Genre* (Cambridge: Cambridge University Press, 1994), p. 119.
3. William Smellie, *Account of the Institution and Progress of the Soceity of Anti-quaries of Scotland* (Edinburgh: William Creech, 1782), pp. 1–2.
4. On this point I am indebted to 'Pedantry and the Scene of History: The Figure of the Antiquary', an unpublished essay by Ina Ferris. I am grateful to her for making it available to me.
5. See Roger L. Emerson, 'The Scottish Enlightenment and the End of the Philosophical Society of Edinburgh', *British Journal for the History of Science* 21 (1988) 33–66.
6. 'Memoirs'; see Hewitt, 31.
7. 'Of Abstraction, Sect. VIII: Use and Abuse of General Principles in Politics', *Elements of the Philosophy of the Human Mind, Stewart*, ii 229.
8. Ibid., 228.
9. See Robert Burns, 'The Dumfries Volunteers' (1795).
10. *Stewart*, ii 228–9.
11. I thank Catherine Jones for help in locating this reference. See also Donald Winch, 'The System of the North: Dugald Stewart and his pupils', in Stefan Collini, Donald Winch and John Burrow, *That Noble Science of Politics: A Study in Nineteenth-Century Intellectual History* (Cambridge: Cambridge University Press, 1983), pp. 23–61. The best recent account of the complex political conditions of the 1790s may be found in John Barrell's *Imagining the King's Death: Figurative Treason, Fantasies of Regicide 1793–1796* (Oxford: Oxford University Press, 2000).
12. *Memorials of His Time* (Edinburgh and London: T. N. Foulis, 1910), pp. 20ff.
13. *Stewart*, ii 220.
14. See Kathryn Sutherland, 'Fictional Economies: Adam Smith, Walter Scott and the Nineteenth-Century Novel', *English Literary History* 54 (1987) 97–127.
15. See Winch, 38, and Bruce P. Lenman, *Integration and Enlightenment: Scotland 1746–1832* (Edinburgh: Edinburgh University Press, 1981), p. 110.

16. *An Inquiry into the Nature and Causes of the Wealth of Nations*, ed. R. H. Campbell, A. S. Skinner and W. B. Todd, *The Glasgow Edition of the Works and Correspondence of Adam Smith* (Oxford: Clarendon Press, 1976), Book 2, Chapter 3, p. 331. See Sutherland, 100–1.
17. *Edinburgh Review* 2 (July 1803) 355.
18. *Edinburgh Review* 3 (October 1803) 156–7.
19. *Edinburgh Review* 12 (July 1808) 449.
20. *Edinburgh Review* 4 (April 1804) 151.
21. *Edinburgh Review* 7 (January 1806) 413.
22. *Edinburgh Review* 12 (July 1808) 402.
23. Ibid., 410.
24. *Edinburgh Review* 13 (October 1808) 36. In his 1794 memoir of Smith, Stewart had coined the phrase to designate the characteristic procedures of Scottish Enlightenment historiography: 'To this species of philosophical investigation, which has no appropriated name in our language, I shall take the liberty of giving the title of *Theoretical* or *Conjectural History*, an expression which coincides pretty nearly in its meaning with that of *Natural History*, as employed by Mr. Hume, and with what some French writers have called *Histoire Raisonnée*' (*Stewart* x 34).
25. *Edinburgh Review* 13 (October 1808) 35.
26. *Edinburgh Review* 6 (July 1805) 447.
27. *Edinburgh Review* 5 (January 1805) 354.
28. *Reflections on the Revolution in France*, ed. Conor Cruise O'Brien (Harmondsworth: Penguin Books, 1969), p. 170. Duff gives a full account of the multiple political possibilities of the rhetoric of chivalry during the Revolutionary period.
29. *Edinburgh Review* 6 (April 1805) 1.
30. See Yoon Sun Lee, 'A Divided Inheritance: Scott's Antiquarian Novel and the British Nation', *English Literary History* 64 (1997) 537–67.
31. *Edinburgh Review* 6 (April 1805) 2.
32. Ibid., 7.
33. Ibid., 12, 13.
34. See Walter Benjamin, *Illuminations* (London: Fontana, 1973), p. 60; Werner Muensterberger, *Collecting: An Unruly Passion: Psychological Perspectives* (Princeton: Princeton University Press, 1994), *passim*, and Susan Stewart, *On Longing: Narratives of the Miniature, The Gigantic, the Souvenir, the Collection* (Durham, NC: Duke University Press, 1999). The British Museum originated in 1753 when the private collections of Sir Hans Sloane were acquired by the government.
35. *On Longing*, 151.
36. *Edinburgh Review* 7 (January 1806) 389.
37. Hewitt, 22, 28.
38. See Susan Manning, 'Walter Scott and Mark Twain', in *International Episodes*, ed. Janet Beer and Bridget Bennett (Manchester: Manchester University Press, 2002).
39. O'Brien, 170, 171.
40. *Edinburgh Review* 7 (January 1806) 396–7.
41. See Sutherland on Scott's subsequent explicit allusion to this commercial frame of reference in *The Heart of Midlothian* and *The Betrothed*; Sutherland, 110–13.

42. *Marmion*, Introduction to Canto I, 290–4.
43. *Marmion*, Introduction to Canto V, 61.
44. O'Brien, 170.
45. *Edinburgh Review* 12 (April 1808) 3.
46. Ibid., 28.
47. Ibid., 13. On this point, see James Watt, *Contesting the Gothic: Fiction, Genre, and Cultural Conflict, 1764–1832* (Cambridge: Cambridge University Press, 1999), p. 134.
48. *Edinburgh Review* 12 (April 1808) 31.
49. *On Longing* 153; Stewart cites James H. Binns's 'The Aesthetics of British Mercantilism', *New Literary History* 11 (1980) 303–21.
50. *Edinburgh Review* 12 (April 1808) 32.
51. Peacock, *Crotchet Castle* (1831), ed. David Garnett (London: Rupert Hart-Davis, 1948), p. 655.
52. *Edinburgh Review* 12 (April 1808) 34–5.
53. Grierson, ii 54.
54. Ibid., ii 66.
55. *Edinburgh Review* 13 (October 1808) 218.
56. Ibid., 220, 221, 218.
57. Ibid., 222.
58. Ibid.
59. *Edinburgh Review* 18 (August 1811) 384–5.
60. Ibid., 384.
61. Jonathan Swift, *Gulliver's Travels* (Harmondsworth: Penguin Books, 1967), pp. 230–1.

6
Jeffreyism, Byron's Wordsworth and the Nonhuman in Nature

Paul H. Fry

In this chapter I wish to suggest a new way of understanding Jeffrey's attacks on Wordsworth and to point out the degree to which these attacks, viewed in this way, influenced Byron's 1821 dispute with Bowles and the earlier Dedication and first Canto of *Don Juan*. I shall claim that Jeffrey baulks at the ascription of ontological importance to the realm of the nonhuman. As an Enlightenment humanist, well versed in the writings of the Scottish successors to Hume and firmly opposed to any and all idealism in philosophy, Jeffrey rejects any valuation of the natural world either for its own sake or for the sake of the allegedly pantheistic claims which hostile readers of Wordsworth and Coleridge always gleefully dismissed as unintelligible. This is not to say that Jeffrey was indifferent to nature, or even that he invariably denied the possibility of poetic interest arising from the investment of nonhuman beings with human feeling. He constantly assumes, however, that the sole purpose of describing the natural world in poetry is to illustrate human characteristics or thoughts, and to enliven metaphors for human feeling.

I

In 1808 the *Edinburgh Review* (but not Jeffrey himself: it was Henry Brougham, as Byron later learned) airily dismissed Byron's first reviewed volume of poems, *Hours of Idleness* (1807), for what they largely were: the adolescent aristocratic pastime indicated in the title. Deeply hurt, Byron took his revenge in *English Bards and Scotch Reviewers*. To surround the Jeffrey assault (featuring a comparison with Jeffreys the Hanging Judge and the *soi-disant* duel with Thomas Moore), Byron padded his poem with mockery that he soon came in varying degrees to regret – attacks on his later allies Scott and Moore, and on Bowles (rather less regretted, and in any case the original lines were written by Hobhouse) – together with amusing broadsides on the Lake School.[1] (Like Jeffrey, Byron was always hard put to find enough fish to fill this pond, or classroom.) While Byron no doubt regretted his attack on Jeffrey, he had little or no occasion to be haunted by it. Despite encouraging a challenge from Jeffrey in the 'Postscript' to the second edition of *English Bards*, he was not further provoked. Although the two appear never to have met (Byron implies as much in his first letter on Bowles), it came to be understood that they took a largely cordial view of each other: as gentlemen, as Liberals and as partial sharers of a national identity.[2] For the next decade Jeffrey wrote several mixed reviews of Byron's publications, much in the tone of the times, praising his copiousness, imagination and originality while censuring his licentiousness and morbidity. Byron never took offence.

Shortly after Byron returned to England in 1811, armed with the two cantos of travelogue *à clef* that made him famous overnight, Jeffrey published a review of Archibald Alison's *Essays on the Nature and Principles of Taste*, in which one can find, in abstract terms (although one suspects Jeffrey had Wordsworth in mind throughout, as so often), the only systematically intelligible basis for his dislike of Wordsworth's poetry.[3] The question of whether Byron read this review, or took special note of it if he did, is perhaps not as important as this preamble would make it seem, because after all many aspects of Jeffrey's critique of Wordsworth were in the air. Wordsworth affected simplicity, he invested vulgar and banal subjects with false, necessarily bathetic feeling, he mistook personal whims and megrims for general truths – all of this everyone had been saying ever since the publication of *Lyrical Ballads* and its controversial Preface. However, in the documents to which I shall be attending here, one finds in addition to the commonplaces, and indeed largely as an elaboration upon them, a particular line of attack, an original and coherent view that is not achieved by other reviewers – even by Hazlitt, whose view of Wordsworth derives largely from his view of Rousseau and forcibly aligns both of them on the Milton side of his great organizing contrast between Milton and Shakespeare. Although Byron would elaborate on Jeffrey's general view of Wordsworth while participating in the quarrel of Thomas Campbell, Isaac Disraeli and Octavius Gilchrist with Bowles' edition of Pope, the basis for his claims in the letter against Bowles is most clearly revealed in Jeffrey's discussion of beauty and taste.

Jeffrey himself must have thought a good deal of this review, as he expanded it for an 1824 *Encyclopaedia Britannica* article on 'Beauty' and made the expanded version the opening piece in the massive 1844 collection of his own work in four volumes, *Contributions to the Edinburgh Review*. In his interesting brief Preface to this collection, he is concerned chiefly to discuss his important decision to preserve the politically partisan flavour of the *Edinburgh* – a decision that had come to a crisis of sorts in 1808 when he decided to decline the Tory Walter Scott's offer to contribute provided that the review henceforth cease to be partisan. The '*Right leg*' of a review, Jeffrey recalls having told Scott in response, is politics, however certain it remains that the left leg is literature.[4] There is undoubtedly a 'politics of' the issues with which I am here concerned, as the firmness of Jeffrey's belief that these branches of endeavour belong to a single body would imply; and although I am somewhat hesitant to say very firmly what such a politics might be (it is belied by exceptions of every kind), Byron does appear to endorse a comparable literary politics or politics of literature in first setting to work on *Don Juan*, and that is one reason why I think it important to conclude with that poem.

II

Jeffrey had corresponded with his friend Alison concerning the 1790 edition of the *Essays* (hence he already had an aesthetic basis for his first attack on Wordworth in 1802), and Alison had, one supposes, revised some passages accordingly for the new edition.[5] Jeffrey's review now appeared partly to publicize Alison and partly to elaborate his own version of the argument, which resolves all points of controversy under a single heading: objects have no inherent aesthetic qualities but appear beautiful or sublime only in association with remembered human feelings or traits of character. There are also hints of the thumbnail history of aesthetics that Jeffrey expanded for the encyclopaedia article, but it is already clear that German developments from Baumgarten to Kant are to be disregarded altogether.[6] Modern readers for whom Kant provides the only real excitement in the history of aesthetics, however, should be aware that the great Continental doctrine of 'multëity in unity' eventually domesticated by Coleridge was already featured as a modestly empiricist idea in English works noticed in Jeffrey's encyclopedia version of the Alison review, especially Francis Hutcheson's *Inquiry Into the Original of Our Ideas of Beauty and Virtue* (1725). So much emphasis indeed was thrown on 'variety' and 'multiplicity' in the eighteenth century that it goes some way towards explaining the outcry against Wordsworth's 'simplicity'.

Two caveats are immediately in order, however. First, Jeffrey does not himself hold that complexity is an aesthetic property of objects any more than any other quality is or can be; nor indeed does he think that the human feelings (for example, contentment) or qualities (for example, innocence) with which objects are associated by taste are necessarily complex either. If this relativizing of baroque, rococo and picturesque standards makes Jeffrey himself seem in some sense Wordsworthian, that is worth bearing in mind – if only to explain why Jeffrey was after all more sympathetic than many others to much of what we call the romantic turn – but it needs to be qualified by a second caveat of crucial importance. It is a simple category mistake to suppose, despite unguarded encouragement from the poet himself, that Wordsworth's representation of the natural or the human world is governed primarily by aesthetic considerations of any kind. Whatever he may say, it scarcely matters to him that 'the permanent and beauteous forms' of nature be either 'beauteous' or even 'forms'; nor are the 'best objects' best in any sense other than in simply constituting the approved rhythm of rural existence. The aesthetic aspect of nature scarcely matters to Wordsworth as a *poet*, that is, however much it may matter to him as a person, as an amateur landscape gardener, and as the author of the *Guide to the Lakes*.[7] As Arnold was still insisting, Mr Wilkinson's spade is not beautiful. But then Wordsworth never thought it was.

All critics including Wordsworth himself agreed that the *medium* of representation must be judged aesthetically, because the purpose of poetry was to give what Coleridge called 'immediate pleasure'. Jeffrey, however, together with virtually all his contemporaries, confuses the medium with the object of representation even while trying, as he does in the review of Alison, to keep them separate. The fallacy arises from the argument whereby one dismisses the 'Dutch School' of painting because of its 'low' subject matter; accordingly, there appears in Jeffrey on Alison (Jeffrey here is quarrelling with Richard Payne Knight) the usual scornful reference to a dunghill, together with the 'filthy and tattered rags of a beggar' and 'the richly fretted and variegated countenance of a pimpled drunkard'.[8] As Jeffrey knew from painterly examples but wished to deny in principle, even a dunghill (like an idiot or a spade or a stunted thorn tree) could be rendered an aesthetic object by introducing such new categories as the ugly or the grotesque, or by expanding the domain of the picturesque.

In short, by subjecting the matter as well as the manner of representation to the standard of 'taste' (the *Excursion* review speaks of 'the errors of early taste'[9]), Jeffrey brings Wordsworth's poetry into focus in a way that cannot be rewarding. He sees that Wordsworth sometimes represents objects (even human beings) just *as* objects, and since he has foreordained that objects lack even the intrinsic qualities normally ascribed to them, this procedure will seem to him doubly absurd – indifference to normative canons of beauty being the less forgivable when their 'social construction', as we might say, is unrecognized or ignored. Wordsworth, in other words, is not entitled to say that an object is beautiful (supposing that that is what he does say) unless he is willing to conform to the agreed upon associations whereby taste comes to be widely shared. In the original Alison article, Jeffrey approvingly quotes 'Tintern Abbey' from memory;[10] the passage on the feelings inspired by the 'uncertain notice' of chimney smoke) in order to suggest that *even* Wordsworth sometimes shares the common taste of humanity.

Moreover, Jeffrey's insistence on the aesthetic neutrality of objects utterly precludes, no doubt unwittingly, any other sort of non-sensory human interest suitable for poetry (natural philosophy aside, that is) in the nonhuman world. Art criticism supplies this prejudice. The tyranny of the commonplace strictures on the Dutch and Flemish, with their embargo on unpeopled landscapes, barnyard imagery and the kitchen genres of *nature morte*, likewise prevented anyone's attending to the more profound – not merely counter-aesthetic – reflections of painters like Chardin on the sheer objecthood of objects, their self-identity and ontological unity. From this divergent standpoint, the fact identified in part by Jeffrey and fully entailed in the logic of his position – the fact that objects lack intrinsic attributes, whether aesthetic *or* semantic – is not what renders them irrelevant to human self-reflection. Rather, this lack is precisely what makes them interesting: objects make us realize with otherwise inaccessible clarity, through the experience of the nonhuman, what it is to be human. Much of Wordsworth's poetry, pre-eminently the structuring of the spots of time and the poetry representing human beings from infants to idiots to dotards in drastically reduced, zero-degree states of consciousness, deliberately underdetermines both the meaning and the appearance of external things in order to disclose, in the space left vacant by the refusal to explain, their being – and thereby our own being, laid bare through the suspension of thought and connoisseurship.[11]

Here is Jeffrey's contrasting position: 'We could almost venture . . . to lay it down as an axiom, that, except in the plain and palpable case of bodily pain or pleasure, we can never be interested in any thing but the fortunes of sentient beings; – and that every thing partaking of the nature of mental emotion, must have for its object the feelings, past, present or possible, of something capable of sensation.'[12] He infers this axiom from his own comments on companion genre scenes, a beautiful English countryside and a sublime 'Welsh or Highland' scene, respectively, which he has composed verbally in order to drive home his – and Alison's – conclusion. What moves us to appreciate the beauty of the English scene is 'the picture of human happiness that is presented to our imaginations and affections': 'comfort, and cheerful and peaceful enjoyment', 'industry', 'piety', 'simplicity', 'health and temperance'. The sublime scene evokes 'primeval simplicity', 'romantic ideas', 'antient traditions', and so on.[13] All very Wordsworthian, one is tempted to say, given the enviable ease with which Jeffrey can pass from the aesthetic into the ethical, from the appeal of the scene to its social significance; until, that is, one is struck as always by Jeffrey's serene anthropocentrism:[14]

> It is man, and man alone, that we see in the beauties of the earth which he inhabits; – or, if a more sensitive and extended sympathy connect us with the lower families of animated nature, and make us rejoice with the lambs that bleat on the uplands, or the cattle that ruminate in the valley, or even with the living plants that drink the bright sun and the balmy air beside them, it is still the idea of enjoyment – of feelings that animate the existence of sentient beings – that calls forth all our emotions, and is the parent of all the beauty with which we proceed to invest the inanimate creation around us.[15]

This still arguably sounds like Wordsworth, composed perhaps with the 'Intimations Ode' echoing in the background; and supposing that this were the case, it would certainly stand as Jeffrey's most subtle challenge to the poet who so persistently troubled his thoughts. Jeffrey here seems almost to identify the issue which, as we shall see, he can only dance around figuratively in his actual Wordsworth criticism. What he appears obscurely to have perceived in Wordsworth, and here to repudiate, is the priority Wordsworth accords to 'the inanimate creation', 'rocks and stone' being two-thirds of the mass that orbits with Lucy. What unifies and levels being in Wordsworth, its 'ground', hence the true object of the imaginative faculty which exists to disclose unity, is the minerality of 'inanimate creation' from which 'sentient beings', all of whom are linked ontically to the world by their own inanimate (that is, somatic) nature alone, are estranged by enlightenment anthropocentrism. In the 'Intimations Ode' almost uniquely in the Wordsworth canon (it is perhaps his least characteristic poem), 'the meanest flower that blows' is the lowest rung on the order of being, with insentient things – earth, ocean, cataracts, and hills – all powerfully humanized. It is possible that Jeffrey here preaches to Wordsworth with his own text, the very text he professed to find unintelligible at the end of his 1807 review.

III

In turning now to the series of reviews in which Jeffrey waged his campaign against Wordsworth, it is helpful to begin with Jonathan Wordsworth's excellent summary of the issues in his facsimile reprint of these reviews.[16] Emphasizing the actual inconsistency in Jeffrey's seemingly invariant themes (belying the claim that the standards of poetry are immutable with which Jeffrey launches his career in the Southey review of 1802), Jonathan Wordsworth stresses the already anachronistic anti-Jacobin agenda of the covert attack on Wordsworth in 1802 (the evidence that this is Jeffrey's main point is perhaps disputable), giving way to the subsequent absurdity of talking in the later reviews about a school of poets being spoiled by 'system' when so little of the work actually under review (Wordsworth poems added to *Lyrical Ballads* by 1807, *The Excursion, The White Doe of Rylstone*, three Coleridge poems) follows the presumed dictates of the offending 'Preface'.[17] This is all that common sense requires by way of commentary, and may admittedly be all that can be said; but it leaves Jeffrey seeming even more negligible than posterity has judged him to be. Perhaps he can seem more respectable when allowed to think philosophically as well as judicially.

The pretext of having Southey's *Thalaba* 'before us', as Judge Jeffreys always says, is, of course, amazingly flimsy. The plaintiff is nearly invisible – though not quite *in absentia*, as we shall see. This in itself should give pause. Why should Jeffrey have been so eager to devote his first effort as a reviewer, in the first issue of the *Edinburgh*, to a sustained rebuke of Wordsworth's 'Preface', 'a kind of manifesto, that preceded one of their most flagrant acts of hostility'?[18] Hostility to what? Why is hostility in the air? Jonathan Wordsworth ascribes it to politics and Jeffrey's xenophobia (Jeffrey marshals the names of Rousseau, Kotzebue and the Schiller of *Die Räuber* among the leading malign influences), but passions can run high about literature as well. Yes, there is also the complaint about affected rusticity. Wordsworth should know better because he has been to college, educated language is self-evidently superior to that of 'inferiors', etc.; but this is all just snide parry and thrust, soon to be the main weapon of the *Quarterly* arbiters but never the chief concern of Jeffrey and his more liberal stable, who made no such scruple about Burns.

In my view, the chief provocation arises from the ontology displaced as aesthetics which had preoccupied Alison and Jeffrey in recent years. If Wordsworth's 'beauteous and permanent forms of nature' can be found valuable in themselves, then the fixed standards Jeffrey announces in the first sentence of his career are not standards of art but standards of nature – and not even human nature but the 'inanimate creation' Wordsworth brings to the fore in deriving authentic passion from the rustic soil. That opinion must be laughed out of countenance because, if taken seriously, it would make the happy standards of civilized taste achieved by enlightenment consensus seem like the arbitrary and capricious hothouse growth Wordsworth says it is in the 'Preface'. Jeffrey's anthropocentric appeal to humanist standards is squarely at odds with Wordsworth's geocentric appeal to humanity, and there will of course be hostility when what is at stake is the very idea of the human itself. Are we 'children of nature',[19] like the school of Wordsworth, or disciples of the 'excellent',[20] as Jeffrey wants us to be? Are we autochthonous, as Lévi-Strauss on the Oedipus myth would have it, or are we born of two human parents, the binary that fixes our place in an unbroken tradition of socially authorized sentience?[21]

Thalaba receives its more or less well-deserved dismissal, but on various grounds scarcely relevant, as all agree, to the opening salvo aimed at Wordsworth. There is, however, one flicker of relevance, cited from a footnote to Southey's poem over which Jeffrey tellingly pauses. 'Mr Southey's partiality to the drawling vulgarity of some of our old English ditties'[22] – the sort of thing that inspired, insofar as anything literary inspired, the *Lyrical Ballads* – is proven from his citation of a ballad in which '[t]he heroine is an old *mare* belonging to John Poulter'.[23] Jeffrey then quotes three stanzas quoted by Southey in which the mare is endowed with human consciousness and treated like one of the Wordsworthian downtrodden in *Lyrical Ballads*. Now, although this ballad indeed has something of the 1798 Wordsworth's tone, Wordsworth never wrote anything quite so straightforwardly Aesopian (excepting his later moral parables in dialogue), not even in *Peter Bell*, 'Hart-Leap Well' or *The White Doe*, poems in which the degree of responsiveness to be imputed to animal consciousness is handled with subtle ambiguity. Nevertheless, Jeffrey has noticed something that will continue to irritate him, namely, the levelling of consciousness effected by the refusal to acknowledge a hierarchy of being, with its description of the human in its nonhuman, somatic registers, and its offsetting personification of the nonhuman: 'the chattering of Harry Gill's teeth [the *teeth* chatter in nonsense syllables, not the person], ... the one-eyed huntsman "who had a cheek like a cherry".'[24] Simon Lee sometimes 'reeled, and was stone blind' (in just those moments the subject-object of a spot of time, both skater and blind beggar), but he was also, in the 1798 text but not later, one-eyed. This cyclopean feature is what Jeffrey notices, bestially estranging the senility of Wordsworth's anti-hero (not an old mare, but almost) as completely as possible from the civilized, binocular perspectives and complexities of enlightenment consciousness.

In 1807 Jeffrey is still exercised at the 'alarming innovation'[25] of *Lyrical Ballads* and its Preface, and relieved to find his 'public duty' in attacking it justified by the disappointing volumes 'before' him.[26] He begins by distancing Wordsworth from the source of autochthonous strength he had earlier apprehended, claiming that 'the new poets are just as great borrowers as the old', drawing merely on 'vulgar ballads and plebeian nurseries' rather than 'their illustrious predecessors'.[27] Having thus shorn the poet's locks of a dangerous strength, Jeffrey turns to the risible subject matter, passing over Mr Wilkinson's spade to begin with 'To a Daisy' (one of the poems Wordsworth wrote with the express purpose of celebrating the being of the ordinary), of which he complains that the conclusion –

> Thou long the poet's praise shalt gain;
> Thou wilt be more beloved by men
> In times to come; thou not in vain
>   Art nature's favourite –

is an 'unmeaning prophecy'.[28] Jeffrey sees that the 'poet' is just this poet, that the daisy's future vogue will be owing to this poem, and that the proof of nature's affection is not qualitative but quantitative (nature produces a lot of daisies: 'The scope of the piece is to say,' Jeffrey rightly says, 'that the flower is found every where'[29]); but he can scarcely approve the profuse egotism shared by poet and nature (for neither of whom is affection sanctioned by men of elegant taste) and calls the prophecy unmeaning because the outcome foreseen is not determined in the slightest by human reason or judgement. The poem just *will* make its way, who knows why, and nature in collusion just *will* make daisies popular for no good reason.

Jeffrey next bridles at the comparison of 'Louisa' with a vigorous wild animal and at the suggestion addressed to the robin, another commonplace object, that 'All men who know thee call [thee] their brother.'[30]

Continuing in this vein, he arrives at the conclusion of the 'Ode to Duty', which he acknowledges to be in 'the lofty vein',[31] albeit a failure. This is an overdue concession that the general fault, the true subversiveness, of Wordsworth is after all neither his simplicity nor his banality. It is (and the main shaft, mentioned above, is reserved for the 'Intimations Ode') his unintelligibility, heralded by the 'unmeaning' part of 'To the Daisy'. Clearly the trouble with Duty from Jeffrey's standpoint is that Wordsworth sees its prototype not in the historical progress of human character but in the rigorous devotion to order and comity reflected in the universe, the 'inanimate creation': 'Thou dost preserve the stars from wrong; / And the most ancient heavens through thee are fresh and strong.'[32] The question of 'The Godhead's most benignant grace' aside, what Wordsworth evokes here is a principle, ostensibly human-centred, that is manifested in and through all modes of being equally. (When he returns to this theme in *The Excursion*, it is the first passage that Jeffrey quotes against him.[33]) All of this the humanist attaching no intrinsic value to natural objects finds simply incomprehensible. The same sense of a naturalized covenant (the perdurable rainbow) linking all created things in 'natural piety' pervades 'My Heart Leaps Up', which Jeffrey quotes entire, witheringly without comment. 'Resolution and Independence' is dismissed chiefly for its vulgar subject, but Jeffrey does scornfully notice the poet's failure to attend to the actual human speech of the leech-gatherer, wincing away perhaps from this hint that it is not as a person but as a composite being (stone, sea-beast and cloud) that the leech gatherer is finally restorative. Vulgarity remains the ostensible chief objection, but one can already see, even while Jeffrey still clings to the idea that the 'system' is the problem, that 'mysticism'[34] is what threatens most.

Only good company, Jeffrey decides by 1814, can cure the malady (here Byron's version of the critique, inverted for *Childe Harold* Canto III, becomes noticeable):

> Solitary musings, amidst such scenes [of lacustrine seclusion], might no doubt be expected to nurse up the mind to the majesty of poetical conception, – (though it is remarkable, that all the greater poets lived, or had lived, in the full current of society).[35]

This passage modulates into the central theme, derived ultimately from Hume, of taste by urbane consensus, 'the few settled and permanent maxims, which form the canon of general taste in all large and polished societies',[36] that concludes the Alison review. When Jeffrey professes not to be able to understand *The Excursion*, it is hard to understand him in turn, given his declaration that nine-tenths of the poem consists in homiletic bromides more prolix than the matter of 'any ten volumes of sermons that we ever perused'.[37] Dull, perhaps, but unintelligible? Only in the last sentence preceding his summary of the poem do we find that the only real difficulty, as usual, concerns the 'inanimate creation': 'His effusions on what may be called the physiognomy of external nature, or its moral and theological expression, are eminently fantastic, obscure, and affected.'[38] He does indeed seem honestly confused here, and it should be said that Wordsworth's treatment of nature in *The Excursion* does lend itself to confusion. For the first time in this poem since the early 1790s, and hereafter for the rest of his career, Wordsworth intermittently lapses back into the 'book of nature topos' (as Curtius calls it[39]) that had dominated the deism-inflected topographical poetry of the eighteenth century. Byron is fooled by, and imitates, the same regression in *Childe Harold* III ('But let me quit man's works, again to read / His Maker's'[40]). Neither Jeffrey nor Byron ever fully realized that for Wordsworth at his most original the natural world encountered without humanist or deist preconceptions cannot be read at all. It should be remembered in extenuation, however, that 'There was a Boy' was the only spot of time they ever had a chance to read – and no doubt they, like most readers, would have leapt to the conclusion that that poem is about communicating with nature, not about the sudden silence of the owls breaking the illusory circuit of communication to anticipate the unknowingness of death.

A further proviso is in order, however: we must presume that both Jeffrey and Byron saw something more in Wordsworth than conventional nature allegory – which is always after all anthropocentric. Their very insistence (apart from Byron's Alpine aberration of 1816) on Wordsworth's unintelligibility and mysticism strongly suggests this. No one ever called Thomson or Beattie or Cowper – or Bowles – unintelligible, even though effusions about nature were in no shortage among them. Both Jeffrey and Byron must in some measure have realized that Nature and Wordsworth did *not* speak '[a] mutual language, clearer than the tome / Of his land's tongue'.[41] It is in any case a different kind of voice that bothers Jeffrey the most:

> The Ninth and last [Book of *The Excursion*] is chiefly occupied with the mystical discourses of the Pedlar; who maintains, that the whole universe is animated by an active principle, the noblest seat of which is in the human soul; and moreover, that the final end of old age is to train and enable us

> 'To hear the mighty stream of *Tendency*
> Uttering, for elevation of our thought,
> A clear sonorous voice, inaudible
> To the vast multitude whose doom it is
> To run the giddy round of vain delight –'[42]

Note that Wordsworth's Wanderer does not here say '*in* a clear sonorous voice'. His curious and interesting assertion is that 'tendency' (the way things incline through time) utters a voice. It is not a voice that says something, just a voice uttering itself, recalling the 'rapturous mystical ode to' the Cuckoo that so exasperated Jeffrey in 1807: 'O Cuckoo! shall I call thee bird, / Or but a wandering voice?'[43] This, however, is one of those moments that almost inadvertently finds the Great Decade resurgent in Wordsworth; and elsewhere his no less 'mystical' but more accessibly theistic belief in a signifying and significant nature apparently makes an easier target: 'We should like extremely to know,' harrumphs Jeffrey concerning the Pedlar's education by nature in Book I, 'what is meant by tracing an ebbing and flowing mind in the fixed lineaments of naked crags.'[44] But only apparently: as in *The Prelude*, this passage, written in 1798, is specifically about the primitive way in which a child experiences nature, the same child who thinks a looming mountain is minatory. For the most part, nonhuman voices in *The Excursion* (*even in The Excursion*) are surrounded by an 'as if' that Jeffrey misses: 'List! – I heard, / From yon huge breast of rock, a solemn bleat; / Sent forth as if it were the Mountain's voice!'[45] Almost better, perhaps, if the mountain did have a voice (as it was revised to do in 1845[46]), a voice that speaks something other than its own being; it would be thus far subdued to Jeffrey's humanism. Among the passages he singles out for praise is the description of a river source, not yet speaking but soon to speak: 'The Mountain Infant to the Sun comes forth / Like human life from darkness.'[47]

The White Doe of Rylstone unfortunately comes before Jeffrey in 1815, the ink of the *Excursion* review scarcely dry, as the sad case of a poet making a pother about a deer, recalling the old mare in the ballad quoted by Southey:[48]

> In consequence of all which, we are assured by Mr Wordsworth, that she [the doe] 'is approved by Earth and Sky, in their benignity;' and moreover, that the old Priory itself takes her for a daughter of the Eternal Prime – which we have no doubt is a very great compliment, though we have not the good luck to understand what it means.[49]

The review of Coleridge's *Christabel, Kubla Khan: A Vision, The Pains of Sleep* in 1816 is the most gratuitously vicious of the whole series. This may be because, as Duncan Wu argues elsewhere in the present volume, it was written at least in part by Hazlitt.[50] This review need not detain us long, as there is very little in it that actually tars Coleridge with the Wordsworth brush (although the *White Doe* is singled out once again for special dispraise); but there is one moment, referring to *Christabel*, in which the glorification of the nonhuman resurfaces: 'We now meet our old friend, the mastiff bitch, who is much too important a person to be slightly passed by'[51] – as if to say, we never left the precincts of the *White Doe* after all.

IV

It was Byron, Jeffrey announces with great ironic to-do, who had the bad taste to recommend *Christabel* for publication. Perhaps, if Jeffrey is indeed the author, this suggests that matters still stood uneasily between them; but Byron in 1816 was hearing far worse things said about him while perhaps imagining worse yet, and in any case he tended at most times to remain aristocratically unruffled in the face of merely bookish disagreements. In the 1820 dedication to *Marino Faliero* of 1820 he told 'Baron Goethe', who had been roughly handled in an 1816 *Edinburgh*, that 'our Critics...are at bottom good-natured fellows – considering their two professions – < studying > taking up the law in Court – and laying it down out of it'.[52] Perhaps in any case Byron accepted the announced verdict on *Christabel*: within a year or two, Coleridge was to join Southey, Wordsworth and Castlereagh in the pantheon of scoundrels lurking throughout the Dedication and first Canto of *Don Juan* (and still present, until he deleted some stanzas at Murray's behest, in Canto Two as well). The addition of Castlereagh to the mix will allow the argument of this paper to gesture in the end, as promised, towards politics. Jumping ahead to 1821 in the meantime, I take up Byron's first *Letter to John Murray, Esqre*, on the *Rev. W. L. Bowles's Strictures on the Life and Writings of Pope* (a second, more personal and less pertinent letter on Bowles went unpublished until 1835) to illustrate the degree to which this politics, or literary politics, resembles Jeffrey's.

True, Byron had lately been in better humour with the *Quarterly* than with the *Edinburgh* because the *Quarterly* had defended Pope against Bowles while Jeffrey in the *Edinburgh* was praising Keats, author of the attack on heroic couplets in 'Sleep and Poetry' which prompted

Byron's outburst of remarks on Keatsian onanism: 'Nobody could be prouder of the praises of the Edinburgh than I was – or more alive to their censure...at present *all the men* they have ever praised are degraded by that insane article.'[53] This may illustrate in passing (only in part because Byron's allegiance to Pope was at least in some respects arguably anomalous[54]) the danger of boiling down any discussion of Regency literary politics to a contrast between the *Quarterly* and the *Edinburgh*. Byron's publisher Murray himself was the publisher of the *Quarterly* and at one time also a suitor, as Byron often reminds him, to become Wordsworth's publisher. However, the occasion of the letter to Murray was not Jeffrey's praise of Keats nor even the offending passage in Keats but Bowles's defence of his commentary on Pope in his 1806 edition of ten volumes. Bowles for his part had recently responded (under the amusingly Jeffreyan title, *Invariable Principles of Poetry*) to comments by Thomas Campbell in his 1819 *Specimens of the British Poets*, and also, in *The Pamphleteer* for October 1820, to a *Quarterly* article by Isaac Disraeli, ostensibly on Spence's *Anecdotes* but really a defence of Campbell and Pope against Bowles (this is the article Byron admired), which Bowles mistakenly believed to have been written by a greengrocer and Pope scholar named Octavius Gilchrist.

Among many other points of controversy to be passed over here, Bowles in the *Invariable Principles* argued that Pope failed to value the natural objects of the external world except as a backdrop to the human scene and as a source of illustration for human transactions. Today, this seems obviously true and scarcely detracts from even the most fervent admiration of Pope. It is taken for granted by Johnson's Imlac in *Rasselas*, who enumerates among the ideal poet's impossibly polymath acquisitions the ability to study 'all the appearances of nature', but only because 'every idea is useful for the enforcement or decoration of moral or religious truth'. Byron assails Bowles with the argument of Jeffrey's Alison review, intermittently alluding and referring to Wordsworth. The greats works of art and architecture, he writes,

are direct manifestations of mind – & *presuppose* poetry in their very conception – – and have moreover as being such a something of actual life which cannot belong to any part of inanimate nature – unless we adopt the System of Spinosa – that the World is the deity.... take away Rome – and leave the Tyber and the seven Hills – in the Nature of Evander's time – let M[r]. Bowles – or M[r]. Wordsworth or M[r]. Southey – or any of the other 'Naturals' make a poem upon them – and then see which is most poetical – their production – or the commonest Guide-book...[55]

Contrast these eighteenth-century *données*, mediated by Alison and Jeffrey, with the following passage in Wordsworth's Preface to *Lyrical Ballads*: having said that the poet's passions are associated with our 'moral sentiments', Wordsworth then speaks in addition of 'our animal sensations', and 'the causes which excite' both. Human events and emotions are prominent on the list of causes, which also includes, however, 'the operations of the elements and the appearances of the visible universe...storm and sun-shine...The revolutions of the seasons...Cold and heat'.[56] The lines are drawn. Bowles sides, albeit less reflectively, with Wordsworth (the questionable models he cites are Cowper and Thomson), while Alison, Jeffrey and Byron seek philosophical reinforcement for what is after all a rearguard opinion. The movement from Johnson's pious rationalism (and Cowper's and Thomson's as well) to Jeffrey's and Byron's humanism is marked by the disappearance of religion from the latter authors' human-centredness; and in this respect Johnson is actually closer to what Wordsworth *believed* himself to be saying (at least in retrospect, he considered the purpose of his poetry to be spiritual) than to Jeffrey. Even for Wordsworth, as the passage from the Preface shows, all things, things even in that ontic nakedness which neither Johnson nor Jeffrey and Byron would understand or appreciate, are to be referred to their role in human consciousness. The difference, by no means an absolute or polar opposition, is the difference between the reinforcement of human self-importance by nonhuman analogues and the disclosure to human reflection of the nonhuman unity, perhaps also the spiritual unity, of all somatic existence – including that of the human body itself.

V

Byron's attacks on Wordsworth and Southey in *English Bards* must certainly have been influenced by Jeffrey's repeated criticisms. (Jeffrey's review of *Poems in Two Volumes* (1807) appeared just a few months before Brougham's review of *Hours of Idleness*.) Byron had already had his first innings with Wordsworth in an undistinguished, only partly negative review of the *Poems*, 1807 (*Monthly Literary Recreations*, July 1807), but the final couplet of the lines on Wordsworth in *English Bards* ('And all who view the "idiot in his Glory" / Conceive the Bard the hero of the story') is much closer to Jeffrey – and to the guiding theme of the

Dedication and the first Canto of *Don Juan*. The only aberration from this viewpoint, again, had been *Childe Harold* III, written during the period of 'exile' in 1816 when Byron's near-paranoid misanthropy, together with Shelley's having force-fed him a diet of Wordsworth, encouraged the misreading of Wordsworth as a lover of legible nature that I have discussed above. Even here, however, Byron turns his back on humanity only to rediscover it in the human face of nature. The governing idea of *Don Juan*, at least up to the point of Juan's expulsion from Spain, is that only humanity is vital and reproductive, whereas all else – including abstracted, reified and autocratic forms of consciousness – is impotent and dead. A 'dry Bob' (Southey), a eunuch (Castlereagh), a pedantic hypocrite (Donna Inez) and three metaphysicians (Plato, Wordsworth and Coleridge) all stand, or fail to stand, in opposition to the polyphiloprogenitive 'lineal sons of Eve' (Jose, Juan, Donna Julia's grandmamma) who 'begat' not only their mixed fate but also the reproductive momentum of the '*Juan* stanza' itself, digression and adultery suggesting themselves as parallel expressions of unregulated human energy.

I do not wish to linger too long on what should be the familiar ground of Byron's critique of Wordsworth in some of its more obvious – and by no means un-Jeffreyan – forms. Much of the Dedication and first Canto are Byron's way of saying 'This will never do' to *The Excursion*, and it is helpful to consider that 'My poem's epic' is asserted in contrast with a poem that also makes epic claims, explicitly so in the 'Prospectus' quoted by Wordsworth in his prose preface to the poem. (Wordsworth: 'the mind of man' is my focus. Byron: 'I want a hero', a more fully human focus, even if 'want' in part means 'continue to lack'.) Byron's prose preface, unpublished until the twentieth century for complex reasons having little to do with its merits and its literary purpose, begins with an attack on the prose preface to 'The Thorn' in order facetiously to introduce his own fictitious narrator, equivalent to Wordsworth's retired sea-captain;[57] but not far away lurks the Pedlar, who likewise consorts, for much of Wordsworth's poem, with 'the curate of the hamlet'.[58] The most telling affinity between those antipodes, the *Juan* narrator and the Pedlar, is their lack of family ties, stressed by Wordsworth (as De Quincey noticed) in the Pedlar's solicitous yet unhelpful role in Margaret's tragedy, and his repeated serene chastisement of the married Poet's indulgence in vicarious grief. To this dramatically interesting feature of the poem Byron's narrator alludes as follows: 'But if there's anything in which I shine, / 'Tis in arranging all my friends' affairs, / Not having, of my own, domestic cares.'[59]

The contempt heaped on 'The Thorn' (*à la* Jeffrey: 'prosaic ravings' passing for poetry) will soon be directed towards the unintelligibility of *The Excursion*, which is linked in turn to that of Donna Inez: 'Her thoughts were theorems, her words a problem, / As if she deem'd that mystery would ennoble 'em.' Byron's quarry is in part the professional jargons ridiculed by his predecessors Smollett and Fielding: the lawyers' 'talk's obscure and circumspect',[60] and, for Byron's plain country squire persona, writing itself, especially bluestocking writing (the link between Joanna Southcott and Wordsworth), is suspect: Julia's friendship with Inez is odd in that 'not a line had Julia ever penn'd'.[61] But the vice infects Juan and Julia themselves, or anyone in whose interest it is to mystify plain facts. Juan falling in love becomes a Laker; hence of the reason for his embarrassment in Julia's presence 'he had no more notion / Than he who never saw the sea of ocean'.[62] This of course leads to the famous comic indictment of 'Plato' ('You're a bore, / A charlatan, a coxcomb – and have been, / At best, no better than a go-between'[63]), but even in the terms of abuse chosen one detects the true object of the attack: Juan in love has become a nature lover, causing finally to surface the indictment of Wordsworth in Jeffrey's review of Alison – and of *The Excursion*:

> Young Juan wander'd by the glassy brooks,
>   Thinking unutterable things; he threw
> Himself at length within the leafy nooks
>   Where the wild branch of the cork forest grew;
> There poets find materials for their books,
>   And every now and then we read them through,
> So that their plan and prosody are eligible,
> Unless, like Wordsworth, they prove unintelligible.
>
> He, Juan (and not Wordsworth), so pursued
>   His self-communion with his own high soul...[64]

Broadly with reference to *The Excursion* ('books', 'read them through'), Juan here becomes the author of the 'Prospectus to *The Recluse*', where somehow 'the Mind of Man – / My haunt, and the main region of my song' (as Blake likewise complained) 'to the external World / Is fitted', all to create 'the spousal verse / Of this great consummation'.[65]

From Byron's point of view, this 'fitting and fitted', as Blake called it, is 'not at all adapted to my rhymes',[66] or is at most soon to be demystified as a perfect fit of a very different kind. 'If *you* think 'twas phil-osophy that this did, / I can't help thinking puberty assisted.'[67] It simply makes no sense, as the logic of Jeffrey's position finally dictates, to be a nature poet, as nature is nothing without a human face: 'He thought about himself, and the whole earth, / . . . and of the many bars / To perfect knowledge of the boundless skies; / And then he thought of Donna Julia's eyes.'[68] *The Excursion* for Byron must remain Wordsworth's 'new system to perplex the sages';[69] Byron shows in this stanza that he has read the Preface with its Prospectus carefully, because of the way in which its scheme incorporates nonhuman things.

When the 'intellectual eunuch Castlereagh' becomes a 'thing', hence-forth called 'it' in the invective that ensues, there can be no more savage indictment, underlaid as it is by the contempt of a humanist for the dehumanized object-world. And how much worse if the object 'thinks', like the horse in 'The Idiot Boy' (a poem full of Byron's *bêtes noires*), which thus seems more human than the idiotic people. Dehu-manization for Byron consists in the objectification of authentic human feeling by 'system', and it is here that nature poetry and excessively calculating politics reveal their common Toryism. It is in this respect, but perhaps in no other, that Jeffrey and Byron can be said to share a Whig interpretation of Wordsworth. Byron may not know it, as in his view 'the Edinburgh Review and Quarterly' alike 'Treat a dissenting author very martyrly',[70] and as there is no doubt much to be said about the difference between moderate and Holland House Whigs; but in this one respect there is common ground.

VI

An important book remains to be written on the 'Regency voice' in English literature. It would account not just for Jeffreyism, but for the whole poetic pantheon that Byron in *Don Juan* (see *Don Juan*, Dedication, stanza 7) creates over against the pretensions of the Lakers: Scott (whose ballads are narrative, not 'lyrical'), Rogers (whose Italy, like Byron's, hides nature under human monuments), Campbell (joined by Byron in attack-ing Bowles), Moore (who joined John Hookham Frere, William Benet Rose and the comic Byron in ennobling the genre of *vers de société* as a sure line of defence against nature poetry) and Crabbe (the rural anti-Wordsworth, as Jeffrey had shown in his 1808 review of Crabbe). An important con-tribution to this end has been Peter Graham's lively and thoughtful '*Don Juan*' *and Regency England* (1990), the first chapter of which concentrates on Byron's critique of Wordsworth in the earliest stanzas of *Don Juan*.

In my view, however, such a book should in some measure come to terms with the issue raised in this paper. Teetering in the balance is the question of whether it means anything to be a thing – whether aesthetic or any other humanized value inheres in things. Wordsworth discovers the ontic unity of the human and the nonhuman in the sheer minerality of things. Coleridge shares this discovery but hates it, arguing that without the shaping spirit of imagination things in themselves are 'fixed and dead'. Shelley turns to advantage the conviction that the natural world is a charnel-house throughout his career. Keats writes 'the poetry of earth'. It is not the case, in fact, that Jeffrey, an exemplary Regency mind, disagrees with any of these views, although of course there is no trace in him of, for example, Shelley's consolatory immaterialism. Jeffrey's insistence that inanimate objects lack innate qualities is just what I have wanted to emphasize. For the whole western world, whether it knew it or not, things had once for all been neutralized and alienated by Kant, who finished the job begun by the apocalyptic imagery of the Bible. But for Jeffrey this was neither a crisis nor a triumph of magnitude, any more than it was for Beau Brummell's fat friend. It merely justified the secular anthropocentrism against which Wordsworth rebelled.

Notes

1. For an account of the origins of this term, or at least its elements, in the first sentence of Jeffrey's 1807 review of Wordsworth, see Peter A. Cook, 'Chronology of the "Lake School" Argument: Some Revisions', *Review of English Studies* 28 (1977) 175–81. Despite what is often said, the term does not appear in the 1802 review of Southey's *Thalaba*.
2. For a comparable view of Byron's underlying approval of Jeffrey, see Muriel J. Mellown, 'Francis Jeffrey, Lord Byron, and *English Bards, and Scotch Reviewers*', *Studies in Scottish Literature* 16 (1981) 81.
3. A recent editor of a Jeffrey selection has also argued that the Alison review provides a basis for Jeffrey's critique of Wordsworth. He points, however, to Jeffrey's insistence at the end of the essay that poets have a special responsibility to be sure that their associations are not merely personal but universal. I take it, though, that this particular complaint had been a commonplace in Wordsworth reviews ever since 1798. See *Jeffrey's Criticism: A Selection*, ed. Peter Morgan (Edinburgh: Scottish Academic Press, 1983), p. 169.
4. *Contributions*, xvii. An interesting brief discussion of this matter, and of the moderately Liberal politics of the *Edinburgh*, appears in Leslie Stephen, *Hours in a Library* (3 vols, London: Smith, Elder, 1909), ii 226–8.
5. A youthful essay on Beauty from the period 1791–2 already reflects Alison's associationist principles and the key discussion of the imagined beautiful and sublime landscapes to be discussed below. For a surviving passage, see Cockburn, i 42–3.

6. That Jeffrey likewise says nothing of Hume in any version of the essay is more surprising, in that 'Of the Standard of Taste' is surely the main source of Alison's associationist aesthetics. In Hume, too, one finds a full exposition of Alison's and Jeffrey's relativism qualified by social consensus—not surprisingly, as no other conclusion can be drawn from associationist views that are not inferred, like David Hartley's, from divine providence.

7. For an account of the negligible role played by form and structure in Wordsworth's view of nature, see my 'Green to the Very Door? The Natural Wordsworth', *Studies in Romanticism* 35 (1996) 535–51.

8. See *Edinburgh Review* 18 (May 1811) 37.

9. *Edinburgh Review* 24 (November 1814) 2.

10. *Edinburgh Review* 18 (May 1811) 29.

11. The view of Wordsworth taken largely for granted here I have set forth more fully in, *inter alia*, *A Defense of Poetry: Reflections on the Occasion of Writing* (Stanford: Stanford University Press, 1995), esp. pp. 91–107; 'Wordsworth in the *Rime*' in *The Rime of the Ancient Mariner*, ed. Fry (Boston: Bedford / St. Martins' Press, 1999), pp. 319–42; and 'Green to the Very Door?' cited above.

12. *Edinburgh Review* 18 (May 1811) 8.

13. Ibid., 13, 14, 15.

14. W. H. Christie also emphasizes Jeffrey's anthropocentrism; see 'Francis Jeffrey's Associationist Aesthetics', *British Journal of Aesthetics* 33 (1993) 260.

15. *Edinburgh Review* 18 (May 1811) 14. While it is irresistible to compare Jeffrey here with Mary Crawford in *Mansfield Park* ('I am like the famous Doge at the court of Lewis XIV; and may declare that I see no wonder in this shrubbery equal to seeing myself in it', *Mansfield Park* (New York: Signet, 1964), p. 164), it should be clear that sorting out the conflicting ideological implications brought to light by the comparison would require an article in themselves.

16. One turns eagerly to James A. Greig's ultra-Jeffreyan *Francis Jeffrey of the Edinburgh Review* (Edinburgh: Oliver and Boyd, 1948), which devotes three chapters to Jeffrey's attacks and much of the rest of the book to laying a groundwork for those chapters; but its only really purpose is to issue in Jeffrey's behalf (and, perhaps, in Scotland's) a *tu quoque* to Wordsworth and his modern admirers by saying that in person Jeffrey was more pleasant and tolerant than Wordsworth.

17. See Jonathan Wordsworth, 'Introduction', *Francis Jeffrey on the Lake Poets*, *passim* (no pp.).

18. *Edinburgh Review* 1 (October 1802) 65.

19. Ibid., 68.

20. Ibid., 67.

21. See Claude Lévi-Strauss, *Structural Anthropology*, trans. Claire Jacobson and Brooke Grundfest Schoepf (New York: Anchor Books, 1967), pp. 211–12.

22. *Edinburgh Review* 1 (October 1802) 78.

23. Ibid.

24. Ibid., 68.

25. *Edinburgh Review* 11 (October 1807) 214.

26. Ibid., 215.

27. Ibid., 218.

28. Ibid., 219.

29. Ibid.
30. Ibid.
31. Ibid., 220.
32. Ibid., 221.
33. *Edinburgh Review* 24 (November 1814) 10.
34. Ibid., 3.
35. Ibid.
36. Ibid.
37. Ibid., 5.
38. Ibid., 6.
39. See Ernst Robert Curtius, *European Literature in the Latin Middle Ages*, trans. Willard R. Trask (Princeton: Bollingen, 1973), pp. 319–26.
40. *Childe Harold's Pilgrimage*, iii 1013–14.
41. Ibid., iii 115–16.
42. *Edinburgh Review* 24 (November 1814) 9.
43. *Edinburgh Review* 11 (October 1807) 225.
44. *Edinburgh Review* 24 (November 1814) 12.
45. Ibid., 16.
46. Greig points this out; Grieg, 220.
47. *Edinburgh Review* 24 (November 1814) 28.
48. Greig, 221–2 suddenly awakens here to the source of disagreement, noting 'the poet's concentration of interest on the doe instead of on the human characters and situations'.
49. *Edinburgh Review* 25 (October 1815) 363.
50. See p. 176 below.
51. *Edinburgh Review* 27 (September 1816) 61.
52. McGann and Weller, iv 546.
53. *BLJ*, vii 229.
54. As Charles Augustin Sainte-Beuve remarked in 'What is a Classic?' (1850), Byron, who slighted even Shakespeare, 'never denied Pope, because he did not fear him; he knew that Pope was only a *low wall* by his side' (see *Criticism: The Major Texts* ed. Walter Jackson Bate [San Diego: Harcourt Brace Jovanovich, 1970], p. 493).
55. Nicholson, 134–5.
56. Owen and Smyser, i 142.
57. A number of commentaries could be cited that stress the importance of 'The Thorn' in Byron's prose introduction, but *The Excursion* in this context goes virtually ignored. See especially Gordon K. Thomas, 'Wordsworth, Byron and "Our Friend the Story-Teller"', *Dutch Quarterly Review* 13 (1983) 200–12; Jerome J. McGann, *Don Juan in Context* (Chicago: University of Chicago Press, 1976), pp. 161–3.
58. Byron cleverly stations himself in this *tableau* as one of the two 'travellers' at a slight distance from the narrator and his auditors. Recalling his trek through the Sierra Morena of 1809, Byron here listens to the narrator's tale, while his companion Hobhouse admires an Andalusian maid. Vis-à-vis *The Excursion*, Byron is the Poet, the Narrator is the Pedlar, and the 'curate of the hamlet' is the Pastor. See McGann and Weller, v 82.
59. *Don Juan*, i 182–4.
60. Ibid., i 260.

61. Ibid., i 524.
62. Ibid., i 559–60.
63. Ibid., i 926–8.
64. Ibid., i 713–22.
65. Quoted by Wordsworth in the Preface to *The Excursion* that Byron would have read in 1815; see Owen and Smyser, iii 7 and *The Poetry and Prose of William Blake*, ed. David V. Erdman (Garden City: Doubleday Anchor, 1970), p. 656.
66. *Don Juan*, i 24.
67. Ibid., i 743–4.
68. Ibid., i 729, 734–6.
69. Ibid., Dedication, 28.
70. Ibid., i 1687–8.

7
Against their Better Selves: Byron, Jeffrey and the *Edinburgh*

Jane Stabler

The relationship between Byron and Jeffrey got off to a monumentally bad start when Byron believed that Jeffrey had been the author of the attack on *Hours of Idleness* which appeared in the *Edinburgh Review* in January 1808. The actual reviewer, Henry Brougham, dismissed Byron's first published volume as 'so much stagnant water', mercilessly exposing the way in which 'the noble author is peculiarly forward in pleading minority':[1]

> It is a sort of privilege of poets to be egotists; but they should 'use it as not abusing it;' and particularly one who piques himself (though indeed at the ripe age of nineteen), of being 'an infant bard,' . . . should either not know, or should seem not to know, so much about his own ancestry.[2]

This hit the mark; Byron was mortified and the episode proved to be of lasting emotional and intellectual significance. When Percy Shelley told him in 1821 that John Keats had been killed by hostile criticism, Byron was inclined to believe him:

> I know by experience that a savage review is Hemlock to a sucking author – and the one on me – (which produced English Bards &c.) knocked me down – but I got up again. – Instead of bursting a blood-vessel – I drank three bottles of Claret – and began an answer – finding that there was nothing in the Article for which I could lawfully knock Jeffrey on the head in an honourable way.[3]

Several critics have pointed out that Byron saw Keats's death in terms of feminine weakness and susceptibility: 'especially in the career of writing, a man should calculate upon his powers of *resistance* before he goes into the arena.'[4] Byron's admission that he had turned to satire because there was no 'lawful' justification for a duel helps to explain why, in *English Bards and Scotch Reviewers*, he fastened on to a particular event in Jeffrey's career in an attempt reassert his own manliness.

The episode concerned Jeffrey's review of Thomas Moore's *Epistles, Odes, and Other Poems*, which castigated the volume as 'a public nuisance'.[5] Outraged at being described as 'the most licentious of modern versifiers', Moore issued a challenge to Jeffrey in August 1806, which was accepted. One of the seconds, however, informed the authorities and the duel was prevented by the timely intervention of the Bow Street Runners. Jeffrey and Moore were bound over to keep the peace, at which point Moore's honour would have been satisfied had it not been for a newspaper report that the pistols confiscated at the scene turned out to be empty. Moore went to great lengths to deny this story but it stuck in popular mythology and Byron recycled it in his mock apostrophe to Jeffrey in the middle of *English Bards and Scotch Reviewers*:

> Can none remember that eventful day,
> That ever glorious, almost fatal fray,
> When LITTLE's leadless pistol met his eye,
> And Bow-street Myrmidons stood laughing by? . . .
> But Caledonia's Goddess hovered o'er
> The field, and saved him from the wrath of MOORE;
> From either pistol snatched the vengeful lead,
> And strait restored it to her favourite's head.
> That head, with greater than magnetic power,
> Caught it, as Danae caught the golden shower . . . [6]

Byron's mixture of hyperbole ('ever glorious') and ironic qualification ('almost fatal') follows the belittling rhetorical style of the *Edinburgh* itself. Specifically, Jeffrey and Moore are unmanned by the *double entendre* of the 'leadless pistol'. The last couplet also uses classical allusion to convey an obscene insult ('golden shower' being the slang term for the sexual act in which one party urinates upon another). In case readers missed the historical allusion, Byron added a note:

> In 1806, Messrs. Jeffrey and Moore met at Chalk Farm. The duel was prevented by the interference of the Magistracy; and, on examination,

the balls of the pistols, were found to have evaporated. This incident gave occasion to much waggery in the daily prints.[7]

The waggish intimation of effeminacy in the image of vanishing balls was made even clearer in the manuscript draft of this note where Byron wrote that 'the balls of the pistols (like the courage of the combattants) had evaporated'. Manliness and personal honour were both at stake. In his prose postscript to *English Bards and Scotch Reviewers* Byron addressed the Edinburgh Reviewers directly informing them that 'Since the publication of this thing, my name has not been concealed; I have been mostly in London, ready to answer for my transgressions, and in daily expectation of sundry cartels; but, alas! "the age of chivalry is over".'[8] With Edmund Burke's *Reflections on the Revolution in France*, Byron struck back at the review which had undercut his own overdeveloped sense of aristocracy. Jeffrey (who had not been the author of the review anyway) did not respond, but Moore wrote to Byron to demand 'the satisfaction of knowing whether you avow the insult', and the circulation of review, satire and newspaper gossip could have led to another dawn meeting at Chalk Farm if Moore's letter had not reached Byron after his departure for an extensive tour abroad.[9]

What the episode suggests is that, from the first, Byron and Jeffrey were engaged in the vigorous early nineteenth-century disputes about the power of print to influence social and cultural codes of behaviour. Byron recognized Jeffrey as an immensely influential cultural critic with a huge dominion over 'the middling class of readers', a class which was to a considerable extent Jeffrey's own creation. As several commentators have pointed out, the *Edinburgh* was the first of a group of periodicals including *Blackwood's*, the *Athenaeum*, the *New Monthly* and *Fraser's* to '[map] out the cultural physiognomy of Britain'.[10] As Klancher has suggested, the authority of the Edinburgh came from the way it fostered a sense of 'total vision', encouraging the middle-class readership to interpret society through literary and philosophical reviews and to realize their own cultural power.[11] Writing and commissioning articles on a wide range of subjects, Jeffrey personified this command of an emergent critical discourse: indeed, as Byron observed, the *Edinburgh Review* was often referred to as 'Jeffrey's Review'.[12] In this respect, as in several others, Jeffrey's literary persona might be seen as a kind of middle-class double of Byron's.

Byron called Jeffrey the 'monarch of existing criticism' and a 'monarch maker'; Jeffrey's reviews drew attention to Byron's '*command*' of readerly sympathy, and were followed up in 1818 by John Wilson's identification of Byron's 'dominion' over the sympathy of the reader, Byron's 'kingly power' and the picture of Byron as 'the undoubting adorer of Power'.[13] The circulation of power in society was a central concern of the *Edinburgh Review* and Jeffrey had a keen sense of his own commanding position. In 1810 he wrote to Francis Horner, 'A certain spice of aristocracy in my own nature withholds me from the common expedient of strengthening myself by a closer union with the lower orders', but he retained a sharp sense of how 'lower order' readers would respond: 'Where I am puzzled the herd puzzle too – and where I grow impatient to know what an author would be at, I reasonably presume that ordinary readers will weary a little also.'[14] Jeffrey recognized that Byron's extraordinary influence came, paradoxically, from his distance from the herd: 'He has too little sympathy with the ordinary… "His soul is like a star, and dwells apart".'[15] This was, however, a high-risk strategy as idolization could – and did – tilt into alienation. English poet and Scotch reviewer recognized a cultural sovereignty which verged on despotism in the sway each exerted over the British reading public. As Whigs, both distrusted absolute monarchical power, but as leaders of Romantic fashion they fostered a literature of power and were involved in a contest to exercise as much influence as possible while claiming the moderate Whig authority of 'checks and balances'.[16]

The proof of the notice Byron and Jeffrey craved came, of course, from the readerly 'herd'. In his 1812 review of Crabbe's *Tales*, Jeffrey noted that:

> In this country, there probably are not less than two hundred thousand persons who read for amusement or instruction among the middling classes of society. In the higher classes, there are not as many as twenty thousand. It is easy to see therefore which a poet should choose to please for his own glory and emolument, and which he should wish to delight and amend out of mere philanthropy. The fact too we believe is, that a great part of the larger body are to the full as well educated and as high-minded as the smaller; and, though their taste may not be so correct and fastidious, we are persuaded that their sensibility is greater.[17]

Jeffrey's confidence in the educated sensibility of the 'middling class' presents a version of the Whig toast to 'Our Sovereign, the People'. Politically and poetically Byron was aware of the power of this potential readership too and when 'Judge' Jeffrey praised the first cantos of *Childe Harold's Pilgrimage,* followed by favourable reviews of *The Giaour,*

The Corsair and *The Bride of Abydos*, Byron was at once astounded and grateful:

> As for Jeffrey, it is a very handsome thing of him to speak well of an old antagonist, – and what a mean mind dared not do. Any one will revoke praise; but – were it not partly my own case – I should say that very few have strength of mind to unsay their censure, or follow it up with praise of other things.[18]

Byron saw Jeffrey as a man who had changed from being 'my worst literary enemy' to one who had 'done the handsome thing by me'.[19] Complementing what he saw as Jeffrey's magnanimous reversal of his position, Byron made strenuous efforts to suppress his assault on Jeffrey in *English Bards and Scotch Reviewers*. Lord Cockburn seems to be quoting from a first hand account when he recorded Byron's subsequent dismissal of the poem as a '*"ferocious rhapsody,"* and a *"miserable record of misplaced anger and indiscriminate accrimony"*'[sic].[20] Although Byron's sense of Jeffrey as an old adversary was mistaken, Byron's letters show that in the figure of Francis Jeffrey he half-perceived and half-created a critical ideal closely akin to his own poetic *mobilité*. The ability to make rapid changes of direction was one of the earliest recognizable features of Byron's poetic texture and Jeffrey was, I think, the reviewer who came closest to understanding the revolutionary importance this had for the development of English poetry. I want now to outline the temperamental coincidences which united the two men.

Neither Jeffrey's nor Byron's Whiggism fitted easily with mainstream politics. Like Byron, Jeffrey moved in and out of favour with Holland House.[21] He was a great talker, a dandy who walked with a limp, was subject to spells of melancholy or *ennui* and was also strangely susceptible to loneliness.[22] Moore's journal of his visit to Scotland in 1825 records the evening Jeffrey confided to him that he 'Cannot bear to stir without his wife & child – requires something living & breathing near him [in bed, something to touch –] & is miserable, when alone'.[23] In a letter to Jane Carlyle in 1831, Jeffrey expressed a quintessentially Romantic awareness of the need for a cosmopolitan demeanour to mask the gulf between his social self and a more private communion with nature:

> It is an especial mercy of Providence, I think, that our House of bondage [that is, Commons] is placed among objects of grandeur and beauty ... I rush out, and walk on the bridge, or place myself at a window in our calm library, and look out on the white moonlight,

and the shadows of the massive trees pencilled so sharp and dark on the turf below, and then muse and start, and back to that hot, glaring tumultuous room again, where I pass for a gay, sarcastic, patient, acute sort of person – and so I am.[24]

Jeffrey's inner sensibilities were not entirely hidden, as this letter suggests, but revealed to a select audience through conversation or epistolary exchange. Such confessional moments were inevitably shaped by Byron's poetry which had, as Jeffrey was well aware, changed the relationship between poet and the nineteenth-century reader. John Wilson's review of *Childe Harold* Canto IV for the *Edinburgh* in June 1818 helped to consolidate and popularize the new dynamics of intimacy. In the case of Rousseau and Byron, Wilson suggested:

> Each of us must have been aware in himself of a singular illusion, by which these disclosures, when read with that tender or high interest which attaches to poetry, seem to have something of the nature of private and confidential communications. They are not felt, while we read, as declarations published to the world, – but almost as secrets whispered to chosen ears. Who is there that feels, for a moment, that the voice which reaches the inmost recesses of his heart is speaking to the careless multitudes around him? Or, if we do so remember, the words seem to pass by others like air, and to find their way to the hearts for whom they were intended, – kindred and sympathizing spirits, who discern and own that secret language, of which the privacy is not violated, though spoken in hearing of the uninitiated, – because it is not understood. . . . we feel as if chosen out from a crowd of lovers.[25]

Wilson's comments help to show how the middling class of readers created its own aristocracy of feeling with Byron's poetry as a form of 'initiation'. To borrow Burke's notion of beautiful servitude, Byron 'made power gentle'. His art enabled individual readers to distinguish themselves from the mass market for poetry of which they were a part. This sense of readerly exclusivity or originality was an aspect of everyday life which the *Edinburgh* disseminated to thousands of people. Jeffrey's early responsiveness to the sense of uniqueness imparted by Byron's poetry, even against his better judgement, shaped his curiously Byronic critique of Byronism.

Byron seems to have sensed the temperamental kinship between himself and Jeffrey, often puzzling over what he felt to be Jeffrey's misreading of his misanthropy and expressing a wish to be better acquainted. In his 1814 journal, for example, Byron meditated upon the known strength of Jeffrey's character:

> I have often, since my return to England, heard Jeffrey most highly commended by those who know him for things independent of his talents. I admire him for this – not because he has praised me ... but because he is, perhaps, the only man who, under the relations in which he and I stand, or stood, with regard to each other, would have had the liberality to act thus; none but a great soul dared hazard it. The height on which he stands has not made him giddy; – a little scribbler would have gone on cavilling to the end of the chapter.[26]

For a moment, Jeffrey anticipates the courage of Manfred on the edge of the Jungfrau, gazing down from a dizzy height on the rest of the world, but maintaining poise and self-awareness. This appreciation of Jeffrey's virtue was shared with Moore as another former antagonist: 'Jeffrey is out with his 45th Number,' Byron wrote to Moore in August 1814. 'He is only too kind to me, in my share of it, and I begin to fancy myself a golden pheasant, upon the strength of the plumage wherewith he hath bedecked me.'[27] And the coincidence of their high esteem for one another in the face of earlier hostilities appealed to Byron's enjoyment of unpredictability: 'Next to *your* being an E[dinburgh] Reviewer, *my* being of the same kidney, and Jeffrey's being such a friend to both, are amongst the events which I conceive were not calculated upon in Mr. – what's his name?'s – "Essay on Probabilities."'[28] Even after his departure from England in 1816, Byron continued to express the hope that one day he would be able to make Jeffrey's acquaintance.[29] They never did meet, nor did Jeffrey succeed in his attempts to enlist Byron among the Edinburgh Reviewers, but Byron entered into the fringe world of pre-publication puffing and review-fixing, and he retained a life-long respect for his 'grand patron' whose critical pronouncements mediated the poet's fraught relationship with the middling class of readers.[30]

What was the substance of Jeffrey's critical pronouncements? Many modern critics have expressed impatience with his judgement. For Thomas McFarland, Jeffrey was 'rarely known to be right about anything'.[31] Donald Reiman summarizes his disappointment with the *Edinburgh* when he claims that 'in no review does Jeffrey or Brougham demonstrate any real understanding of the new trends in poetry during the period', and he refers disparagingly to the 'banality' of Jeffrey's poetic principles, depicting him as 'the greatest plot summarizer of them all'.[32] But Jeffrey did much more than merely summarize Byron's plots or cavil about his pernicious moral effects. The line adopted by the *Edinburgh* in its first review of Byron's poetry – 'It is a sort of privilege of poets to be egotists' – opened up the possibility of a more aesthetic, less stridently moral approach to poetry. In many ways, Jeffrey's scepticism and his awareness of critical relativity made him peculiarly sensitive to the more radical instabilities of Byron's verse.

Jeffrey first recognized the unsettling tendency of Byron's poetic surface in his review of *Childe Harold's Pilgrimage* Cantos I and II. There, he found 'flashes of emotion and suppressed sensibility that occasionally burst through the gloom'.[33] This experience of sudden appearance and disappearance would characterize Jeffrey's readings of Byron's poetry throughout his career. In *Childe Harold* I and II Jeffrey identified a 'singular turn of sentiment which we have doubted whether to rank among the defects or the attractions of this performance'.[34] In this particular case, he was worried about the political tenor of Byron's reflection on the vanity of 'Battle's minions'. But there was something else as well. The idea of the 'singular turn' captured Byron's ability to move abruptly from one sentiment to another. Jeffrey's commentary on the linear progress of the poem registers the full force of these shifts:

> After this, there is a transition to the maid of Saragoza, and a rapturous encomium on the beauty of the Spanish women; in the very middle of which, the author, who wrote this part of his work in Greece, happens to lift up his eyes to the celebrated peak of Parnassus – and immediately, and without the slightest warning, bursts out into the following rapturous invocation.[35]

Other reviewers noticed and objected to the transitions of the poem as well, but Jeffrey saw these moments as the defining trait of a new sort of poetry.

The *Edinburgh Review* developed the idea of poetic velocity as a measure of cultural change and over the course of a decade it sustained a poised, ambivalent response to Byron's mobile poetic surface. At the beginning of this critical dialogue, Anna Laetitia Barbauld detected a superior intelligence self-consciously displayed in both *The Giaour* and in Jeffrey's review of it: 'And do you understand the poem at first read-ing?' she wrote to ask her friend, Mrs Beecroft, '– because Lord Byron and the Edinburgh Reviewers say you are very stupid if you don't, and yet the same Reviewers have thought proper to prefix the story to help your apprehension'.[36] Jeffrey's remarks about 'persons of slender sagacity ... liable to be perplexed by an ellipsis'[37] were almost certainly directed at the other reviewers who had wrestled unsuccessfully with the plot. In the month before Jeffrey's review appeared, the *Monthly Review*, for example, outlined the story of the poem with 'considerable hesitation'.[38] Jeffrey's review also teased conservative critics like William Roberts, who deplored the use of the fragment form and equated it with the work of 'those who, in the language of Mr. Burke, are expert in "arrangements for general confusion"'.[39] While Jeffrey welcomed the fragment as a relief from long poems suggesting that 'the greater part of polite readers would now no more think of sitting down to a whole Epic, than to a whole ox', Roberts disapproved of the 'patronage which we observe with surprise some of our reviewing fraternity have conferred'.[40] But beyond his liberal toleration for the fragment, what Jeffrey's reading consistently highlighted was the alliance of Byron's 'power' with abruptness. While many critics regarded the sudden jumps in the story as flaws which needed to be excused (the *Satirist* argued that 'nothing can be more fatal to the effect of any composition ... than such repeated interruptions as those in "the Giaour"'[41]), Jeffrey realized the way in which Byron's poetry created a new licence for itself:

> The whole poem, indeed, may be considered as an exposition of the doctrine, that the enjoyment of high minds is only to be found in the unbounded vehemence and strong tumult of the feelings. ... The images are sometimes strained and unnatural – and the language sometimes harsh and neglected, or abrupt and disorderly; but the effect of the whole is powerful and pathetic.[42]

In this passage, it sounds as if Jeffrey, too, is attempting to separate the flawed parts from the whole, but towards the end of his review, we find a more contradictory and suggestive passage:

> The sterner and more terrible poetry which is conversant with the guilty and vindictive passions, is not indeed without its use both in purging and in exalting the soul: But the delight which it yields is of a less pure, and more overpowering nature; and the impressions which it leaves behind are of a more dangerous and ambiguous tendency. Energy of character and intensity of emotion are sublime in themselves, and attractive in the highest degree as objects of admiration; but the admiration which they excite, when presented in combination with worthlessness and guilt, is one of the most powerful corrupters and perverters of our moral nature; and is the more to

be lamented, as it is most apt to exert its influence on the noblest characters. The poetry of Lord Byron is full of this perversion; and it is because we conceive it capable of producing other and still more delightful sensations than those of admiration, that we wish to see it employed upon subjects less gloomy and revolting than those to which it has hitherto been almost exclusively devoted.[43]

Although the trajectory of this reading still inclines towards moral exhortation, it contains within it recognition of an amoral admiration for energy and intensity. This apprehension of the 'ambiguous' effects of volatility is also, fascinatingly, linked with questions about class. Jeffrey's careful distance from Holland House Whiggism was supported by a sense that the 'noblest characters' were peculiarly susceptible to exhibitions of instability. Jeffrey's diagnosis of 'perversion' in Byron's poetry carried an awareness of Byron's ability to turn or deflect the emotions driving his readers (an early manifestation of Byron's art of digression). This experience was primarily one of palpable disruption and movement with the connotations of wickedness coming afterwards. In analysing the combination of delight, danger in Byron's poetry and connecting it with a morally 'ambiguous tendency', Jeffrey defined the revolutionary texture of Byron's writing which most other critics (with the exception of Hazlitt) struggled to comprehend.

After his review of the first cantos of *Childe Harold's Pilgrimage*, Jeffrey sustained his attentiveness to poetic speed, patterns of abrupt movement and forms of conflict in Byron's work. In April 1814, shortly after his return from America, he reviewed *The Bride of Abydos* and *The Corsair*. His recent experience of a new form of government probably contributed to the overview of evolving civilization which preceded his remarks on the poems themselves. Jeffrey's long-term view of poetry as reflecting and partaking in social transformation provides a context for his close reading of Byron's verse narratives. As before, he discovers 'rapidity' and an 'abrupt' style 'hurrying on . . . not always very solicitous about being comprehended by readers of inferior capacity'.[44] This style is portrayed as an 'experiment' to adapt the heroic couplet to 'all the breaks, starts and transitions of an adventurous and dramatic narration'.[45] He declared the experiment to be a complete success, showing that 'the oldest and most respectable measure that is known among us' is capable 'of vibrations as strong and rapid as those of a lighter structure'. The use of the word 'vibrations' here reveals the extent to which Jeffrey's associationist aesthetics were combined with his sense of social change.[46]

For Jeffrey, the new poetry of strong emotion rendered it in unprecedented physical detail for the reader: 'The minds of the great agents must
be unmasked for us – and all the anatomy of their throbbing bosoms
laid open to our gaze…the crossing and mingling of their opposite
affections, must be rendered sensible to our touch.'[47] Jeffrey's image of
an anatomy of passion shows that, despite his early criticism of Joanna
Baillie's dramatic work, he was stimulated by the new explorations of
irrationality. Even as his eighteenth-century critical inheritance taught
him to be wary of courting emotional extremity, Jeffrey prepared his
readers for the arrival of the Nietzschean superhero.

In Jeffrey's historical overview, human beings (especially 'the more
powerful spirits') flinch from monotony and vulgarity:

> a disdain and impatience of the petty pretensions and joyless ele-
> gancies of fashion will gradually arise: and strong and natural sensations
> will again be sought, without dread of their coarseness. … This is the
> stage of society in which fanaticism has its second birth, and political
> enthusiasm its first true development – when plans of visionary
> reform, and schemes of boundless ambition are conceived, and
> almost realized by the energy with which they are pursued – the era
> of revolutions and projects – of vast performances, and infinite
> expectations.[48]

'This is the age to which we are now arrived,' Jeffrey proclaimed.
Although he displays some caution about the human 'avidity for strong
sensations',[49] his welcome for a poetry of 'muscular force and beauty'[50]
is unmistakable and ought to be contrasted with the conservative rejec-
tion of such developments as appeared, for example, in the *Critical
Review* when it reviewed *The Corsair* in February 1814:

> The last half century has produced as great a revolution in the world
> of fiction as of fact. Within that time established customs have been
> set aside, grave opinions derided, and the bounds of poetic licence
> extended beyond the limits of ordinary vision. Lord Byron is one of
> the mighty spirits who lead the revolt.[51]

The features of this modern school of poetry were listed as

> an unsparing contempt of all kind of rule and minor adaptation; a
> disproportionate attention to some favourite train of associations; and

a proud disregard to every species of arrangement and development, which tamely infers the propriety of beginning, middle, and end.

While conservative critics were beginning to harden their objections to Byron's sudden transitions into disapprobation of a 'jacobin' style, Jeffrey's analysis of the poetry was more thoughtful. He detected 'radically incongruous' unions of cultivated feeling and 'uncontrouled' manners in other writers such as Southey, Scott and Campbell, but he found that Byron's poetry was the only variety which combined this startling mixture within a factually accurate context: 'Lord Byron, we think, is the only modern poet who has set before our eyes a visible picture of the present aspect of scenes so famous in story.'[52] This element of fact would become increasingly important to Byron and while many readers objected to the incursion of quotidian detail or satiric contemporary allusion, Jeffrey seems to have welcomed the mixture as a check on sweeping singularity or uniformity. After the publication of this review, Byron expressed his warmest admiration for Jeffrey and in February 1815 wrote in the hope of establishing 'personal friendship':

> I shall be now most happy to obtain and preserve whatever portion of your regard you may allot to me. The whole of your conduct to me has already secured mine, with many obligations which would be oppressive, were it not for my esteem of him who has conferred them. I hope we shall meet before a very long time has elapsed; and then, and now, I would willingly endeavour to sustain your good opinion.[53]

This letter negotiates the difficult territory between Byron's manly pride and Jeffrey's lack of prejudice and is full of Byron's awareness of Jeffrey's legal training, talking of the critic's 'judgment' and 'public sentence' together with Byron's desire to 'acquit' himself. The formality of the letter, however, does not prevent us from sensing the strong attraction Byron felt towards Jeffrey – as when he writes of 'the pleasure [he] should derive from the power of exciting and the opportunity of cultivating' Jeffrey's friendship. Byron had many friends who doubled as literary advisers – for example, William Gifford, the editor of the *Quarterly Review*. But while Gifford exerted a more 'fatherly' strain of correction over Byron's work, Jeffrey seemed to represent the voice of a firm but fair older brother. His steadying influence was nowhere more evident than in the review which marked the year of Byron's divorce from the English public.

In the *Edinburgh* for December 1816 (published in February 1817) Jeffrey reviewed *Childe Harold's Pilgrimage* Canto III and *The Prisoner of Chillon*. The reception of these works in most periodicals was shadowed by the scandal of Byron's personal life. Jeffrey was as uneasy as everyone else about the public exposure of domestic circumstances and he passed over poems such as 'Fare thee well' with the observation that 'not even the example of Lord Byron, can persuade us that they are fit for public discussion'.[54] But in a review that focused on the consistency of Byron's publications to date, Jeffrey defused the expectation that there was anything new or sensational in Byron's 1816 poems. While many reviewers plunged immediately into hysterical indictments of Byron's culpability in the separation scandal, Jeffrey set out to present him as a model of stability compared with the Lake School. The opening of the piece pours gallons of cold water on frantic contemporary speculation about Byron's sanity:

> though he is sometimes abundantly mystical, he never, or at least very rarely, indulges in absolute nonsense – never takes his lofty flights upon mean or ridiculous occasions – and, above all, never dilutes his strong conceptions and magnificent imaginations with a flood of oppressive verbosity. On the contrary, he is, of all living writers, the most concise and condensed; and, we would fain hope, may go far, by his example, to redeem the great reproach of our modern literature – its intolerable prolixity and redundance.[55]

We can only appreciate the heroic degree of level-headedness and restraint involved in saluting Byron's 'nervous and manly lines' in 1816 by comparing Jeffrey's language with the violent declamations of other reviewers at the same time. In April 1816 the *British Critic* summarized Byron's poetry as the 'feverish and fretful workings of a confined and selfish sensibility', adding: 'The querulous acrimony of proud and peevish misanthropy bear no more comparison to the real feeling of a poetic mind, than the morbid convulsions of an hysterical female, to the active exertions of a powerful and manly frame.'[56] While Tory magazines demonized the poet, Jeffrey trod a fine line between highlighting Byron's uniqueness ('a sort of demoniacal sublimity, not without some traits of the ruined Archangel') and protesting that his singularity had grown a little too familiar ('But it is really too much to find the scene perpetually filled by one character'[57]). As if to balance this criticism of a limited range of characters, Jeffrey drew attention to the continuing experience of 'the sudden flash of those glowing thoughts' and the 'abrupt and irregular diction' in Byron's poetry.[58] Canto III, for example, is said to open with 'a burst of grand poetry',[59] and the closing address to Byron's daughter is, according to Jeffrey, 'extremely beautiful' in contrast to reviewers such as that in the *British Critic* who dismissed it as 'written in bad taste, and worse morality'.[60]

While Jeffrey asserted the necessity that a poet should be a 'Moral Teacher', he identified the moral problem of Byron's poetry to be exactly the source of its aesthetic success. The inextricability of negative and positive qualities is evident in the subject and the texture of his poetry: Jeffrey pondered the moral implications of Byron's demonstration that 'all these precious gifts of dauntless courage, strong affection, and high imagination, are not only akin to Guilt, but the parents of Misery; – and that those only have any chance of tranquillity or happiness in this world, whom it is the object of his poetry to make us shun and despise'.[61] Once again, the seductive power of Byron's poetry is that it creates its own élite. In his review of Cantos I and II, Jeffrey had suggested that the character of a misanthropical hero was 'piquant' and that 'the best parts of the poem . . . are those which embody those stern and disdainful reflexions'.[62] Now, in Canto III, he contemplated the social cost of Byron's misanthropy:

> Even our admiration is at last swallowed up in a most painful feeling of pity and of wonder. It is impossible to mistake these for fictitious sorrows, conjured up for the purpose of poetical effect. There is a dreadful tone of sincerity, and an energy that cannot be counterfeited in the expression of wretchedness and alienation from human kind, which occurs in every page of this publication. . . . We certainly have no hope of preaching him into philanthropy and cheerfulness; but it is impossible not to mourn over such a catastrophe of such a mind, or to see the prodigal gifts of Nature, Fortune, and Fame, thus turned to bitterness, without an oppressive feeling of impatience, mortification and surprise.[63]

Byron expressed surprise at this response and wrote to ask Moore to tell Jeffrey 'that I was not, and, indeed, am not even *now*, the misanthropical and gloomy gentleman he takes me for, but a facetious companion, well to do with those with whom I am intimate, and as loquacious and laughing as if I were a much cleverer fellow'.[64] Byron's after-reflection on the review is interesting: 'I suppose now I shall never be able to shake off my sables in public imagination', as if aware that Jeffrey's opinion would set a seal on the matter.

Jeffrey's lament over the 'catastrophe' of Byron's mind may be seen to have captured the poet's imagination as much as that of the reading public. Byron read the review in March 1817 just after completing the first draft of *Manfred* and submitting it for Gifford's approval. When Gifford found the third Act to be weak, Byron agreed to revise it, making the Abbot into a more credible ethical and intellectual opponent for Manfred. In the new Act III, the exhortation of the Abbot ('why not live and act with other men?'[65]) is strongly reminiscent of Jeffrey's socio-critical opinions even as they echo Ophelia's elegy for Hamlet:

> This should have been a noble creature: he
> Hath all the energy which would have made
> A goodly frame of glorious elements,
> Had they been wisely mingled; as it is,
> It is an awful chaos...[66]

The reshaping of the Abbot into a companion who remains with Manfred up to the moment of his death also reflects the character of the reviewer Byron felt had 'stuck by' him.[67] When he came to review *Manfred*, Jeffrey pointed to the continuing interest in tyrannical power: 'The noble author...still deals with that dark and overawing Spirit, by whose aid he has so often subdued the minds of his readers.'[68] But although he found in Manfred the same soul as in Harold, Conrad and Lara, he also detected 'the fiercer traits of its misanthropy subdued, as it were, quenched in the gloom of a deeper despondency'. Again Jeffrey contemplated the way in which Byron's art created its own rules: 'To object to the improbability of the fiction is, we think, to mistake the end and aim of the author.'[69] Discussing the appearance of the Witch of the Alps, Jeffrey notes again that 'improbability is swallowed up in... beauty'.[70] At the end of the review, he acknowledges that, as a proper drama or a finished poem, 'it is far too indistinct and unsatisfactory. But we take this to be according to the design and conception of the author.'[71] Repeatedly, Jeffrey positioned himself as a critic who could appreciate the exceptional licence of genius and this extended to the moral questions in the work as well.

Like other reviewers, Jeffrey was cagey about the possibility of an incestuous union between Manfred and Astarte, referring with legalistic circumlocution to the fact that she is 'too nearly related to be lawfully beloved'.[72] Later in the review he is more direct, listing among the faults of the work 'the painful and offensive nature of the circumstance on which its distress is ultimately founded...incest, according to our modern ideas – for it was otherwise in antiquity – is not a thing to be at all brought before the imagination.'[73] Jeffrey's parenthetical acknowledgement that things were different 'in antiquity' marks a crucial intellectual difference between his objections and the prurient biographical revulsion of other journals. Indeed, the anthropological evidence of changing religious and social attitudes to incest is one of the most important philosophical underpinnings of Byron's next metaphysical drama, *Cain*. But in Jeffrey's reviews of Byron's dramas in general and *Cain* in particular, his intellectual sympathy with Byron reached a crisis-point.

Having encouraged Byron towards dramatic writing as early as 1814, readers might have expected a favourable review from Jeffrey when *Marino Faliero* was published. Ironically, Jeffrey claimed to be disappointed because (amongst other reasons) Byron had chosen a story 'as if in wilful perversity ... without love or hatred – misanthropy or pity'.[74] But he found some passages to admire, such as the one in which Lioni 'contrasts the tranquillity of the night scene which lies before him, with the feverish turbulence ... he has just quitted'.[75] In *The Prophecy of Dante* (published with the play) Jeffrey encountered a more recognizably Byronic mode with its ability to sift the reading public into 'common readers' and 'those who are qualified to enter into its spirit, and can raise themselves to the height of the temper in which it is conceived'.[76] The review finished positively, declaring the poem to be 'the work of a man of great genius',[77] but Jeffrey's next report on 'Lord Byron's Tragedies' was much less favourable: 'I have at last administered a little cruel medicine,' Jeffrey wrote to Charles Wilkes in April 1822.[78]

Jeffrey began with the suggestion that English drama lost its way when it began to harbour 'an unreasonable and undue dread of criticism'.[79] He echoed the liberal views of Percy Bysshe Shelley in, for example, the Preface to *The Revolt of Islam* when he adds:

> we are convinced that no modern author will ever write with the grace and vigour of the older ones, who does not write with some portion of their fearlessness and indifference to censure. Courage, in short, is at least as necessary as genius to the success of a work of imagination.[80]

Byron might at first seem to fulfil the requirement of fearlessness, but Jeffrey suggested instead that he was more than usually vulnerable to audience reactions: 'instead of proving that he is indifferent to detraction, [he] shows only, that the dread and dislike of it operate with more than common force on his mind'.[81] This observation goes to the heart of Byron's relationship with his reading public. Jeffrey points out that Byron does not display 'superiority to censure, but aversion to it', and it links with his earlier sense that the Byronic hero is 'averse indeed from mankind'.[82] While Jeffrey had a role in defending the originality of *Manfred*, Byron's return to more traditional forms caused the understanding between poet and critic to collapse.

Jeffrey had ended his review of *Marino Faliero* and *The Prophecy of Dante* with a call to Byron to 'digest his matter a little more carefully, and somewhat concentrate the potent spirit of poetry'.[83] Superficially at least, this is what the *Three Dramas* volume appeared to do, but Jeffrey saw Byron's attempts to re-establish the Unities as 'mere caprice and contradiction':

> He, if ever man was, is *a law to himself* – 'a chartered libertine;' – and now, when he is tired of this unbridled license, he wants to do penance within the *Unities!* This certainly looks very like affectation.[84]

This was shrewd criticism. Jeffrey was much closer than he knew to Byron's reactive aesthetic principles. The return to the Unities was, in part, because Byron had become weary of too much liberty. The campaign against the Lake School also led to his involvement with the Pope/Bowles Controversy in which, as Paul Fry points out elsewhere in this volume,[85] Byron exhibited his most Jeffreyan aspects. Jeffrey's suggestion that the dramas amounted to little more than a critical flounce was echoed by Hazlitt in *The Spirit of the Age* where he claimed that Byron

> is not contented to delight, unless he can shock the public. He would force them to admire in spite of decency and common sense. . . . He is to be 'a chartered libertine,' from whom insults are favours, whose contempt is to be a new incentive to admiration. His Lordship is hard to please: he is equally averse to notice or neglect, enraged at censure and scorning praise.[86]

But while Jeffrey saw Byron to be vainly at odds with his reader throughout the volume, he was most disturbed by *Cain*. In *Cain*, in particular, Byron seemed to embody the argumentative traits of Jeffrey's own philosophy and profession, only to turn away from Jeffrey's sociability into a 'system of resolute misanthropy'.[87] The drama manifests great 'power', but Jeffrey regretted its publication as it 'may be the means of suggesting the most painful doubts and distressing perplexities, to hundreds of minds that might never otherwise have been exposed to such dangerous disturbance'.[88] The inference is clear: Jeffrey (and select readers) possess the intellectual equipment to be able to encounter the drama without being undermined or overwhelmed, but there is a 'lower order' whose experience of power and beauty might not be contained as aesthetic experience.

Jeffrey (unlike other reviewers) '[acquitted] Lord B...of any wish to corrupt the morals, or impair the happiness of his readers'.[89] Rather, Byron's poetry identified one of the hazards of the *Edinburgh*'s success in extending the readership. Jeffrey recognized that Byron's 'haste to obliterate' the sentiments he evoked was part of that 'hurrying' style he had always admired. But he resisted both the scepticism of *Cain*, and its manifestation in the texture of *Don Juan* where the author repeatedly impersonates what is 'sweet and lofty' until 'he casts off the character with a jerk – and, the moment after he has moved and exalted us to the very height of our conception, resumes his mockery at all things serious or sublime'.[90] Jeffrey's self-consciously 'exaggerated'[91] objections to the sudden changes in *Don Juan* which he had appreciated in other contexts are, perhaps, due to a realization of the extent to which Byron's poetry shadowed his own art and the extremes to which special pleading might lead. This possibility is especially evident if we examine Hazlitt's estimate of the 'sceptical indifference'[92] of the *Edinburgh* and of Jeffrey's style. Hazlitt depicts Jeffrey as the master of 'speculative doubts, of checks and drawbacks'; he is prone to a 'too restless display of talent.... He cannot rest on one side of a question: he is obliged by a mercurial habit and disposition to vary his point of view...there are always *relays* of topics; the harness is put to, and he rattles away as delightfully and as briskly as ever.'[93] This is reminiscent of nothing so much as the narrator of *Don Juan* ('I rattle on exactly as I'd talk'[94]). As if to point to Byron, Hazlitt concluded his portrait of Jeffrey with the assertion that 'He has not been spoiled by fortune – has not been tempted by power':[95] the unspoken other half of this comparison is Hazlitt's view of Byron as 'the spoiled child of fame as well of fortune'.[96]

Jeffrey and Byron began their critical relationship at odds with one another and that is how it ended. In June 1822 Byron complained that 'even' Jeffrey has 'risen up against me and my later publications'[97] and, briefly, he contemplated direct confrontation with the *Edinburgh Review*:

it will be difficult for me not to make sport for the Philistines by pull-
ing down a house or two – since when I once take pen in hand – I

must say what comes uppermost. . . . I have not the hypocrisy to pretend impartiality – nor the temper (as it is called) to keep always from saying – what may not be pleasing to the hearer – or reader.[98]

Even as he struck back at Jeffrey, Byron deployed the *Edinburgh*'s rhetoric of independence, simultaneously dismissing and keeping an eye on the 'Philistine' audience. As Hazlitt showed, Jeffrey, the 'master of the foils', also drew on a rhetoric of performative opposition. For a brief, exhilarating period Byron and Jeffrey turned the arena of print culture into duelling ground, theatre and courtroom, where, as Jeffrey remarked ruefully and admiringly, poets are 'not very often safe advocates'.[99]

Notes

1. *Edinburgh Review* 11 (January 1808) 285.
2. Ibid., 288.
3. *BLJ*, viii 102.
4. *BLJ*, viii 103.
5. *Edinburgh Review* 8 (July 1806) 456.
6. *English Bards and Scotch Reviewers*, 464–7, 490–5.
7. McGann and Weller, i 407.
8. Ibid., 263.
9. Dowden, i 135. By the time Byron returned, Moore felt that family responsibilities prevented him from reissuing the challenge. Rogers acted as mediator and Byron and Moore became firm friends.
10. Jon P. Klancher, *The Making of English Reading Audiences 1790–1832* (Madison: The University of Wisconsin Press, 1987), p. 52.
11. Ibid., 68–73.
12. Nicholson, 82.
13. *BLJ*, iv 87, iii 209; *Edinburgh Review* 23 (April 1814) 199; 30 (June 1818) 88, 99, 117.
14. Letter to Francis Horner, 20 July 1810, Cockburn, ii 129. Letter to Archibald Alison, 29 July 1808, quoted in Peter F. Morgan, 'Francis Jeffrey as Epistolary Critic', *Studies in Scottish Literature* 17 (1982) 116–34, p. 126.
15. *Edinburgh Review* 36 (February 1822) 420.
16. For a discussion of Byron's style in relation to Whig rhetoric, see Malcolm Kelsall, *Byron's Politics* (Brighton: Harvester Press, 1987).
17. *Edinburgh Review* 20 (November 1812) 280.
18. *BLJ*, iv 92.
19. Ibid., ii 119, iv 156.
20. Cockburn, i 199.
21. Jeffrey's Don Pedro Cevallos article and *English Bards and Scotch Reviewers* article were both regarded as *faux pas* by Holland House. For discussion of Jeffrey's Whiggism, see Flynn, 95–134.
22. Jeffrey's dandyism was foregrounded in Lockhart's *Peter's Letters to his Kinsfolk*. David Bromwich, however, suggests that 'Byron's dandyism . . . eluded

Jeffrey entirely' (see 'Romantic Poetry and the *Edinburgh* Ordinances', *Year-book of English Studies* 16 (1986) 1–16, p. 5). Cockburn records that Jeffrey had a 'contracted limb, which made him pitch when he walked' (Cockburn, i 200).

23. *The Journal of Thomas Moore*, ed. Wilfred S. Dowden (6 vol, Newark: University of Delaware Press, 1984), ii 852.

24. Quoted in Peter F. Morgan, 'Principles and Perspective in Jeffrey's Criticism', *Studies in Scottish Literature* 4 (1967) 179–83, p. 185. Morgan sees Jeffrey writing 'in semi-Wordsworthian vein', but the 'start' and the idea of 'passing' for a 'gay, sarcastic' person make this self-portrait much closer to the Byronic persona of *Childe Harold* III (admittedly when Byron is in his most Wordsworthian mode). See Jeffrey's review of *Marino Faliero*, p. 161 above.

25. *Edinburgh Review* 30 (June 1818) 90. The linkage between Byron and Rousseau was made by several reviewers. See Theodore Redpath, *The Young Romantics and Critical Opinion 1807–1824* (London: Harrap, 1973), p. 30.

26. *BLJ*, iii 252–3.

27. *BLJ*, iv 152.

28. *BLJ*, iv 201.

29. *BLJ*, v 185.

30. *BLJ*, ix 63–4; ix 173.

31. Thomas McFarland, *The Masks of Keats: The Endeavour of a Poet* (Oxford: Clarendon Press, 2000), p. 39.

32. Donald Reiman, *The Romantics Reviewed* (8 vol, New York: Garland, 1972), B ii 832, 918, 910.

33. *Edinburgh Review* 19 (February 1812) 467.

34. Ibid., 469.

35. Ibid., 470.

36. *The Works of Anna Laetitia Barbauld* with a Memoir by Lucy Aikin (2 vol, London: Longman, 1825), ii 96–7.

37. *Edinburgh Review* 21 (July 1813) 299–300.

38. *Monthly Review* 71 (June 1813) 202.

39. *British Review* 5 (October 1813) 136. Roberts refers to the poet 'frittering, mincing, comminuting and subdividing' in order to puzzle 'all persons of "slender sagacity"'.

40. *Edinburgh Review* 21 (July 1813) 299; *British Review* 5 (October 1813) 133.

41. *The Satirist* 13 (July 1813) 86.

42. *Edinburgh Review* 21 (July 1813) 301.

43. Ibid., 309.

44. *Edinburgh Review* 23 (April 1814) 205–6.

45. Ibid., 206.

46. See W. H. Christie, 'Francis Jeffrey's Associationist Aesthetics', *British Journal of Aesthetics* 33 (1993) 257–70.

47. *Edinburgh Review* 23 (April 1814) 203.

48. Ibid., 200.

49. Ibid.

50. Ibid., 202.

51. *Critical Review* 4th series, 5 (February 1814) 144.

52. *Edinburgh Review* 23 (April 1814) 205.

53. *BLJ*, xi 188.

54. Private discussion was another matter, and Moore's letter to Jeffrey of 23 May 1816 salivates over the possibility of 'a day's talk with you about Lord Byron, about *Glenarvon*, about all the extraordinary topics that are agitated "usque ad nauseam" in this town!' (Dowden, i 394).
55. *Edinburgh Review* 27 (December 1816) 278.
56. *British Critic* 2nd Series, 5 (April 1816) 436.
57. *Edinburgh Review* 27 (December 1816) 279. The *British Critic* complained of the same thing in much less measured language: 'Wherever we turn, the same portrait meets our eye... there is really a limit beyond which human patience ceases to be a virtue. ... What is Lord Byron to us, and what have we to do either with his sublimity or his sulks?' (*British Critic* 2nd Series, 6 (December 1816) 609–10).
58. *Edinburgh Review* 27 (December 1816) 278.
59. Ibid., 293.
60. *British Critic* 2nd Series, 6 (December 1816) 617.
61. *Edinburgh Review* 27 (December 1816) 280.
62. Ibid., 29 (February 1812) 467.
63. Ibid., 27 (December 1816) 309–10.
64. *BLJ*, v 186.
65. *Manfred*, III i 124.
66. Ibid., III i 160–4.
67. In April 1817 Byron wrote to Murray, 'I joy in the success of your Quarterly – but I must still stick by the *Edinburgh* – Jeffrey has done so by me I must say through everything – & this is more than I deserved from him' (*BLJ*, v 204).
68. *Edinburgh Review* 28 (August 1817) 418.
69. Ibid., 419.
70. Ibid., 425.
71. Ibid., 430.
72. Ibid., 420.
73. Ibid., 429–30.
74. Ibid., 35 (July 1821) 272.
75. Ibid., 279.
76. Ibid., 285.
77. Ibid.
78. Letter to Charles Wilkes, 13 April 1822, Cockburn, ii 200.
79. *Edinburgh Review* 36 (February 1822) 417.
80. Ibid., 418.
81. Ibid., 419.
82. Ibid., 28 (August 1817) 419.
83. Ibid., 35 (July 1821) 285.
84. Ibid., 36 (February 1822) 422–3.
85. See pp. 136–8 above.
86. Wu, vii 140.
87. *Edinburgh Review* 36 (February 1822) 451–2.
88. Ibid., 437.
89. Ibid., 451.
90. Ibid., 450.
91. Ibid., 451.
92. Wu, vii 192.

93. Ibid., 195, 197.
94. *Don Juan* xv 19.
95. Wu, vii 198.
96. Ibid., 140.
97. *BLJ*, ix 173.
98. Ibid., 168.
99. *Edinburgh Review* 36 (February 1822) 438.

8
Rancour and Rabies: Hazlitt, Coleridge and Jeffrey in Dialogue

Duncan Wu

Given Hazlitt's involvement with Coleridge and Wordsworth from an early stage of his life, and admiration for Wordsworth's poetry, it may at first seem surprising that he should have found a secure berth for most of his journalistic career with the *Edinburgh Review*. After all, by the time Hazlitt began to contribute in February 1815, Jeffrey had established the grounds of his opposition to the Lake School.[1] First articulated in October 1802 in a detailed critique of Southey's *Thalaba the Destroyer*, they were repeated periodically thereafter – in October 1807 in a review of Wordsworth's *Poems in Two Volumes*, in August 1811 in a review of the dramatic works of John Ford, in February 1812 in a review of John Wilson's *The Isle of Palms*, and most notoriously (and unmissably) in that of *The Excursion* of November 1814. The first issue to which Hazlitt contributed was that published immediately after November 1814, so he would probably have read it while writing the first of his *Edinburgh Review* articles.

There were good reasons for Hazlitt's readiness to appear in its pages. He was a jobbing journalist and the *Edinburgh* was among the foremost periodicals of the time; by 1809 no fewer than 9,000 copies of each number were printed quarterly, to be jointly published in Edinburgh (by Constable) and London (by Longman), many passing through several hands. To be among its writers was not only a mark of distinction, but to be given a prominent platform from which to articulate one's opinions. As a professional writer, Hazlitt would have appreciated the fact that Jeffrey was the most generous of his various employers, offering 'ten sterling pounds per sheet'.[2] (He is said to have received 50 guineas for his review of *Biographia Literaria*.)[3]

Beyond that, Hazlitt and Jeffrey had other things in common. Hazlitt's father and Jeffrey were both graduates of Glasgow University though of different generations, Jeffrey having attended the 'Old College' as it was known three decades after Hazlitt Senior. None the less the connection is significant as it aligns both Hazlitts with the tradition that informed the *Edinburgh* – one eloquently accounted for by Philip Flynn in his essay in this volume, and outlined in the Hazlittian context by Tom Paulin and Uttara Natarajan.[4]

Not only do these factors provide a context within which to understand Hazlitt's involvement with the *Edinburgh Review*, they also inform the way in which we might read two of his most important contributions to it – those on Coleridge. This article narrates the story behind Hazlitt's reviews of Coleridge in the *Edinburgh* to reveal that he, Coleridge and Jeffrey were engaged in a kind of three-handed dialogue from 1816 to 1817. In order to explain this affair, it is necessary for me to begin with some discussion of 'The Recluse' and its background.

When Hazlitt visited Alfoxden in 1798 on the occasion later memorialised in 'My First Acquaintance with Poets', he had with him the manuscript of his then unfinished *Essay on the Principles of Human Action*, which would be published in 1805. It sets out in plain terms the philosophy that underpinned his life's work. It hinged on a psychological insight – that the volition to action originated from within the mind, as the product of the imaginative faculty, independent of sense impressions. Ever since Locke, philosophers had been wrestling with the problem of demonstrating how moral knowledge might be acquired through the exercise of the senses – it was taken to be the product of an act of perception. The many philosophers who had shaped the curriculum at Glasgow – not least Hutcheson, Hume, and Adam Smith – had placed this at the centre of their work. Hazlitt's masterstroke was to separate perception and imagination, arguing that moral judgement originated from the imagination alone, which was innate. Love of the self and love of others are similarly rooted within the mind, and actuated by it, he proposed.

No manuscript of Hazlitt's *Essay on the Principle of Human Actions* is known to exist today, but it would be reasonable to conjecture that the one he took to Alfoxden in May 1798 contained a version of this idea. If so, it placed him on a collision course with Wordsworth and Coleridge who (like the Scottish Enlightenment thinkers) were Lockeans in so far as they accepted the umbilical connection between perception and the moral faculty. Not surprisingly, they argued with him about it. In the Advertisement to *Lyrical Ballads* (1798) Wordsworth noted: 'The lines entitled Expostulation and Reply, and those which follow, arose out of conversation with a friend who was somewhat unreasonably attached to modern books of moral philosophy.'[5] That 'friend' was Hazlitt, and the tone of Wordsworth's comment, especially that delicate phrase, 'unreasonably attached', alerts us to his suspicion of philosophical enquiry in the wake of his disillusionment with Godwinism, as well as to whatever unease he may have felt towards Hazlitt's notions. There may have been more than unease; their 'conversation' was actually a disagreement, Hazlitt recalled in 'My First Acquaintance with Poets':

> I got into a metaphysical argument with Wordsworth, while Coleridge was explaining the different notes of the nightingale to his sister, in which we neither of us succeeded in making ourselves perfectly clear and intelligible.[6]

Hazlitt's belief that the moral sense arose from within the mind and had no other source contradicted the guiding theory of 'The Recluse', adopted as the central project of Wordsworth's poetic career in January 1798.[7] As devised by Coleridge, 'The Recluse' was intended to propose that love of nature would lead, necessarily and universally, to love of mankind. In order to bear out the connection between perception and the moral faculty, it depended on a combination of associationist and idealist philosophies (derived from Hartley and Berkeley). That connection is reiterated throughout Wordsworth and Coleridge's 1798 poetry and correspondence. For instance, when in March 1798 Coleridge sent a copy of some lines of blank verse towards 'The Recluse' to his brother George in March 1798, he declared:

> I love fields & woods & mounta[ins] with almost a visionary fondness – and because I have found benevolence & quietness growing within me as that fondness [has] increased, therefore I should wish to be the means of implanting it in others – & to destroy the bad passions not by combating them, but by keeping them in inaction.[8]

With this statement Coleridge sets himself up as the exemplar of the visionary process at the heart of their project. The conceit of 'The Recluse' was that beautiful objects in nature would necessarily, through association, arouse benevolent and virtuous feelings within the mind, prompting the individual to seek for similar 'beauties' in other people. A universal awakening of such instincts in humanity at large would lead, so Wordsworth and Coleridge hoped, to a millenarian brotherhood and the property-less society envisaged by Godwin.

Hazlitt visited Alfoxden in May 1798. It was an intoxicating experience, as he describes in 'My First Acquaintance with Poets', where he recalled that Dorothy Wordsworth allowed him

> free access to her brother's poems, the *Lyrical Ballads*, which were still in manuscript, or in the form of *Sibylline Leaves*. I dipped into a few of these with great satisfaction, and with the faith of a novice.[9]

Hazlitt doesn't refer to 'The Recluse' in this essay, a fact that might lead us to suppose that he was shown only the *Lyrical Ballads* and nothing else. But there is no reason to doubt that he knew of it and read parts of it.[10] In all likelihood he was told of it by Coleridge on their first meeting in Shrewsbury in January. Hazlitt's talent for intellectual cut-and-thrust was well established on that occasion, doubtless in the context of philosophical debate – as Coleridge confirmed in a postscript to a letter to John Wicksteed of 9 March 1798: 'I have therefore opened my letter to beg that you will tell young Mr Haseloed that I remember him with respect due to his talents.'[11]

If Hazlitt was not told of 'The Recluse' in January, it would have been perverse had Coleridge withheld the information in May, as it was well known to the Wordsworth circle by March.[12] The 'metaphysical argument' mentioned in 'My First Acquaintance' could hardly have been conducted without reference to it. The fact that he was discussing philosophical ideas with Wordsworth and Coleridge indicates that he was apprised of its central thesis and, having formulated an alternative theory, argued the case with them. By the time the argument took place, it is probable that Hazlitt not only knew of 'The Recluse' but had seen drafts towards it. That is the most likely explanation for Wordsworth's reference to Hazlitt's 'unreasonable' attachment to works of philosophy, and the reiteration of his view in 'Expostulation and Reply':

> Nor less I deem that there are powers,
> Which of themselves our minds impress,
> That we can feed this mind of ours,
> In a wise passiveness.
>
> (ll. 21–4)

In 'The Recluse', the 'impressing' of sense perceptions on the mind would be claimed as the process by which the moral character is established. It was a direct response to Hazlitt's argument that benevolence and virtue existed within the mind independently of its perceptions. Rattled by this, it is not surprising to find Wordsworth reiterating the thesis of 'The Recluse' in 'The Tables Turned':

> Sweet is the lore which nature brings;
> Our meddling intellect
> Mishapes the beauteous forms of things;
> –We murder to dissect.
>
> Enough of science and of art;
> Close up these barren leaves;
> Come forth, and bring with you a heart
> That watches and receives.

(ll. 25–32)

These stanzas comprise a forceful rebuke to the young Hazlitt. Wordsworth tells him that his learning (which included the ideas of Hutcheson, Locke, Adam Smith, Shaftesbury and others) had led him to neglect the unwritten 'lore' of the natural world, to which he was a stranger. By focusing on the 'barren' leaves of dead philosophers, Hazlitt had blinded himself to the morally improving influence of nature – the very thing he was attempting to deny. Wordsworth believed he knew the truth of this because he felt it was something of which he had been guilty, during his flirtation with Godwinism.

If all this seems obvious, it is necessary to state because Hazlitt's failure to mention 'The Recluse' in 'My First Acquaintance' has led commentators to take the view that in May 1798 he regarded Wordsworth solely as the co-author of *Lyrical Ballads*. A widespread lack of awareness of 'The Recluse' among romanticists has inclined them to look no further than 'My First Acquaintance' for evidence of what transpired on that fateful visit to Alfoxden. And yet 'The Recluse' was almost certainly the primary subject of discussion. It remained central to Hazlitt's understanding of Wordsworth and Coleridge's literary aspirations from 1798 onwards, and bears heavily on his later opinion of them.

Publication of *The Excursion* on 17 August 1814 should have represented the fulfilment of Wordsworth's poetic ambitions, but it didn't. Reviews were either lukewarm or, like Jeffrey's, damning. It was no surprise that Jeffrey was unsympathetic; he came from a different school of thought. To him, the moral sense was a learned, shared thing, common to most people in society. Rejecting teleological arguments for the moral sentiments, he preferred the pragmatic view that they were part of the observable 'facts' of human life. Nor did he subscribe to theories of perfectibility or millenarianism; such notions were not for down-to-earth, common-sense Caledonians. Not surprisingly, then, he was impatient with the messianic ambitions of 'The Recluse', and criticized the 'tissue of moral and devotional ravings' in *The Excursion:*

> Moral and religious enthusiasm, though undoubtedly poetical emo-
> tions, are at the same time but dangerous inspirers of poetry; nothing
> being so apt to run into interminable dulness of mellifluous
> extravagance, without giving the unfortunate author the slightest
> intimation of his danger.... All sorts of commonplace notions and
> expressions are sanctified in his eyes, by the sublime ends for which
> they are employed; and the mystical verbiage of the methodist pulpit
> is repeated, till the speaker entertains no doubt that he is the elected
> organ of divine truth and persuasion.[13]

Hazlitt's philosophy was distinct from Wordsworth and Coleridge's, at least in 1798, but there is no reason to think that he shared Jeffrey's impatience with the metaphysical preoccupations of *The Excursion.* Indeed, they are praised in his own *Examiner* review.[14] Nor is there reason to think that he agreed with Jeffrey's argument that Wordsworth's talents were misguided. His *Spirit of the Age* goes out of its way to hold Jeffrey guilty of 'some capital oversights',[15] citing his treatment of *Lyrical Ballads* first and foremost. It is likely that Hazlitt regarded Jeffrey's review of *The Excursion* as unfairly critical.[16] As Wordsworth's poetry was a controversial matter, he tended to steer clear of the subject when writing for the *Edinburgh.* For all that, it is symptomatic of Hazlitt's disillusionment with Wordsworth and Coleridge that by 1815–16 he was willing to ally himself with their chief critic.

He first reviewed Coleridge's *Lay Sermons* – on the strength of no more than an announcement by the publisher that it was forthcoming – in *The Examiner* in September 1816. He pulled no punches, accusing Coleridge of unintelligibility, fancifulness and of writing nonsense:

> He is without a strong feeling of the existence of any thing out of
> himself; and he has neither purposes nor passions of his own to
> make him wish it to be. All that he does or thinks is involuntary;
> even his perversity and self-will are so. They are nothing but a necessity
> of yielding to the slightest motive. Everlasting inconsequentiality
> marks all that he attempts. All his impulses are loose, airy, devious,
> casual.[17]

According to Hazlitt, Coleridge is ruled by whatever 'involuntary' – that is to say, unconscious – inclinations flutter through his mind. Devoid of the governing mechanisms that form the human personality, he is a slave to 'the slightest motive'. Hazlitt goes further than merely to suggest that Coleridge suffers from a behavioural disorder; he implies that Coleridge is wrapped in a kind of perpetual opium-dream – and the article contains a number of reminders, for those in the know, of his addiction.

Coleridge read the *Examiner* piece and was deeply hurt by it. Just over a week after its publication he described it as 'a most brutal attack, as unprovoked as it is even to extravagance false, on me both as a man and an author'.[18] He went on to ascribe its harshness to his knowledge of the alleged incident in Keswick, when Hazlitt appears to have assaulted a young local woman.[19] In another letter on 25 September Coleridge told the same correspondent: 'As to Hazlitt, I shall take no notice of him or his libels – at least with reference to myself.'[20] For the time being this was true. He went on to say that Hazlitt had 'a wicked Heart of embruted Appetites'[21] – an amplification of his earlier reference to the Keswick incident. As time went on, Coleridge would (at least in private) reiterate and elaborate that connection.[22]

On 12 November[23] Jeffrey published an unreservedly critical review of *Christabel, Kubla Khan* and *The Pains of Sleep*. Until now, the identity of its author(s) has remained a matter of debate. It was not Thomas Moore, as E. L. Griggs thought.[24] Perhaps, as Jonathan Wordsworth believes, it was by Jeffrey[25] – but against that we must take into account Jeffrey's own comment on *Christabel*: 'I did not review it.'[26] On the other hand, its criticism of Coleridge's 'raving and driv'ling'[27] echoes Jeffrey's attack on the 'moral and devotional ravings' of *The Excursion*, and little that appeared in the *Edinburgh* was not either revised or rewritten by him. At the very least, he endorsed its account of the volume as 'one of the most notable pieces of impertinence of which the press has lately been guilty; and one of the boldest experiments that has yet been made on the patience or understanding of the public'.[28] In effect, the *Christabel* review consolidates the criticisms made by Jeffrey in earlier attacks on Wordsworth – or rather, as the reviewer has it, on 'the new school, or, as they may be termed, the wild or lawless poets'.[29]

I shall return shortly to the matter of attribution, but for the moment the important thing is that, whoever wrote it, its publication on 12 November 1816 marked the point at which Jeffrey joined the debate with Coleridge that Hazlitt had begun with his (p)review of *Lay Sermons* in September. Indeed, one of the features of 'Kubla Khan' to which the

Edinburgh drew attention was the very thing Hazlitt had ridiculed earlier: 'The lines here given smell strongly, it must be owned, of the anodyne; and, but that an under dose of a sedative produces contrary effects, we should inevitably have been lulled by them into forgetfulness of all things.'[30]

This review put Coleridge and Hazlitt in conversation, indirectly, through a mutual friend. That much is clear from a letter written by Coleridge to R. H. Brabant on 5 December, in which he reports Hazlitt's response to the distress caused by these attacks:

> His reason I give in his own words – 'Damn him! *I hate him*: FOR I am under obligations to him.' – When he was reproached for writing against his own convictions, and reminded that he had repeatedly declared the Christabel the finest poem in the language of it's size – he replied – 'I grumbled part to myself, while I was writing – but nothing stings a man so much, as making people believe Lies of him.' – You would scarcely think it possible, that a monster could exist who boasted of guilt and avowed his predilection for it.[31]

Coleridge and Hazlitt had several acquaintances in common, but the most likely intermediary was Charles Lamb, who told Wordsworth of the *Examiner* attack shortly after its publication and in the same letter praised the quality of Hazlitt's conversation before noting that he had 'seen Colerge. but once this 3 or 4 months'.[32] In November Lamb encountered Coleridge again 'in the street',[33] and it may have been on that occasion that he told him of Hazlitt's comment.

If Lamb was indeed the intermediary, the discussion at which Coleridge expressed disquiet at Hazlitt's preliminary *Examiner* attack published 8 September can be dated to about 17 September and probably before 23 September when Lamb told Wordsworth about it. The meeting at which Hazlitt told Lamb how much he hated Coleridge must have occurred within a couple of weeks of publication of the *Edinburgh* notice of *Christabel* on 12 November. Throughout November and December Lamb saw Hazlitt socially on a regular basis despite the fact that, as he mentioned to Wordsworth, Hazlitt made 'a cut at me a few months back'.[34] (When Henry Crabb Robinson 'broke altogether with Hazlitt' in late December, he was rebuked by Charles and Mary Lamb, who told him: 'We cannot afford to cast off our friends because they are not all we wish'.[35])

During that conversation with Hazlitt in November, Lamb evidently pointed out the discrepancies between the reviews of the *Christabel* volume in the *Edinburgh* and *The Examiner*, both of which he thought Hazlitt had written. Consistency was a prized virtue to Hazlitt, and had he not been responsible for the review in the *Edinburgh* it would have been the correct thing for him to have disowned it. Not only did he fail to do so, but he even went so far as to tell Lamb, 'I grumbled part to myself, while I was writing – but nothing stings a man so much, as making people believe Lies of him' (that is, of Coleridge).[36] In other words, he not only admitted having written the *Christabel* review, but said that he took pleasure in its anticipated result. Lamb and Coleridge were given direct licence by Hazlitt to conclude that he was its author, even if it meant conceding that he had written 'against his convictions' as one who had 'repeatedly declared the Christabel the finest poem in the language of it's size'.[37]

We must therefore conclude that although Jeffrey revised it, perhaps quite drastically, it was originally Hazlitt's.[38] Jeffrey's involvement as the mere editor of the periodical in which it appeared was in his view ample justification for the later declaration that he was not the author. On the other hand, in considering Hazlitt's contributions to the *Edinburgh* as attempts to initiate, or engage in, dialogue with Coleridge, we do well to remember that Jeffrey was not merely party to it, but actively involved. It was standard practice in the offices of the *Edinburgh* for him to recast much of what appeared in its pages, and all of Hazlitt's contributions are believed to contain such revision.[39] 'Do what you please with the article,' Hazlitt told Jeffrey on one occasion.[40] In fact, several articles the published texts of which 'are demonstrably not' by Hazlitt[41] are known to have been first written by him. The confusion surrounding authorship of the *Christabel* review points to a situation of this kind, but the strongest clue of all is the fact that Hazlitt refused to disown it when confronted by Lamb.

Lamb then met Coleridge and reported Hazlitt's uncompromising remarks, probably in November (if Marrs' dating of Mary Lamb's letter is correct).[42] That Hazlitt's words were repeated verbatim to Coleridge, and reported in that form to Brabant, makes it likely that Lamb reported them soon after they were spoken.

Coleridge continued to refrain from responding in print; if he hoped that Hazlitt would tire of venting his spleen, he could not have been more wrong. As a matter of fact, Lamb's report of Coleridge's hurt feelings may have given Hazlitt encouragement. When chided by Henry Crabb Robinson at Basil Montagu's on 22 December, Hazlitt was unrepentant: 'Coleridge he seemed very bitter against.'[43] The next number of the *Edinburgh* (for December 1816) carried Hazlitt's review of the first of the *Lay Sermons*, published as *The Statesman's Manual* in December. Hazlitt had already previewed it in the *Examiner* (on the strength of an advertisement), and then written a preliminary review of the published text, also in *The Examiner* of 29 December. So that when, in a letter dated 3 January 1817, he wrote to Jeffrey proposing that he write another for the *Edinburgh*, he was requesting a third crack of the whip. For the purposes of the present discussion it is necessary to concentrate on the review in the *Edinburgh*, as Jeffrey had a hand in it. In his letter Hazlitt promised to have the review in Jeffrey's hands by 21 January.[44] After Jeffrey had inflicted on it a number of 'retrenchments and verbal alterations'[45] it was printed in the *Edinburgh* for December 1816, published in London on 24 February 1817. How extensive were Jeffrey's revisions is questionable. In his account he says they were entered 'just as I was setting off, in a great hurry, for London, on professional business, in January',[46] which might suggest that they were not extensive and that the article as published is largely Hazlitt's.

The December number of the *Edinburgh* also carried a review of a book about Napoleon (which John Murray mistakenly took to be by Hazlitt[47]) and, immediately before it, the notice of *The Statesman's Manual*. It continued Hazlitt's *ad hominem* attacks on his former mentor.

> Plain sense and plain speaking would put an end to those 'thick-coming fancies,' that lull him to repose. It is in this sort of waking dream, this giddy maze of opinions, started, and left, and resumed – this momentary pursuit of truths, as if they were butterflies – that Mr Coleridge's pleasure, and, we believe, his chief faculty, lies. He has a thousand shadowy thoughts that rise before him, and hold each a glass, in which they point to others yet more dim and distant. He has a thousand self-created fancies that glitter and burst like bubbles. In the world of shadows, in the succession of bubbles, there is no preference but of the most shadowy, no attachment but to the shortest-lived.[48]

No one who read this can have doubted its implication. The references to a 'waking dream', the 'glass' held by Coleridge's 'shadowy thoughts' and the 'world of shadows', speak of addiction – whether to alcohol, opium, or both. Hazlitt's Coleridge is a lost soul engulfed in a perpetual hallucination, which leaves him incapable of logic, intellectual consistency, or rational thought. Hazlitt goes on to say that 'His fancy is stronger than his reason; his apprehension greater than his comprehension'.[49] The point is that Coleridge is lost in an insubstantial, unreal world.

These observations are sharpened by their relation to Coleridge's early poetry – a context of which Hazlitt was well aware. It had been the aspiration of the conversation poems and 'Religious Musings' that the visionary would, by an act of perception, engage with the Deity, 'We and our Father ONE!'[50] The notion of the perceiving mind as essentially passive would inform the philosophy of 'The Recluse' and much of Wordsworth's poetry. As I have already indicated, it had not been to Hazlitt's taste even in 1798 – and, as if to show what he thought, the fate to which he assigns the Coleridge of 1816 is a horrible parody of it. Coleridge has become a grotesquely exaggerated version of that earlier ideal self, trapped in an unending act of perception – unhappily not the transcendental experience described in 'Religious Musings'. On the contrary, it is characterized in terms of 'shadows', 'butterflies', a 'giddy maze' and a 'succession of bubbles'. The mature poet caricatures the mystic of earlier years. In the 1790s, Wordsworth and Coleridge valorized the philosopher-poet by concocting 'The Recluse' as 'the *first* and *only* true Phil[osophical]. Poem in existence', as Coleridge described it to Wordsworth in 1815.[51] By comparison, Hazlitt's 1816 lampoon of Coleridge is incapable of sequential thought of the most elementary kind: 'Mr Coleridge accordingly has no principles but that of being governed entirely by his own caprice, indolence, or vanity; no opinion that any body else holds, or even he himself, for two moments together.'[52] Hazlitt's Coleridge takes the idea of a passively receptive mind to its extreme, making it inert, a slave to whatever whims pass before it. This was a comically heightened but logical outcome to a philosophy that welcomed the mind's sublimation in a larger whole. Although Coleridge understood Hazlitt's attacks exclusively within the context of the Keswick débâcle, they none the less enshrined Hazlitt's reservations about Coleridgean thought.

These remarks sound more like Hazlitt than Jeffrey, but Hazlitt knew that his editor would approve. His father and Jeffrey shared a Caledonian education in the sceptical, common-sense tradition of Thomas Reid, which held the idealism of Berkeley's 'world of spirits' to be erroneous and misguided.[53] Like Coleridge, Jeffrey had looked into the associationist philosophy of Hartley, but instead of placing it at the heart of his system, concluded that the theory of vibratiuncles belonged to the realm of what Dugald Stewart called 'metaphysical romances' – theories 'which it is difficult to confute, because it is impossible to comprehend them'.[54] Jeffrey was instinctively suspicious of metaphysics and, in a review of Stewart, could comment scathingly on 'the absolute nothingness of the effects that have hitherto been produced by the labours of the philosophers of mind'.[55] A few years earlier, reflecting on an idealist view derived from Berkeley, he judged that 'To deny the existence of matter and of mind, indeed, is not to philosophize, but to destroy the materials of philosophy'.[56] No wonder he took exception to the 'moral and devotional ravings' of *The Excursion* and the 'raving and driv'ling' of *Christabel*.

Again, the cadences of the next paragraph sound more like Hazlitt than Jeffrey, but they articulate sentiments Hazlitt knew Jeffrey would endorse:

> Our Lay-preacher, in order to qualify himself for the office of a guide to the blind, has not, of course, once thought of looking about for matters of fact, but very wisely draws a metaphysical bandage over his eyes, sits quietly down where he was, takes his nap, and talks in his sleep – but we really cannot say very wisely. He winks and mutters all unintelligible, and all impertinent things. Instead of inquiring into the distresses of the manufacturing or agricultural districts, he ascends to the orbits of the fixed stars, or else enters into the statistics of the garden plot under his window, and, like Falstaff, 'babbles of green fields:' instead of the balance of the three estates, King, Lords, and Commons, he gives us a theory of the balance of the powers of the human mind, the Will, the Reason, and – the Understanding: instead of referring to the tythes or taxes, he quotes the Talmud; and illustrates the whole question of peace and war, by observing, that 'the ideal republic of Plato was, if he judges rightly, to "the history of the town of Man-Soul" what Plato was to John Bunyan:' – a most safe and politic conclusion![57]

One reason why this paragraph must be Hazlitt's is that it begins with an item of privileged information: Coleridge's principal mode of composition at this time was dictation. At this period Coleridge was dictating his 'Opus Maximum', the much-heralded 'Logosophia', to J. H. Green and Anne Gillman in his lodgings at Highgate.[58] Somehow, Hazlitt learnt of these goings-on (perhaps through Lamb), and guessed that *The Statesman's Manual* was produced in that manner. He has caricatured the situation, turning the inspired philosopher into an inebriated addict mumbling nonsense in his slumbers. Hazlitt's victim is doubly benighted: he wears a metaphysical blindfold. By implication, an infatuation with outlandish ideas, as much as intoxication, has rendered him incapable of comprehending what is going on before him. He is oblivious to the high taxes levied by the government to pay for the Napoleonic Wars and conceives of war only in the context of a far-fetched comparison between Plato and Bunyan.

These criticisms should be placed firmly within the context of Hazlitt's acquaintance with Wordsworth and Coleridge since 1798, for that was the context in which Hazlitt himself saw them. While writing the review in the *Edinburgh* Hazlitt dashed off 'Mr Coleridge's Lay-Sermon' for *The Examiner*, an early version of a recollection of his first meeting with Coleridge in Shrewsbury, which would be reworked for 'My First Acquaintance with Poets' in 1823. This was Hazlitt's *fourth* piece of writing on *The Statesman's Manual*. It was published on 12 January 1817, less than two weeks before the review in the *Edinburgh*, and is intimately connected with it:

> I begin to suspect that my notions formerly must have been little better than a deception: that my faith in Mr Coleridge's great powers must have been a vision of my youth, that, like other such visions, must pass away from me; and that all his genius and eloquence is *vox et preterea nihil*: for otherwise how is it so lost to all common sense upon paper?[59]

There is genuine sadness in Hazlitt's question. In 1798 it had appeared that Wordsworth and Coleridge would revolutionize the world and that the egalitarian aspirations of 'The Recluse' could be realized. That his former mentors had forsaken their early visions and hopes now led Hazlitt to believe that his faith in them had been a delusion. No wonder he told Lamb that when he first read *The Excursion* 'he actually cried because he was disappointed, and could not praise it as it deserved'.[60] Robinson, who recorded that anecdote, did not believe it, but there is every reason to think it true. Hazlitt had been present when 'The Recluse' was being discussed in 1798. He knew how far short of those aspirations Wordsworth had fallen, and his tears were shed not only on that account, but for his own youthful belief in them. The attacks on Coleridge of 1816–17 are an elegy on those hopes; that is why they went hand in hand with Hazlitt's reminiscences of 1798.

When composing his 'Lectures on the English Poets' in 1818, Hazlitt wrote, and then deleted, a important note about Coleridge unpublished until the Pickering and Chatto edition of his works in 1998:

> He is the earliest friend I ever had, & I will add to increase the obligation, that he is the only person from whom I ever learnt any thing in conversation. He was the only person I ever knew who answered to

my idea of a man of genius, & that idea at the time I first became acquainted with Mr. Coleridge was somewhat higher than it is at present.[61]

Lamb was correct to realize that in Hazlitt's criticisms 'there is a kind of respect shines thro' the disrespect that to those who know the rare compound (that is the subject of it) almost balances the reproof, but then those who know him but partially or at a distance are so extremely apt to drop the qualifying part thro' their fingers'.[62] It was true; Hazlitt respected Coleridge and Wordsworth as they had once been. He respected the man he looked up to in 1798, who taught him through his conversation. And he respected the poet of *Lyrical Ballads* with whom he had debated the principles of 'The Recluse'. By the same token, he detested what they had become. It is true, as David Bromwich has observed, that Hazlitt had personal reasons for turning against Coleridge,[63] but his feelings were driven primarily by the unwelcome knowledge that the visionary radicals of the 1790s had become toadying sycophants, that they had neither kept faith with their former selves nor fulfilled their early promise. He understood that the abandonment of their principles could have only an adverse effect on their art.

By the time the *Edinburgh* published Hazlitt's review of *The Statesman's Manual*, Jeffrey and Hazlitt had become identified as joint accusers, at least in the mind of their principal victim. When John Murray asked him if he had seen the review, Coleridge responded:

I have not seen either the Ed. or the Quart. last Reviews – the Article against me in the former was, I am assured, written by Hazlitt. Now what can I think of Mr Jeffries, who knows nothing personally of me but my hospitable attentions to him, and from whom I heard nothing but very high-seasoned Compliments, and who yet can avail himself of *such* an instrument of his most unprovoked Malignity toward an inoffensive man in distress and sickness–. As soon as I have read the Article (and the Loan of the Book is promised me) I shall make up my mind whether or not to address a Letter publicly to Mr Jefferies – or in the form of an Appeal to the Public – concerning his proved pre-determined Malice.[64]

Coleridge was not entirely correct in referring to Jeffrey's 'high-seasoned Compliments'; their private correspondence of 1808 concerning *The Friend* had been a frank one on both sides, with Jeffrey admonishing Coleridge for affectation, particularly in his phrasing – although it was true that Jeffrey had written: 'I am really interested in your success.'[65] Coleridge was right to the extent that that brief contact had been cordial, with no suggestion of the strongly negative opinions expressed in 1816 and 1817. Coleridge's reference to 'pre-determined Malice' effectively strips Hazlitt of critical impartiality, suggesting that he had made up his mind about Coleridge's work before he looked at it. It is echoed in a notebook entry which probably dates from this moment:

<blockquote>

To Hazlitt & Jeffery

'Therefore you speak unskillfully: or if your knowlege be more, it is much darkened in your malice.'

Measure for Measure—[66]

</blockquote>

The context of the quotation doesn't help Coleridge's cause: it is the Duke's comment to Lucio, in response to some well-founded criticisms of his conduct. What both the letter and the notebook entry serve to underline is that Coleridge now understood himself to be in dialogue with two men – Hazlitt and Jeffrey – and that his response should extend beyond private correspondence or conversations with mutual acquaintances. The idea of composing a public letter to Jeffrey that could appear in a newspaper (perhaps *The Courier*) soon went by the board, for a better opportunity was at hand. About three-quarters of the finished *Biographia Literaria* had been in print since October 1815, but publication could not take place until the remaining sheets had been filled. Coleridge had been working on them since summer 1816, and by February 1817 it remained only to revise what had originally been composed as the final chapter (24). As he laboured on it in the early spring of 1817, Coleridge turned the conclusion of his literary life into a public rebuff of Hazlitt and Jeffrey. This was the last work he did for *Biographia* before publication in July 1817.[67]

Critics tend not to recognize the oddity of this act of self-justification in *Biographia* – not surprisingly, perhaps, as there is more important material elsewhere. It has to be said that the concluding chapter is not only inconclusive but, as a defence, ineffective. It appears in the context of a disquisition on the 'abuse' which greeted *Christabel* on publication:

<blockquote>

In the Edinburgh Review it was assailed with a malignity and a spirit of personal hatred that ought to have injured only the work in which such a Tirade was suffered to appear: and this review was generally attributed (whether rightly or no I know not) to a man,

</blockquote>

who both in my presence and in my absence, has repeatedly pronounced it the finest poem of its kind in the language.[68]

Coleridge repeats the point made by Lamb the previous autumn – that Hazlitt's attack in the *Edinburgh* was inconsistent with his praise elsewhere. And he is still under the impression that Hazlitt was responsible for the review of *Christabel*; evidently this was composed prior to June 1817, by which time someone had (mis)informed him that Thomas Moore was its author.[69]

Coleridge then passes to a defence of *Zapolya* before turning to Hazlitt's treatment of *The Statesman's Manual*. He makes a distinction between Hazlitt as the author responsible for the attacks on him, and Jeffrey as his 'employer'.

> But I can truly say, that the grief with which I read this rhapsody of predetermined insult, had the Rhapsodist himself for its whole and sole object: and that the indignant contempt which it excited in me, was as exclusively confined to his employer and suborner.[70]

What makes the remainder of this defence so peculiar is that Coleridge veers off at a tangent, refuting a charge of infidelity to his religious principles, quoting at length from a passage in *The Statesman's Manual* dealing with miracles (for which he provides further elucidation), and then rebutting the accusation that he denied the Unitarians to be Christian (something Hazlitt had done no more than imply). The concluding paragraph of the chapter (and of *Biographia* as a whole) draws largely on a marginal note scribbled into Coleridge's copy of Böhme's *Works*,[71] with no bearing on Hazlitt's attacks. In short, chapter 24 fails to demolish the charges laid against him, particularly that of political apostasy, says nothing about the personal jibes made by Hazlitt and disregards what bearing they may have had on his earlier writing or ideas. As a defence, it is largely irrelevant to what Hazlitt and Jeffrey had said of him; the ripostes he was providing in letters to such friends as Francis Wrangham were more to the point.[72] Perhaps, in truth, he really did feel more grief for 'the Rhapsodist' than anger; and perhaps, in any case, Hazlitt's arguments were unanswerable.

Coleridge's volume was read eagerly by the Hazlitt circle on publication. Godwin raced through it within the week,[73] and by 24 July Leigh Hunt had seen it. Hunt even went so far as to allude to chapter 24 and its 'response' when asking Jeffrey for a commission to review *Sibylline Leaves*: 'But, perhaps, as he [Coleridge] has made some direct observations on the *Edinburgh Review* in his *Literary Life* (just published also), he may require a more particular notice than a new contributor to that work could give him.'[74] This indicates that he suspected Jeffrey would prefer Hazlitt to review *Biographia*, and that in turn would suggest that Hazlitt too was aware of the contents of chapter 24 by the time Hunt wrote this letter. Jeffrey must have been in touch with Hazlitt in short order because Hazlitt's review of *Biographia* was in the post on 12 August.[75] During the ensuing weeks word must have leaked out that Hazlitt had written it, as Southey was aware of his authorship by 4 September.[76] The *Edinburgh Review* for August was published in London on 17 September, when it was trailed in the *Morning Chronicle* and the *Courier*.

Hazlitt's review, revised by Jeffrey, possessed all the virtues which *Biographia* chapter 24 lacked. It was precise, detailed and sharp. Of all the articles on Coleridge in the *Edinburgh*, this was probably the most coherent and well thought-out. Its theme was apostasy. But before developing that idea it offered, on its fourth page, a marvellous Hazl-ittian diatribe recapitulating the complaints of earlier articles:

> If the study of Mr Bowles's poems could have effected a permanent cure of that 'preposterous' state of mind which he has above described, his gratitude, we admit, should be boundless: But the disease, we fear, was in the mind itself; and the study of poetry, instead of counteracting, only gave force to the original propensity; and Mr Coleridge has ever since, from the combined forces of poetic levity and metaphysic bathos, been trying to fly, not in the air, but under ground – playing at hawk and buzzard between sense and nonsense, – floating or sinking in fine Kantean categories, in a state of suspended animation 'twixt dreaming and awake, – quitting the plain ground of 'history and particular facts' for the first butterfly theory, fancy-bred from the maggots of his brain, – going up in an air-balloon filled with fetid gas from the writings of Jacob Behmen and the mystics, and coming down in a parachute made of the soiled and fashionable leaves of the Morning Post, – promising us an account of the Intellectual System of the Universe, and putting us off with a reference to a promised dissertation on the Logos, introductory to an intended commentary on the entire Gospel of St John.[77]

It may have been, as Hazlitt believed, that the common-sensical Jeffrey had a tendency to dull down his prose, but this elegant piece of mockery has Hazlitt's paw-marks all over it, as its allusions suggest. The phrase 'in a state of suspended animation' is taken from the Preface to *Christabel*, where Coleridge had described his poetic powers as having been, since 1800, 'till very lately, in a state of suspended animation'.[78] The 'fine Kantean categories' are mentioned in *Biographia* chapter 9.[79] The allusion to 'history and particular facts' reiterates the charge that Coleridge was such a metaphysician that he was unaware of political injustices before him, as well as alluding to the disquisition in *Biographia* chapter 10.[80] It was a fine Hazlittian stroke to propose that Coleridge had maggots in his brain, one that he would level at Shelley in 1821, by way of portraying him as a 'philosophic fanatic'.[81] (It was also true, of course, that both Shelley and Coleridge took opium.) The 'air-balloon filled with fetid gas' alludes to intoxication of some kind, as well as to experiments of 1799 in which Humphry Davy dosed Coleridge with laughing-gas.[82] Jacob Behmen, or Böhme, is mentioned several times in *Biographia*, not least in relation to pantheism.[83] And Coleridge's involvement with the *Morning Post* is mentioned in *Biographia* chapter 10.[84] Whether or not Hazlitt was aware of it, Coleridge was even now at work on his long-promised *Logosophia* or *Opus Maximum*, the great work that would provide a focus for his entire *oeuvre*.

But the central issue, of which Hazlitt was determined not to lose sight, was Coleridge's failure to live up to his early radicalism. Having quoted the extensive note at the end of *Biographia* chapter 3, he launches into a diatribe about Coleridge's 'lamentable affectation of surprise at the otherwise unaccountable slowness of good men in yielding implicit confidence to a party...who could with impunity, and triumphantly, take away by atrocious calumnies the characters of all who disdained to be their tools, – and rewarded with honours, places, and pensions all those who were'.[85] (The subsequent criticism of Wordsworth and Kant is likely to be Jeffrey's, as it espouses views that Hazlitt did not hold – not least the notion that Kant's philosophy comprised 'absurdities that have not even the merit of being amusing'.[86] What is significant is that, although he cannot have agreed with such criticisms, Hazlitt was content for them to be incorporated into the review.)

In some ways the most important element of the review was the portrait of Burke which was entirely Hazlitt's, later extracted in *The Champion* for 5 October 1817 and then in his *Political Essays* (1819).[87] It is a digression on the theme of apostasy. When Burke is said to have 'constructed his whole theory of government...not on rational, but on picturesque and fanciful principles',[88] the mention of fancy draws an implicit comparison with Coleridge. Hazlitt goes on to answer

Coleridge's claim in *Biographia* chapter 10 that Burke's principles remained the same between the American War and the French Revolution:[89]

> Mr Burke, the opponent of the American war – and Mr Burke, the opponent of the French Revolution, are not the same person, but opposite persons – not opposite persons only, but deadly enemies. In the latter period, he abandoned not only all his practical conclusions, but all the principles on which they were founded.[90]

So, likewise, has Coleridge. And Hazlitt's concluding view of Burke as 'a man of fine fancy and subtle reflection; but not of sound and practical judgment – not of high or rigid principles' could equally well apply to Coleridge, as he had portrayed him. Indeed, Coleridge's praise of Burke is held, by implication, to explain his failings.

What makes this a particularly intriguing review is that Jeffrey felt it necessary to answer *Biographia* chapter 24 in a lengthy footnote. For the first and only time, he addressed Coleridge directly, as himself. In doing so he reveals much, including his first and only encounter with Coleridge in the Lakes in 1810. He denies knowledge of Hazlitt's first review of *The Statesman's Manual* in *The Examiner*, and replies directly to the charge made by Coleridge: 'I never employed or suborned any body to abuse or extol it or any other publication.'[91] In particular, he is at pains to deny the accusation of 'pre-determined Malice': 'Nay, I was not even aware of the existence of the Lay Sermon itself, when a review of it was offered me by a gentleman in whose judgment and talents I had great confidence, but whom I certainly never suspected, and do not suspect at this moment, of having any personal or partial feelings of any kind towards its author.'[92] For all Jeffrey's plain-speaking, could he really have been unaware of Hazlitt's strong feelings towards Coleridge, and their relation to the annus mirabilis of 1798? So he claimed.

Jeffrey's exculpatory note recalling his visit to Southey and Coleridge in 1810, and vindication of his reviewer, is an important source of information for an understanding of this exchange. But as I have already suggested, it was not entirely straightforward. Jeffrey was technically correct to deny that he had reviewed *Christabel*, but he had commissioned Hazlitt's review, revised it and bore some of the responsibility for it. And at least one contemporary reader realized that the note gave a little too much away in another respect: on 6 October Henry Crabb Robinson noted that Jeffrey 'confesses enough to fix on himself the imputation of gross flattery and insincerity towards Coleridge. He says that he saw Coleridge liked compliments, and therefore gave them.'[93]

After a final skirmish with the metaphysical sections of *Biographia* (in which Coleridge's metaphysics are said to be 'a dead weight on the wings of his imagination'[94] – another judgement that sounds like Hazlitt's), the review cocks a final snook in Coleridge's direction: 'Till he can do something better, we would rather hear no more of him.'[95]

That was not quite the end of this strange, three-sided conversation, which at this point attracted the attention of a fourth participant. On 24 September, just over a week after the *Edinburgh Review* had appeared in London, the *Courier* newspaper published an article entitled 'The Edinburgh Review'. It was a two-and-a-half column refutation of Hazlitt's principal arguments about apostasy as related to Southey and Burke, featuring a sustained critique of the French Revolution and its sympathizers:

> The French revolution was the anarchy of a mob, frenzied by the writings of Voltaire, Rousseau, Mirabeau, &c. Mr. Burke soon foresaw the excesses to which it would lead, and warned the world against them. . . . During the American war he was for a moderate reform of abuses that might remove well-founded complaints. – During the French Revolution, he opposed all Reform, from the apparent danger of its letting in universal suffrage, anarchy and ruin, upon us.

Not only was Burke innocent of the charge of inconsistency, but so, the author argues, are Coleridge and Southey. A good deal of space is given over to the exoneration of Southey, in particular, from the charge of being a turncoat – so much so, that it seems to bear more on Hazlitt's reviews of *Wat Tyler* and *A Letter to William Smith, Esq. M.P.*[96] Who was the author? The prime suspect must be Southey himself. Besides the fact that the article served his interests more than Coleridge's, he was in the habit during this period of making occasional contributions to the *Courier* – some signed, some not. Moreover, from the moment he heard of Hazlitt's review of *Biographia* – as early as 4 September (well before publication) – he lobbied John Murray to let him write a reply for the *Quarterly*: 'I am very ready to undertake it – *omnibus viribus* – beginning very quietly, proceeding clearly and discretely so as to make the readers on our side, and lastly laying it on with a willing hand and a cat and nine tails.'[97] The only reason for Southey's desire to respond to a review he had not yet seen was that his true motive was to respond to some he *had* – those of his own works.[98]

Whoever wrote it, this marked the end of the dialogue between Hazlitt, Jeffrey and Coleridge. Not that Hazlitt was finished; portraits of Coleridge, Wordsworth, Southey and Jeffrey would appear in *Spirit of the Age* (1825). He would have no further contact with the Lakers on a social level, and it would appear that the affair caused strains with mutual friends. Henry Crabb Robinson cut him over it, and Hazlitt was conspicuously absent from the 'immortal' dinner given at Haydon's on 28 December, probably because Wordsworth was present. The relationship with Jeffrey was sufficiently robust to continue until Hazlitt's death. In 1830 he would write to him from the Soho rooming-house where he lodged: 'I am dying: can you send me 10£, and so consummate your many kindnesses to me?'[99] All the same, after the review of *Biographia* Jeffrey commissioned no further reviews from Hazlitt on Coleridge. For all its infelicities, *Biographia* chapter 24 had achieved one thing: it made it hard for Jeffrey to claim impartiality on Hazlitt's behalf again.[100]

There is no evidence that Coleridge saw Hazlitt's review of *Biographia* or the subsequent article in the *Courier*. His feelings were raw and exposure to either would only have aggravated them further. In February 1818 he was still ranting, in a letter to James Perry, about 'Hazlitt's rancor and rabies against Southey, Wordsworth, and myself!'[101] And it certainly caused friction between him and Lamb; in January 1818 he said that he had avoided the Lambs as they were frequently in Hazlitt's company.[102] One of the saddest things about the episode is that Coleridge never understood its cause. From the outset his reaction was one of bewilderment and hurt. So far as he could see, he had made all the 'efforts of friendship...which a Brother could not have demanded',[103] and his reward was unremitting public criticism.

Nor can Jeffrey have fully comprehended the debate; indeed, it may have been even less clear to him than to Coleridge. As editor he was able to appropriate the charges laid at Coleridge's door by revision of Hazlitt's copy. But he did so from the perspective of the Glasgow-educated dominie that he was. The grounds of his opposition to the Lake School as laid down in his articles on Southey and Wordsworth were derived from aesthetic ideas that were part of the culture into which he was born. Of course, he would have recognized that the dialogue represented a clash between that culture and what he regarded as the intellectually enfeebled metaphysics favoured by the Lakers, but he apparently knew nothing of Hazlitt's early involvement with them and therefore cannot have perceived the dynamics of the fracas as it unfolded. His reviewer, he remarked, was 'a gentleman in whose judgment and talents I had great confidence, but whom I certainly never suspected, and do not suspect at this moment, of having any personal or partial feelings of any kind towards its author' (that is, Coleridge). If taken at face value (and I find no evidence to discredit it), this can mean only that the full context of these reviews was not available to Jeffrey. He and his journal were tools with which Hazlitt subjected his former mentor to ridicule in the most public of forums.

Only Hazlitt could have understood fully what his attacks, the involvement of Jeffrey, and Coleridge's response, represented. Over the course of the nine-month-long spat, he had been responsible for no less than four hostile attacks on *The Statesman's Manual*, one on *Christabel* and one on *Biographia Literaria* – three of which had appeared in the *Edinburgh Review*, one of the most prestigious and widely read periodicals of the day. He had not shied away from blame, admitting to the Coleridge circle that he was responsible for the *Christabel* review and publicly declaring his involvement with Coleridge in 1798 in the third of the *Examiner* pieces. If Jeffrey missed that, it was not Hazlitt's fault. In declaring his interests, Hazlitt went a long way towards explaining what the dialogue with Coleridge was about. Throughout it he returns to one subject: infidelity to deeply held principles. As he recalled in 'My First Acquaintance with Poets', he had known Coleridge when his egalitarian ideals had been inextricably intertwined with the artistic future he planned with Wordsworth. At Alfoxden 'The Recluse' had seemed within Wordsworth's reach, and with it the just society for which they all yearned. By 1816 the fruits of that time were to Hazlitt's eye a blighted harvest – the imperfect *Excursion*, the unfinished *Christabel* and the 'psychological curiosity' published as *Kubla Khan*. Those works were incapable of alleviating poverty and deprivation; indeed, Wordsworth's poem was dedicated to the wealthiest landowner in Cumberland whose corrupt interest he would support in the 1818 elections. The extent of Coleridge's indifference to the causes he had formerly espoused is clear when the contents of *The Statesman's Manual* and *Biographia* are placed in context. Neither has anything to say about the suspension of habeas corpus by the government on 4 March 1817 or the accompanying Act laying stringent penalties on the mere utterance of treasonable or seditious words. During that summer the government used *agents provocateurs* to expose ringleaders of popular uprisings in Yorkshire, Nottinghamshire and Derbyshire – who, once revealed, were summarily executed.

Hazlitt spoke out against these matters in his political essays;[104] his former mentors spoke up too, on the other side. And they wrote privately, as well as publicly. On 19 March 1817 Southey wrote privately to Lord Liverpool, the prime minister, urging that he clamp down on free speech:

> But if juries, either from fear or faction . . . give their verdict in the
> very face of facts, I beseech you do not hesitate at using that vigour

beyond the law which the exigence requires, and which your own personal safety requires as much as the vital interests of the country.[105]

Southey does not refer to Hazlitt by name, but does single out *The Examiner* as a particular danger. Laws, he says, however repressive, are 'altogether nugatory while such manifestoes as those of Cobbett, Hone, and the Examiner, &c., are daily and weekly issued, fresh and fresh, and read aloud in every alehouse where the men are quartered, or where they meet together'.[106] The government hardly needed encouragement. On 5 May William Hone would appear in court for 'blasphemous and seditious libels, being Parodies on the Catechism, the Litany and the Creed of St. Athanasius'.[107] While Southey's letter cannot be held responsible for Hone's first trial (or the two further ones that followed) a pledge of support from no less than the poet laureate exonerated Liverpool and his government from any doubts their draconian measures might have occasioned. Coleridge also wrote to Liverpool on 28 July 1817, enclosing a copy of *Biographia;* he refrained from speaking as bluntly as Southey had done, confining himself largely to metaphysical observations on his own work, in a letter of which Liverpool remarked: 'I cannot well understand him.'[108] None the less, both Southey and Coleridge had written in support of Liverpool, and in Southey's case the communication had been sent in the hope that suspension of habeas corpus would be followed by the arrest and perhaps transportation of the government's critics. So far had they drifted from their earlier beliefs that they were willing to deliver their former allies to the forces of oppression. Hazlitt was correct to mark them down as turncoats. The twist in this tale is that he knew of their letters and seems to have read them, because he quotes the phrase, 'vigour beyond the law' (in the above quotation) in his review of Southey's *Letter to William Smith, Esq. M.P.*[109]

Despite the asperity of Hazlitt's observations on Coleridge, all his attacks were on the record and available for his victim to refute as he could. Their appearance in the *Edinburgh Review* was useful because the protection of such a popular and respected journal lent them a credibility not vouchsafed by less 'respectable' publications such as *The Examiner.* Any personal context that informed them was to some extent irrelevant since they were written so as to blend seamlessly with Jeffrey's attacks of earlier years. Indeed, Jeffrey was pleased to endorse and embellish Hazlitt's reviews while remaining unaware of what underlay them. Only Hazlitt seemed fully cognisant of that, and only he seems completely to have understood the implications of this unique three-handed dialogue of 1816–17.

Notes

1. These are discussed by Paul Fry in his chapter in this volume, pp. 124–42.
2. Byron, *English Bards and Scotch Reviewers*, 70. Byron wasn't impressed but, as McGann and Weller observe, this was more than other periodicals paid.
3. Morley, i 209.
4. See Tom Paulin, *The Day-Star of Liberty: William Hazlitt's Radical Style* (London: Faber, 1998), Uttara Natarajan, *Hazlitt and the Reach of Sense: Criticism, Morals, and the Metaphysics of Power* (Oxford: Clarendon Press, 1998), and my '"Polemical Divinity": William Hazlitt at the University of Glasgow', *Romanticism* 6.2 (2000) 163–77.
5. Cornell, *LB* 739.
6. Wu, ix 106.
7. The course of this 'adoption' was uneven. Wordsworth attempted to release himself from the obligation in 1799, and again in 1803, but by February 1804 it was firmly accepted as his life's work; his shifting attitudes are traced in my *Wordsworth: An Inner Life* (Oxford: Blackwell, 2002), chapters 5–8.
8. Griggs, i 397.
9. Wu, ix 103.
10. In May 1798 this would have included 'Not useless do I deem', 'The Ruined Cottage' MS B, 'The Pedlar', 'In storm and tempest', 'A Night-Piece', 'The Discharged Soldier' and 'The Old Cumberland Beggar'.
11. Griggs, i 394.
12. On 11 March 1798 Wordsworth told James Losh that he had 'written 1300 lines of a poem which I hope to make of considerable utility; its title will be *The Recluse or views of Nature, Man, and Society*' (*EY* 214). See also his letter to James Webbe Tobin of 6 March, which refers to '1300 lines of a poem in which I contrive to convey most of the knowledge of which I am possessed' (*EY* 212).
13. *Edinburgh Review* 24 (November 1814) 4.
14. 'The power of his mind preys upon itself. It is as if there were nothing but himself and the universe. He lives in the busy solitude of his own heart; in the deep silence of thought' (Wu, ii 327).
15. Wu, vii 194.
16. This is much the view taken by Jones, 155.
17. Wu, iv 110.
18. Griggs, iv 669.
19. This episode is discussed by Michael Foot, 'Hazlitt's Revenge on the Lakers', *The Wordsworth Circle* 14 (Winter 1983) 61–73.
20. Griggs, iv 685–6.
21. Ibid., 686.
22. News of the *Examiner* article spread round the Wordsworth circle through Lamb, who told them of it in a letter of 23 September; see Marrs, iii 224.
23. The review appeared in the *Edinburgh Review* for September, which was not advertised as published until 12 November. An advertisement appeared in the *Morning Chronicle* for that date.
24. The attribution appears in a footnote at Griggs, iv 668, but is disproved by Moore's letter to John Murray of 24 December 1816 which states that he

'gave up my intention' of reviewing *Christabel* when he learnt of Coleridge's poverty; see Dowden, ii 407. It is worth adding that in June 1817 Coleridge believed Moore to have been the culprit, but this was a mistake (see Griggs, iv 736).

25. It appears as Jeffrey's in Professor Wordsworth's volume, *Francis Jeffrey: On the Lake Poets* (Poole: Woodstock Books, 1998).
26. In his lengthy note to Hazlitt's review of *Biographia*; *Edinburgh Review* 28 (August 1817) 510.
27. *Edinburgh Review* 27 (September 1816) 66.
28. Ibid.
29. Ibid., 59.
30. Ibid., 65.
31. Griggs, iv 693.
32. Marrs, iii 225. Lamb apparently refers in his letter to Hazlitt as 'H——'.
33. Marrs, iii 233. In fact it is Mary Lamb who reported this encounter, but it is highly likely that she was with her brother when the meeting took place.
34. Marrs, iii 224–5. The 'cut' appeared in a note to Hazlitt's review of Southey's *The Lay of the Laureate*, which appeared in *The Examiner*, 14 July 1816; see Wu, iv 90–1.
35. Sadler, ii 40.
36. Griggs, iv 693.
37. Ibid.
38. This runs counter to the conclusion of Stanley Jones, who states that the author was Thomas Moore; see his *Hazlitt: A Life* (Oxford: Oxford University Press, 1991), p. 223. Jones appears not to have seen Moore's letter to Jeffrey of 23 May 1816, or that to Murray of 24 December, which indicate conclusively that Moore was innocent.
39. Such is the implication of the final line of Hazlitt's poem, 'The Damned Author's Address to his Reviewers': 'Teach me, great Jeffrey, to be dull!' (See *William Hazlitt to his Publishers, Friends, and Creditors: Twenty-Seven new Holograph Letters*, ed. Charles E. Robinson (York: Keats-Shelley Memorial Association, 1987), p. 30).
40. See Stanley Jones, 'Some New Hazlitt Letters', *Notes and Queries* 222 (1977) 336–42, p. 337.
41. Howe, xvi 420.
42. The dating is conjectural; see Marrs, iii 232.
43. Morley, i 201.
44. See Sikes, 164.
45. Jeffrey's account as given in the note to Hazlitt's review of *Biographia*, *Edinburgh Review* 28 (August 1817) 512.
46. Ibid.
47. See his letter of 22 February to Blackwood, Murray papers. Blackwood replied that he had heard that the author was actually John Allen. This is the attribution given by W. A. Copinger, *Bibliographiana no. 2* (privately printed, Priory Press: Manchester, 1895), p. 27.
48. *Edinburgh Review* 27 (December 1816) 446.
49. Ibid., pp. 446–7.
50. Coleridge, 'Religious Musings', 51.

51. Griggs, iv 574.
52. *Edinburgh Review* 27 (December 1816) 446.
53. For more on Jeffrey's epistemology see Flynn, chapter 2.
54. As quoted by Flynn, p. 56.
55. *Edinburgh Review* 17 (November 1810) 184.
56. *Edinburgh Review* 7 (October 1805) 175.
57. Ibid., 445.
58. See his letter to Daniel Stuart of 7 October 1815; Griggs, iv 591. I am grateful to Richard S. Tomlinson for information about Coleridge's use of dictation at this period.
59. Wu, iv 121.
60. Morley, i 202.
61. Wu, ii 379n7.
62. Marrs, iii 224–5.
63. Coleridge twice blocked him from gaining a patron; see Bromwich, 266–7.
64. Griggs, iv 706–7.
65. See Deirdre Coleman, 'Jeffrey and Coleridge: Four Unpublished Letters', *The Wordsworth Circle* 18 (1987) 39–45, p. 44.
66. *Notebooks* iii 4323. Coburn dates the entry to 1816–17.
67. It was advertised, with *Sibylline Leaves*, in the *Morning Chronicle* on 11 July.
68. CC *Biographia*, ii 239.
69. See Griggs, iv 736.
70. CC *Biographia*, ii 242.
71. Several of the marginalia in these volumes date from June and July 1817; see CC *Marginalia*, i 555.
72. See for instance letters to Murray (26 March 1817) and Wrangham (5 June); Griggs, iv 716–17, 734–7.
73. The entry of 16 July 1817 in Godwin's diary, 'Coleridge ça la', presumably refers to *Biographia*.
74. *The Correspondence of Leigh Hunt*, ed. Thornton Leigh Hunt (2 vols, London: Smith, Elder, 1859), i 102.
75. Sikes, 176.
76. He mentions it in a letter to John Murray; see *New Letters of Robert Southey*, ed. Kenneth Curry (2 vols, New York: Columbia University Press, 1965), ii 171.
77. *Edinburgh Review* 28 (August 1817) 491.
78. *Christabel: Kubla Khan, A Vision; The Pains of Sleep* (London: John Murray, 1816), p. v.
79. See CC *Biographia*, i 142.
80. See esp. CC *Biographia*, i 219.
81. Wu, vi 130.
82. This was reported in Davy's *Researches Chemical and Philosophical; chiefly concerning nitrous oxide, or dephlogisticated nitrous air, and its respiration* (London: J. Johnson, 1800).
83. CC *Biographia* i 246.
84. Ibid., i 212.
85. *Edinburgh Review* 28 (August 1817) 493.
86. *Edinburgh Review* 28 (August 1817) 498. Hazlitt's thoughts on Kant were less critical than those expressed in the review; see Natarajan, *Hazlitt and the Reach of Sense*, pp. 158ff.; Bromwich 241–5.

87. Wu, iv 210–13.
88. *Edinburgh Review* 28 (August 1817) 506.
89. CC *Biographia* i 191.
90. *Edinburgh Review* 28 (August 1817) 503.
91. Ibid., 512.
92. Ibid.
93. Morley, i 209.
94. Ibid., 514.
95. Ibid., 515.
96. These were published in *The Examiner*, March and May 1817; see Wu, iv 157–94.
97. Curry, ii 171.
98. Southey was still hoping for the chance to write the article for the *Quarterly* in late October (see Curry, ii 176). This does not reduce the chances of his having made a preliminary attempt on the subject in the *Courier*.
99. Sikes, 378.
100. None the less, when commissioned by Jeffrey to write about Defoe in a review of January 1830, Hazlitt found himself discoursing again on the subject of apostasy; see Howe, xvi 364–93.
101. Griggs, iv 831. Coleridge was still complaining of Hazlitt's 'hatred of me' in 1819; see CC *Literature*, ii 294.
102. Griggs, iv 798.
103. Ibid., iv 735.
104. See, for instance, the two essays 'On the Spy-System' and 'On the Treatment of the State Prisoners', Wu, iv 194–201.
105. Charles Duke Yonge, *The Life and Administration of Robert Banks, Second Earl of Liverpool, K.G.* (3 vols, London, 1868), ii 299.
106. Ibid., p. 298.
107. *The Examiner* no. 489 (11 May 1817) p. 303.
108. Ibid., pp. 300–7. The letter is reprinted in Griggs, iv 757–63.
109. See Wu, iv 183 and 406–20.

9

Women and the *Edinburgh Review*

Stuart Curran

The last third of the eighteenth century witnessed a wholly unprecedented influx of women writers into the publishing industry of Great Britain, some of them not just making noticeable inroads but also creating for themselves household names and even occasionally fortunes. The ground had thus been long charted, and at the beginning of the nineteenth century when a group of young liberal men presumed to set on its ear the conservative political and artistic culture of Edinburgh, it might have been expected, as part of their programme of reform, that they would champion women authors and their principal causes. They already had an example, after all, in the literate openness Joseph Johnson displayed during the 1790s in his stewardship of the *Analytical Review*, which prominently employed Mary Wollstonecraft to hector her sister novelists into providing contemporary fiction with intellectual backbone and moral fibre. But, conversely, no women wrote for the *Edinburgh Review*, and, more surprisingly still, relatively few were critically noticed in its pages. In the early years, where women did enter its precincts as the subject of reviews, the young men seemed not quite sure what to make of this transgressive incursion through the doors of their fraternal club.

It was not that there seemed a deliberate programme of exclusion or partiality. In the first issues of the *Edinburgh Review* women authors entered its lists in the guise of various genres and were reviewed by diverse voices. The tone, however, is uniformly supercilious and virtually dismissive. Dr Thomas Brown led the opening charge in the initial number, condescending with a strained paternal kindness to Amelia Opie's 1802 volume of verse by placing it within traditional female stereotypes:

She is therefore wholly unfit for that poetry, which endeavours to reason while it pleases; and, powerful as she is in solitary pathos, we do not think that she is well fitted for bringing before us the connected griefs and characters of the drama.[1]

Valuing her verse only where she expresses unadorned simplicity, Brown offers a litany of forms where Mrs Opie 'has *attempted*' success but consistently falls short, ending with a gendered reconfiguration of traditional eighteenth-century couplets:

> The regular heroic couplet she has also *attempted*; but a line of ten syllables is too large for the grasp of her delicate fingers. . . . It is in the smaller verse of eight syllables, which requires no pomp of sound, and in the simple tenderness, or simple grief, to which the artlessness of such numbers is best suited, that the power of Mrs Opie's poetry consists . . .[2]

The final sentence of the review notes the poet's 'marriage to a celebrated artist', alluding to John Opie, director of the Royal Academy of Art, and thus giving an impression of using this notice to curry favour with the cultural elite in London, if that could ever be the outcome of such demeaning rhetoric. Or perhaps we should construe the opposite, the review constituting a gesture of near-defiance of that southern establishment. Whatever the case, the pattern continues in the second number, with Francis Jeffrey, who had cut his teeth on 'the Lake School' in the first issue, taking on the hapless wife of Edinburgh's foremost physician and medical scholar, John Hunter. 'These poems have some merit,' he begins,

> but their beauties are not of the very highest order. They are chiefly remarkable for a modest simplicity, both of thought and expression; and are composed, in general, with an unambitious plainness, that aims only at the natural representation of moderate affection; and escapes the dangers of extravagance, by renouncing all pretension to magnificence, force, or novelty.[3]

This notion of a woman's sphere in poetry is much the same as that employed by Brown in the previous number, though the tone is strikingly nastier, so much so that one wonders whether some personal animus against Dr Hunter were motivating Jeffrey. In this age, men were challenged to duels over lesser insults than Jeffrey's ensuing foray: 'Though, in general, but little disposed to venture out of the safe and beaten track, she has been sometimes tempted to transgress into originality.'[4] In a critique that is little more than an extended list of minute nit-picking, Jeffrey never mentions the fact that Franz Josef Haydn had set a number of Anne Hunter's poems during his residence in Great Britain in the 1790s, an honour which the author mentions in a prefatory note has encouraged their publication.

Later in the same volume Sydney Smith weighed in with a review of even less principle, since neither the author nor subject were in any sense current.[5] His text was the *Reflexions sur le Divorce* by Suzanne Necker, originally published just before her death in 1794. The only indication that this is not a new work is the abbreviation 'Nouv. Edit.' in the headnote. It is clear from the start that Smith regards the French assembly's liberalization of the laws covering divorce as bad policy, but, from the character of the review, it is scarcely possible to discern that the treatise shares the same opinion. The entire notice is geared towards Madame Necker's use of classical citations and allusions, which Smith, with a preening display of his own facility in the classics, terms 'second-rate erudition',[6] and it ends by cautioning against the 'dangerous' example such a work sets for a woman aspiring to learning: 'She may be a sort of prodigy in her own circle, without having acquisitions beyond those of a boy of sixteen.'[7] As with the censure launched in the first volume against the poetic aspirations of wives of male luminaries, one senses a curious undercurrent in the way in which Smith takes up the French department in the *Edinburgh Review*. The attack on Madame Necker in January 1803 seems, indeed, to be a preliminary skirmish before his full-scale assault on her daughter in the first number of Volume 2, three months later. His subject is Germaine de Staël's novel *Delphine* in the translation published by Mawman:

> This dismal trash, which nearly dislocated the jaws of every critic among us with gaping, has so alarmed Bonaparte, that he has seized the whole impression, sent Madame de Staël out of Paris, and, for aught we know, sleeps in a nightcap of steel, and dagger proof blankets. To us it appears rather an attack against the Ten Commandments, than the government of Bonaparte, and calculated not so much to enforce the rights of the Bourbons, as the benefits of adultery, murder, and a great number of other vices, which have been somehow or other strangely neglected in this country, and too much so (according to the apparent opinions of Madame de Staël) even in France.
>
> It happens, however, fortunately enough, that her book is as dull as it could have been if her intentions had been good . . . [8]

Smith ends his review by reinforcing the latter stricture: 'this celebrated lady would have been very guilty, if she had not been very dull.'[9]

Sydney Smith's dislike of *Delphine*, of course, could have many rationale sources underlying it. By audaciously creating royalist protagonists only a decade after the Terror, Staël might have seemed to a contemporary liberal as espousing a reactionary politics. And a minister of the Church of England assuredly might be expected to frown heavily on the easy sexual morality represented in the novel. Still, the masculinist rhetorical stance is pervasive, and it is a tone that Smith seems unable to shake off even when he comes to a work that sits squarely within his own political sensibilities as a supporter of liberal Irish causes. Although a later time would know very well how to apportion the relative contributions of Richard Lovell and Maria Edgeworth to the *Essay on Irish Bulls* (1801), Smith, reviewing it in the fourth number of the *Edinburgh Review*, immediately (and wrongly) surmises 'that the male contributions exceed the female, in a very great degree'.[10] And so Smith continues under this assumption:

> it is of considerable importance, that the character of a nation should not be degraded; and Mr Edgeworth has great merit in *his* very benevolent intention of doing justice to the excellent qualities of the Irish. It is not possible to read *his* book, without feeling a strong and a new disposition in their favour.[11] (my emphasis)

Thus having managed in successive issues of the periodical to single out and almost dismiss the two women authors that the *Edinburgh Review* would subsequently come to champion might be considered something of a perverse achievement on Sydney Smith's part. But, in truth, it is indicative of a lack of editorial control that might seem surprising to a later time that would assume that the political and cultural programme of the *Edinburgh Review* was consistent from the start. That assumption is not incorrect, but what these examples strongly suggest is that it is predicated wholly on reviews written by men about men and for men. In its early days women were simply beyond the pale of the periodical's intellectual authority.

At a certain point the dismissive treatment of women authors must have begun to be apparent to the cadre of contributors as well as to the editor, Francis Jeffrey. In the same fourth number in which Smith credits Richard Lovell Edgeworth with his daughter's creativity, Francis Jeffrey at last takes up the case of Scotland's foremost contemporary woman, and the tone abruptly shifts. The first volume of Joanna Baillie's *Plays on the Passions* had been published to considerable notice in 1798, and thus their claims for literary recognition were already well established by the time Jeffrey, using the second volume as pretext, essayed a general critique of the project in July 1803. As the leading article and at eighteen pages, this was by far the most extensive treatment of a woman author to this point in the periodical's development. It is by no means an unquestioning encomium: indeed, Jeffrey's strong and well-articulated objections to the system on which Baillie was constructing her dramas are sufficiently cogent to be still cited in the critical literature two centuries later. But the questions are formulated within and balanced by a high respect for Baillie's intrinsic achievement.

> Upon the whole, then, we are pretty decidedly of opinion, that Miss Baillie's plan of composing separate plays upon the passions, is, in so far as it is at all new or original, in all respects extremely injudicious; and we have been induced to express this opinion more fully and strongly, from the anxiety that we feel to deliver her pleasing and powerful genius from the trammels that have been imposed upon it by this unfortunate system. It is paying no great compliment, perhaps, to her talents, to say that they are superior to those of any of her contemporaries among the English writers of tragedy; and that, with proper management, they bid fair to produce something that posterity will not allow to be forgotten.[12]

It could be argued that Jeffrey had little choice in his treatment of Baillie, even that, given her status as a living monument to Scottish culture, his animadversions against her system were as close as he could get to repeating his attack on the system underlying the Lake Poets in his inaugural review. Supporting such an argument would be the general drift of Jeffrey's later treatment of her *Miscellaneous Plays*[13] and the third instalment of *Plays on the Passions*,[14] which, though surely of considerable length, contained an increasingly open deprecation of her dramaturgy. Even so, whether by choice or cultural constraint, the *Edinburgh Review* had at last found a woman it had to take seriously, and from this point on those responsible for its course appear to have sought for a means of integrating women writers into the general contours of the periodical's own system. Maria Edgeworth, stepping out from the shadow of her father's imprimatur, led the way.

All in all, after Sydney Smith's misattributions of the *Essay on Irish Bulls*, Maria Edgeworth was reviewed six more times in the *Edinburgh Review*, with the notices becoming increasingly lengthy and laudatory over the span of thirteen years. Francis Jeffrey appears to have written them all.[15] The account of *Popular Tales*[16] sets the agenda to which the *Edinburgh Review* will return again and again: 'The design of these tales is excellent, and their tendency so truly laudable as to make amends for many faults of execution,'[17] it begins. Maria Edgeworth's importance as a novelist is to address her works 'to that great multitude who are neither high-born nor high-bred'.

> It is for this great and most important class of society that the volumes before us have been written; and their object is, to interest, amuse and instruct them by stories founded on the incidents of common life, and developed by the agency of ordinary characters...
>
> But in the great and respectable multitude of English tradesmen, yeomen, and manufacturers – in that most important part of our population which consists of the well-educated in the lower and middling orders of the people, we do believe that there is so much good sense and good principle, as to secure the favourable reception of a work which professes to interest them by a picture of their own condition, to make them proud of their independence, and cheerful in their submission, and to point out the happiness which is placed within the reach of all who are industrious and affectionate.[18]

Eventually, Edgeworth's series of *Tales of Fashionable Life* will force Jeffrey to broaden his frame of reference, but in the early reviews his centring attention on bourgeois readers and their values rather against the expectations of an aristocratic and privileged elite reveals a cultural allegiance of a kind discernible in the more overtly political reviews in which the program of the *Edinburgh Review* is generally carried forward. One senses in that concern a quasi-Victorian ethos desiring to come to the fore a generation early. Even more is this the case when it is linked with the value Jeffrey most honours in Edgeworth's *oeuvre*, her distinctive breed of moralism.

In his review of *Leonora*[19] two years later, although he thinks the novel a comparatively weak production, Jeffrey expands on his admiration for Maria Edgeworth:

> We are partial, indeed, we will confess, to Miss Edgeworth; for we think the public very greatly indebted to her; and conceive that she has come nearer the true tone of moral instruction than any other writer we are acquainted with....

We do not know any books that are more likely to be useful than most of those she has published; and while we willingly do all we can to promote their notoriety, we earnestly exhort her to multiply their number.[20]

Here at his conclusion, Jeffrey reverts to his earlier review of the *Popular Tales* to drive his point home:

> We rather wish she would write more moral tales; for though it requires some resolution to dissuade the author of Belinda from delineating the character of fashionable life, we are satisfied that she will do most good by continuing the former publication. By works like Belinda or Leonora, she can only hope to correct the vices, or abate the follies of three or four persons of fashion: by improving the plan of the Moral Tales, she may promote the happiness and the respectability of many thousands in all ranks of society.[21]

What recommends Maria Edgeworth, then, is not her imaginative genius, nor her construction of fictional character, though Jeffrey does at least honour both, but her utility. So, indeed, he explicitly states in beginning an undiluted panegyric upon the achievement of the first of her *Tales of Fashionable Life* three years later.[22]

> If it were possible for reviewers to *envy* the authors who are brought before them for judgement, we rather think we should be tempted to envy Miss Edgeworth; – not, however, so much for her matchless powers of probable invention – her never-failing good sense and cheerfulness – nor her fine discrimination of characters – as for the delightful consciousness of having done more good than any other writer, male or female, of her generation.[23]

Jeffrey underscores this hyperbolic introduction in his concluding paragraph, calling Edgeworth's writings 'beyond all comparison, the most useful of any that have come before us since the commencement of our critical career'.[24]

That this is not our customary ground for considering fiction of the Romantic period may easily be discerned by considering whether any reader would ever think to speak in such terms of the 'utility' of the novels of either Jane Austen or Walter Scott. But the demands on literature of such fervent utilitarianism will, we must remember, assert itself even more fully in the 1820s and 1830s in periodicals, such as the

Westminster Review or *Fraser's Magazine*, that we associate with the next generation's dispensation. What Jeffrey's enthusiasm allows us to see this early is how closely linked it originally is to the aims of evangelical religion and Dissenting values – values peculiarly embedded in the character of Presbyterian Edinburgh – and to an emerging literary realism behind which always lurks the implicit desire for social improvement. Rather than too hastily reacting against Jeffrey's judgements as only marginally concerned with literature as a form of art rather than sociology, we should instead perhaps credit him with discerning Edgeworth's actual centrality to her culture and, just as important, to the middle-class orientation and values increasingly expected of its literature.[25]

There is another important aspect of Edgeworth's hold over Jeffrey's critical tastes, the Irish setting of much of her fiction. Although the treatment of Irish affairs is treated separately in this volume,[26] the concern is of some import for our understanding of how very 'useful' Edgeworth was not just to improving the English-speaking world in general but, more directly, to supporting the particular interests of the *Edinburgh Review*. '[T]he calmer spirits of the South can hardly yet comprehend the exhilarating effect which her reappearance uniformly produces upon the saturnine complexion of their Northern Reviewers,' Jeffrey writes, as he undertakes a notice of *Patronage*.[27] This remark is, however, more than a witty tweaking of English tastes: it suggests, indeed, a sense of underlying identity between the interests of Ireland and of Scotland in dealing with their far-off, hegemonic capitol, an identity that is an important aspect of the alternative voice the *Edinburgh Review* sought to project. Jeffrey's continual praise of Edgeworth's feel for local colour and ideolect – for instance, in regard to *Ennui*: 'The Irish characters are inimitable; – not the coarse caricatures of modern playwrights – but drawn with a spirit, a delicacy, and a precision, to which we do not know if there be any parallel among national delineations'[28] – evinces his respect for the endurance, and desire for the advancement and further enfranchisement of, a non-English culture and character within Great Britain. Indeed, part of Edgeworth's utility in this regard might have been the very fact that her Irishness allowed the *Edinburgh Review* to promote its multicultural agenda without raising accusations of mere Scottish jingoism.

If this overarching British enlargement of the sphere of concern animating the editorial interests of the *Edinburgh Review*, however shrewd it may play itself out, may be thought almost predictable from our hindsight, the other major venture into an alternate cultural model undertaken by the periodical was truly audacious, and this enterprise was likewise carried out through the agency of a woman, the same Germaine de Staël ridiculed by Sydney Smith in the second volume barely six months into the career of the periodical. A salient difference in the case of de Staël is that her centrality to the mission of the *Edinburgh Review*, rather than merely demonstrating the intellectual domination of Francis Jeffrey as appears to have been the case with Maria Edgeworth, seems to have resulted from a common editorial decision to which a variety of participating reviewers acceded. That is to say, John Playfair undertook the critique of *Corinne*;[29] Francis Jeffrey assigned himself the enormous leading articles on *De la Litérature considerée dans ses Rapports avec les Institutions Sociales*[30] and the posthumous *Considérations sur les Principaux Événemens de la Révolution Françoise*;[31] and James Mackintosh was given both *Reflexions sur le Suicide*[32] and *De L'Allemagne*.[33] It is not straining for significance to underscore that all these works are read from French editions, which are lavishly quoted from in all these reviews, even though both *Corinne* and *On Germany* had prominent London imprints and were largely read by the British in translation. And although de Staël's credentials as a highly vocal opponent of Napoleon and her residence in Britain during the preparation of *On Germany* for John Murray in 1813 gave her an unassailable political and cultural position in the country, the character of the reviews she received in the *Edinburgh Review* testifies to much more than notoriety as a reason for such concentrated and extensive notice.[34]

The *Edinburgh Review*, which saw in Maria Edgeworth the embodiment of a reformist multicultural Britain, discerned in Madame de Staël a linked attribute, one, indeed, that she went out of her way to exemplify almost mythically, that of a pan-European cosmopolitanism set against both encrusted monarchic autocracy and Napoleonic empire. The first paragraph of John Playfair's encomium on *Corinne* ends by centring the novel geographically across Europe:

> the difference of national character is the force that sets all in motion; and it is Great Britain and Italy, the extremes of civilized Europe, that are personified and contrasted in the hero and heroine of this romantic tale.[35]

These distinctively national timbres are reverted to further along in Playfair's exposition: 'Corinna is represented as excelling in the character of an *Improvisatrice*, so peculiar to Italy, and so intimately connected with the flowing and sonorous language of that country.'[36] Not only does de Staël thus evince an intimate knowledge of Italy and its culture, but she is equally at home in Britain:

> Madame de Staël, as appears from almost every part of this work, has studied with great care the character and manners of the English. She has done so also with singular success; and, though all her notions may not be perfectly correct, we believe that hardly any foreigner, who has not resided long in England, ever approached so near to the truth.[37]

The breadth of de Staël's reach across cultures, both ancient and modern, clearly impressed Jeffrey as well, but in his 50-page engagement with *De la Litérature considerée dans ses Rapports avec les Institutions Sociales*, one discerns as well an almost programmatic expansion of his current obsession with Maria Edgeworth. Indeed, he begins on the subject of the novels that have brought Germaine de Staël fame from what he calls 'this frivolous generation':[38]

> the bolder among them already venture to insinuate that the author of Delphine and Corinne is falling fast into dotage and morality. For ourselves, we must say that we are not exactly of that opinion. We look upon this as, upon the whole, the best and least exceptionable of all Mad. de Staël's publications; and we look upon her as beyond all comparison the first female writer of her age.[39]

Acknowledging that 'there may be others whose writings are of more direct and indisputable utility'[40] (the cause he had last extolled in Edgeworth just six months before), none the less, in Staël Jeffrey discerns a writer acutely sympathetic to the larger literary perspective of the *Edinburgh Review*, which is, one surmises, what justifies his extended and deeply personal engagement with this volume:

> We are not acquainted, indeed, with any writer who has made such bold and vigorous attempts to carry the generalizing spirit of true philosophy into the history of literature and manners, or who has thrown so strong a light upon the capricious and apparently unaccountable diversity of national taste, genius, and morality, by connecting them with the political structure of society, the accidents of climate and external relation, and the variety of creeds and superstitions.[41]

Although Jeffrey expresses himself as much less sure than his subject of the inevitability of progress in human civilization, one senses his identification with the ends to which Staël aspires as a writer, for they replicate those he would wish to be understood as upholding as an editor. In a long digression on the difference between the useful and the merely pleasurable in literature, Jeffrey all but writes his credo as a public literary servant.

> It is quite true, as Mad. de Staël observes, that the power of public opinion, which is the only true and ultimate guardian either of freedom or of virtue, is greater or less exactly as the public is more or less enlightened; and that this public never can be trained to the habit of just and commanding sentiments, except under the influence of a sound and progressive literature. . . . When life is considered as nothing more than an amusement, its termination is contemplated with far less emotion, and its course, upon the whole, is overshadowed with deeper clouds of *ennui*, than when it is presented as a scene of high duties and honourable labours, and holds out to us at every turn – not the perishable pastimes of every passing hour, but the fixed and distant objects of those serious and lofty aims which connect us with a long futurity.[42]

Jeffrey's powerful sense of identification with de Staël, so wholly contrasting with the view of her with which Sydney Smith introduced her to the pages of the *Edinburgh Review*, receives its clearest articulation in his encounter with her posthumous publication, *Considérations sur les Principaux Événemens de la Révolution Françoise*,[43] which he envelopes with hyperbolic praise from first to last:

> No book can possibly possess a higher interest than this which is now before us. It is the last, dying bequest of the most brilliant writer that has appeared in our days. . . .
> We cannot stop now to say all that we think of Madame de Staël: – and yet we must say, that we think her the most powerful writer that her country has produced since the time of Voltaire and Rousseau – and the greatest writer, of a woman, that any time or any country has produced.[44]

Yet, at the end of the review, Jeffrey sounds an ominous note, repositioning Germaine de Staël within the very rigid categorization of gender that her own example had so wholly subverted, thinking himself justified, as he puts it, 'in ascribing to its lamented author that perfection of masculine understanding, and female grace and acuteness, which are so rarely to be met with apart, and never, we believe, were before united'.[45]

With Germaine de Staël's death and Maria Edgeworth's retirement from the lists of British fiction, both of which occurred in 1817, the sudden and surprising prominence of women's voices in the *Edinburgh Review* ceases. There are occasional revivals of concern with the distaff: Jeffrey pens yet another retrospective of de Staël in October 1821, and in 1824–5 there are two reviews of Lady Morgan in which, as issues are raised concerning the social organization of Ireland, one detects the faint echo of the earlier veneration of Maria Edgeworth in these pages. But after the first two decades of the nineteenth century, the *Edinburgh Review* had lost its centrality as a forum for liberal and multicultural causes, and women were too wholly entrenched in the literary landscape of Great Britain to require the intervention of the periodical press for their support. Perhaps, however, we may see in the *Edinburgh Review*'s struggle to come to terms with the prominence of women in British letters something of a parable for the larger struggle in the culture. The initial dismissiveness had given way to respect, though the complete absence of notices of female writers in the periodical between November 1825 and October 1829, when Francis Jeffrey, about to retire as editor, signs off with an encomium on Felicia Hemans as the embodiment of female poetic virtues, might suggest that it was a respect still rather grudging in its nature.

Notes

1. *Edinburgh Review* 1 (October 1802) 115.
2. Ibid.
3. *Edinburgh Review* 1 (January 1803) 421.
4. Ibid.
5. I am following the identifications to be found in the *Wellesley Index to Victorian Periodicals, 1824–1900*, ed. Walter E. Houghton (London: Routledge & Kegan Paul, 1966). Smith is listed as the reviewer in this case, but with a question mark after his name to suggest that the identification is not definitive.
6. *Edinburgh Review* 1 (January 1803) 487.
7. Ibid., 495.
8. *Edinburgh Review* 2 (April 1803) 172. The treatment of Bonaparte here is of a piece with the deliberate deflation of his image practised, it would appear, as a political policy by the *Edinburgh Review*: see John Clive, *Scotch Reviewers: The 'Edinburgh Review', 1802–1815* (London: Faber & Faber, [1957]), pp. 96–7.
9. Ibid., 177.
10. *Edinburgh Review* 2 (July 1803) 398.

11. Ibid., 401.

12. Ibid., 277.

13. *Edinburgh Review* 5 (January 1805) 405–21.

14. *Edinburgh Review* 19 (February 1812) 261–90.

15. The *Wellesley Index* places a question mark after his name for the review of *Popular Tales* (*Edinburgh Review* 8 (July 1804) 329–37) and, offering the possibility of Charles Kinnaird as alternative author, also for that of *Patronage* (*Edinburgh Review* 21 (January 1814) 416–34). There is, however, such a consistency of voice and sentiment throughout these notices, even to the point of a consistent cross-referencing of earlier remarks in later reviews, that I find it hard to believe that anyone beside Jeffrey was involved in their production.

16. *Edinburgh Review* 4 (July 1804) 329–37.

17. Ibid., 329.

18. Ibid., 329, 330–1.

19. *Edinburgh Review* 8 (April 1806) 206–13.

20. Ibid., 211, 213.

21. Ibid., 213.

22. *Edinburgh Review* 14 (July 1809) 375–88.

23. Ibid., 375–6.

24. Ibid., 388.

25. It is only fair to note that, in his last review, of *Harrington* and *Ormond*, Jeffrey objects to the excessive moralism of these tales (*Edinburgh Review* 18 (August 1817) 393). Other readers, it should be added, were much less tolerant of the utilitarian cast of Edgeworth's fiction: for an account of their critique, and a suggestive reading of how Scott reconfigured the utilitarian ethos into a public arena, see chapter 2 of Ina Ferris's *The Achievement of Literary Authority: Gender, History, and the Waverley Novels* (Ithaca, NY: Cornell University Press, 1991): 'Utility, Gender, and the Canon: The Example of Maria Edgeworth', pp. 60–71. On the centrality of Edgeworth to a particular school of realistic fiction that our dual emphases on Austen and Scott have eclipsed, see Michael Gamer's foundational monograph, 'Maria Edgeworth and the Romance of Real Life', included in a collection devoted to the subgenres of Romantic fiction in *Novel: A Forum on Fiction* 34:2 (Spring 2001) 233–68.

26. See Timothy Webb's essay, pp. 58–81, above.

27. *Edinburgh Review* 22 (January 1814) 416.

28. *Edinburgh Review* 14 (July 1809) 380.

29. *Edinburgh Review* 11 (October 1807) 183–95.

30. *Edinburgh Review* 21 (February 1813) 1–50.

31. *Edinburgh Review* 30 (September 1818) 275–317.

32. *Edinburgh Review* 21 (July 1813) 424–32.

33. *Edinburgh Review* 22 (October 1813) 198–238.

34. A useful, recent account of how Germaine de Staël fits with the interests and values of Regency Britain will be found in Joanne Wilkes, *Lord Byron and Madame de Staël: Born for Opposition* (Aldershot: Ashgate, 1999).

35. *Edinburgh Review* 11 (October 1807) 183.

36. Ibid., 191.

37. Ibid., 192.

38. *Edinburgh Review* 21 (February 1813) 1.
39. Ibid., 2.
40. Ibid.,
41. Ibid., 2–3.
42. Ibid., 7, 8.
43. *Edinburgh Review* 30 (September 1818) 275–317.
44. Ibid., 275.
45. Ibid., 317.

Index